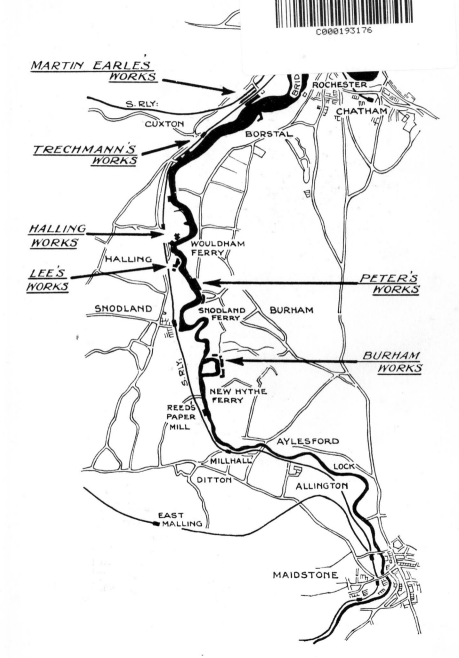

MARTIN EARLE'S WORKS

S. RLY:

CUXTON

TRECHMANN'S WORKS

HALLING WORKS

LEE'S WORKS

HALLING

SNODLAND

S. RLY:

REED'S PAPER MILL

EAST MALLING

BRID

ROCHESTER

CHATHAM

BORSTAL

WOULDHAM FERRY

PETER'S WORKS

SNODLAND FERRY

BURHAM

BURHAM WORKS

NEW HYTHE FERRY

AYLESFORD

MILLHALL

LOCK

DITTON

ALLINGTON

MAIDSTONE

The Medway from Rochester to Maidstone.

The maps of the Thames and Medway used as endpapers are reproduced from the A.P.C.M.'s 'Handbook for Bargemen, Lightermen, Tugmen and Coasting Captains' compiled by Charles T. Perfect, 1930 edition.

US BARGEMEN

TO JOAN
who first came alongside in *Dione*

Us Bargemen

A. S. BENNETT

Author of 'June of Rochester' and 'Tide Time'

MERESBOROUGH BOOKS
1980

Further copies of this book may be obtained through your local bookshop, or direct from the publisher, Meresborough Books, 7 Station Road, Rainham, Kent, ME8 7RS, at £7.95 post free.

Reprints of A. S. Bennet's first two books, 'June of Rochester' and 'Tide Time', are being considered. The publisher would be pleased to hear from anybody who would like details when available.

Printed and bound by Tonbridge Printers Ltd., Tonbridge, Kent.

CONTENTS

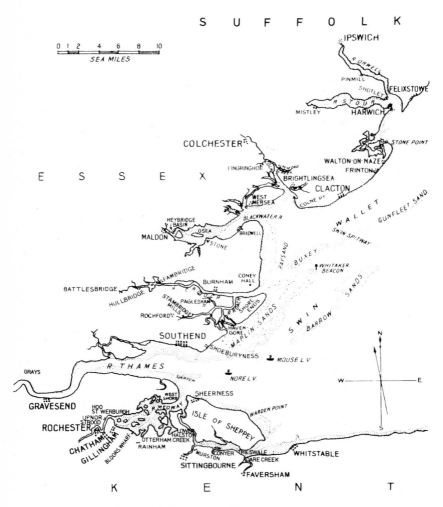

THE EAST COAST FROM ROCHESTER TO IPSWICH

Chapter One

'THE NORE'

I always felt that one day we should go back afloat. Dorothy must have known it too, but the first time she showed any hankering after the old way of life since we abandoned our little old topsail barge *June* at the end of the war and came to live on the Sea Wall at Whitstable, was in the summer of 1947 as we sat by the open window watching the sun go down across the bay.

The entire western sky was afire and the flats a shimmering blaze of colour when, into all this brilliance, there crept a Faversham barge on the first of the flood, silhouetted over by the Sheppey shore, each sail set in a dainty purposeful curve.

"I've been thinking," Dorothy murmured as if hypnotized by the beauty of it. "You know, I wouldn't mind having another barge."

I looked up quickly. "You really mean it?"

"M'm. After all, we'll have to make a move sometime or other."

That was true for we were outgrowing our house. Peter was running about now and Elizabeth had been at school these three years past. They slept at either end of a real outsize in ship's bunks, but already their feet were over-lapping; soon Peter would have to move into the spare room, when there would be no place for my books and papers.

Dorothy inclined towards a cottage in the country. There would have to be schools for the children of course, and a train to London. We would want shops close handy and a creek for a boat. I did come across an empty farm-house on Faversham Creek that might have done, but before Dorothy had a chance to see it vandals broke in and set the place on fire.

And now Dorothy was talking of going afloat again. It had to be a sailing barge, of course. There never was another craft that could equally well make a passage down channel in the middle of winter or poke up some narrow gut above bridges to a lonely berth in the midst of meadows. Only a barge could load a stack of hay or straw some twelve feet up the mast and turn up Swin for London River, as countless Essex stackies have done almost from time immemorial. And all this with a crew of two or at the most three.

Those smaller river barges, too, were wonderfully handy craft. There were hundreds in the Medway cement works alone serving Lee's, Peters', West Kent, Burham Cement and all the other works above Rochester Bridge. They never towed up through, but shipped a huffler at Strood and stood on boldly for the centre arch, dropping their gear at the very last moment by surging the stayfall round the windlass barrel. Once through it was all hands on the windlass to rig her again and keep sailing. Those handy well-kept cement barges shot Rochester

Bridge week after week, year in year out, and thought nothing of it. Whole fleets of them went through on every tide.

June had been a little old bluff-bowed Burham cement barge. She was never a racer even in her prime, but for all that she was wonderfully handy and with mizzen sheeted to a great barn door of a rudder she could turn to windward in those tortuous upper reaches almost in her own length. We bought her in 1933 when the Medway cement works were closing down — £50 complete with boat. We kept the gear in her, and for another £200 or so had the cement-encrusted hold lined out and turned into cabins.

She was a comfortable old barge and we spent seven very happy years on board, wintering in London or the Medway, fitting out each Spring, then sailing away down Swin to spend the summer months on the Essex sea borders, wherever there was a train to be had for London.

It was strange how that barge making up past Shell Ness while the setting sun bathed the world in a rich ethereal glow served to bring back memories of those *June* days; taking the evening tide up Maldon River with the ancient town silhouetted on the hill-top against the saffron afterglow of the western sky; or weatherbound in Colne towards the end of a summer gale, with a few fitful gleams of late evening sunshine breaking through the scudding clouds to gleam wanly on troubled waters and light up the fleet of loaded barges with sudden warmth.

So often too we seemed to come blowing into Harwich at the end of a long day's sail only for the breeze to fine away in the Orwell, so that we drifted up to the beautiful land-locked anchorage at Pin Mill, while the trading barges made the most of a fair tide and sailed on, Ipswich bound, into the path of the setting sun.

June was only a 75-ton barge which was small by modern standards but quite large enough for the two of us to handle. Of course, ours was mostly summer sailing and sometimes little more than ditch crawling. A favourite summer berth was Battlesbridge where barges still traded with corn. Sometimes we carried a fair breeze easterly up through Burnham anchorage but more often than not we had to turn to windward all the way up the Crouch to the barge mooring above Hullbridge and there wait for the flat calm of the early morning tide to poke up the last few winding reaches. The local huffler reckoned the best breeze for Battlesbridge was none at all.

And there was that unforgettable night when we came over the Spitway in company with a whole fleet of Ipswich and Mistley barges crosstacking to and fro as the silvery moonbeams danced and twinkled on the water, while every now and then, borne faintly on the breeze, came that time-honoured greeting: "Where you for?"

Those were happy, care-free days. Just occasionally though we were caught out, as that morning we came out of Harwich to sneak a passage up the coast to Maldon, only to meet a real snorter of a south-wester off the Naze. *June* had the length to drive through the short, steep seas in the Wallet but we had water

10

Whitstable Harbour, Yacht Club, Reeves Beach and 'The Nore' with white windows.
(Douglas West)

slobbering over the foredeck, and every now and then our bluff bows would punch into a sea to send spray high into the foresail. We were glad to bear up and run into Colne.

Yet another time, with friends on board, we threshed into Harwich on a dark night through driving rain that stung and blinded and made navigation a hazardous business. The ebb was pouring out and it was past one o'clock in the morning before we made our anchorage under the lee of Shotley. We were wet and tired and the canvas was too sodden for more than a rough stow. Then Dorothy called to us from the companion hatch. Down below all was quiet and peaceful. There was warmth and comfort and a wonderful smell from the galley that set our mouths a-watering as we hurriedly stripped off dripping oilskins and sou'westers. On the table was a great steaming meat pie. It should have been for our supper hours before; no wonder we were hungry. Presently, as we sat back with a wonderful sense of well-being, Dorothy set before us an apple pudding and a pot of tea. We fell to again, more slowly now, until at last plates were pushed away and each of us sprawled back luxuriously replete, ready for bed....

That was the charm of it, a yacht we could handle ourselves, yet large enough to afford all the creature comforts and amenities of a home. It was the unconventional way of life that had always appealed to us and now, after ten years ashore, Dorothy was getting the urge again to go afloat.

"It's a pity in many ways we ever abandoned *June*," she said thoughtfully. "Oh, I know she wanted a lot of doing up but she was no worse off than lots of other yacht barges at the end of the war."

"No," I said. "She was too far gone. What was the use of patching her up? She'd have been nothing but a very old barge at the end of it."

"M'm." Dorothy was still unconvinced. "We could have used her as a houseboat for the summer months even if she never sailed again."

I still shook my head. "It wouldn't have worked. She'd have broken our hearts in the end. No, we did the right thing in letting her go. This house was a wreck don't forget. We couldn't have managed both."

Dorothy sat silent for a while, still gazing out across the flats. The Faversham barge had passed the remains of the old, war-time boom guarding the East Swale and was picking up her mainsail. Soon she would be bringing up at the mouth of the Creek.

"That might have been us," Dorothy said softly.

"And why not?"

She looked up. "What, with barges at their present prices? We'd never afford it."

"Oh I don't know. We have this place to sell. After all houses have gone up too."

"What do you think it's worth then?"

"I should say about £2,500."

"Do you really? It's not very large you know."

"I don't suppose you'd get anything cheaper, not with a view like this."

"There's no garden."

"That's an attraction for some of us," I grinned. "Besides who'd want a garden with the whole of Whitstable Bay out there?"

"The trouble is," said Dorothy thoughtfully, "the sort of people this house would appeal to usually haven't got the money. Besides, even if we do sell "The Nore" what are the chances of finding another little barge like *June*?"

"But we wouldn't want another like *June*. Those little river barges seem to have gone, anyway. No, I'd like something a bit bigger. A 100-ton barge wouldn't be all that much heavier to handle; in fact she'd be much the same size as *June* with deeper sides and beam of seventeen feet or so. She'd be all that stiffer in a breeze and give more room down below."

"She'd have to have a low keelson, too," Dorothy added, whereupon I grinned for this had always been her *bête noir*. A barge is completely flat-bottomed, hence the inside keelson to take the place of a keel and forming a backbone through the middle of the hold. In the older barges it was usually a massive baulk of pitch pine standing some eighteen inches high, but this had been replaced in others by a far less obtrusive steel girder.

"All right," I conceded. "We'll look for a grain barge with a tall hatch coamings and a shallow steel keelson and a hold that hasn't been knocked about by grabs so we shan't have to panel out below. As for the pitch pine ceiling we'll have that buffed up and polished, with rugs instead of carpets. And her top will have to be good. No more leaky decks."

Dorothy laughed. "That's altogether too much to expect. I've never seen a deck yet that didn't leak at times — usually over somebody's head."

12

"All right," I said. "You win. At any rate we'll see the decks are sound and the covering boards are good. I'm not so keen on pumping as I was, so she'll have to be pretty tight."

"And wherever are you going to find such a wonderful barge may I ask?"

"You'll see. Something or other is sure to turn up."

"What about a barge that's already converted? It would save a lot of trouble if we could just walk straight aboard."

I shook my head. Many of the pre-war conversions that lay empty during the war were little better than *June* at the end of it, although some had been patched and changed hands at soaring prices. The few barges that had been lived on during the war were in better shape but they were not for sale. Few were worth considering. As for the post-war conversions, many were in poor condition when they came off war service, both as regards hull and gear. It was hardly surprising, for practically all the handy barges were taken up for powder work or mine spotting and spent the war years swinging at their moorings.

"No," I said. "If we do go afloat again we'll pick out the barge we want and plan it ourselves as we did with *June*, only this time we'll have a good solid job, with built-in furniture and electric light and everything else you want."

"M'm. It sounds all right but you won't find it so easy as before the war. I don't suppose we'll ever come across another barge like *June*."

"But we don't want a barge like *June*," I repeated. "You've got to remember she was sixty-five years old when we bought her. Besides, we'd want more room below decks to cope with the children."

Dorothy sat up with a start. "Good heavens!" she exclaimed. "I'd forgotten all about Elizabeth and Peter."

"I didn't hear anything. Surely they're asleep."

"No. No. I was just wondering how they'd get on aboard a barge," she said, but I scoffed at her doubts, for children are naturally sure-footed and readily take to the sea provided they are not continually chided. Elizabeth thought nothing of balancing on the gunwale when I first took her sailing and several times I had to bite my lips to keep myself from shouting. But *June's* boat which we kept off the house was as safe as houses and far too heavy for Elizabeth to turn over. Peter was less impulsive and showed an instinctive boat sense. They wore life belts, of course, but neither ever put a foot wrong. As I told Dorothy we were far more likely to tumble in ourselves, but she was not easily convinced.

"It's all very well for you to talk," she said. "They've only been out with you in the boat for an hour or two at the time, but don't forget I'd have them on my hands all day."

"Well, others seem to have brought up families on board barges. Besides, nearly all the places we used to visit in *June* dried out most of the day."

"And that's another thing. We'd have to have a permanent berth of our own somewhere or other. That's a must."

I nodded agreement, whereupon Dorothy's eyebrows rose and she gave a superior little smile as she would at one of Elizabeth's more incredulous stories.

13

Peter and Elizabeth on the steps of 'The Nore'.

"That doesn't sound like you," she declared. "You were always so restive. As soon as ever we'd got in somewhere you were all for sailing the very next weekend. I don't think I could ever go on as we did in the old days. I never was all that keen on sailing anyway. That's one reason why I used to look forward to the winter so as to get settled in."

It was my turn to smile. "You and your log fires! Why, you even reckoned there was an autumn nip in the air before summer was through."

"Log fires, m'm. I think that's one of the nicest smells."

Dorothy was no hard-bitten sailor really. Very few women are. They take to the water because they hate to disappoint their menfolk. Some never do become enured and the arrival of a family usually gives them the opportunity to drop out gracefully; others like Dorothy accept fair weather sailing for all the associations that go with it, such as blue skies and the tang of the sea, quiet moon-lit nights in a lonely anchorage, and the pleasure of making new friends. But few come to understand or appreciate the art of sailing. Dorothy would never be a sailor, yet she used to steer a barge to windward as well as most men, for she kept her a good full-and-by, which is how a barge should be sailed.

"No," she said. "I liked to feel we could move around in *June* and I didn't mind the sailing so long as it was fine, but not when it came on to blow. It was all too worrying then. What I'd have liked was a wharf in the country with an orchard to come back to and tie up any time we wanted. You know, some place we call our own and relax and grow roots."

14

"That's all right," I said quickly. "There's no reason why you shouldn't have your wharf." I meant it, too, for my own outlook had changed in some ways since the war. Coastal Forces may have had something to do with it. Possibly it was no more than *anno domini*. While I still begrudged time spent away from the sea, I no longer had to be sailing all the time to enjoy it. I wanted to get back into the world of barging again instead of just standing on the fringe, but there was more to it than the purely personal pleasure of ownership. There was all the association of barging; getting to know owners, surveyors, shipwrights, watermen and the great multitude of folk whose lives have been wrapped up with sailing barges. Above all I hankered after that easy cameraderie of bargemen them- selves, which is so difficult of attainment for a landlubber. Anyone with sufficient application can study the historical development of the sailing barge through the centuries by delving into the archives of museum and library, but the really fascinating human story of barge life can only be learned from years of contact with the men who sailed them. The only satisfactory way was to live afloat. It was easy then, for there never was a bargeman moored up alongside so taci- turn or reserved that he would not talk barges by the hour from the fastness of his own hatch top or quarter rail.

It was difficult putting all this into words. Not that it mattered really for Dorothy must have realized with a woman's intuition how much I missed the old way of life.

"There's one thing though," she said. "You mustn't forget you're that much older now. So am I and we'd find just as much work aboard a barge as ever there was. You couldn't count on much help from me with the children on my hands."

"I've not forgotten," I replied. How could I? There was the fitting out each year — sheer hard, back-breaking work of lowering gear on deck, unbending sails and dragging them ashore, scraping and varnishing spars, heaving sails on board again, with our faces, clothes and hair all plastered with red ochre and fish oil, then bending on again and rigging. There was ironwork to be chipped, decks to be dressed and any amount of painting both above and below; the sides had to be cleaned off and tarred — all this packed into the six weeks between Easter and Whitsun.

It was the same old grind each year, working all hours both early morning and late at night, until I grew physically sick with it all and cursed myself ever to start on such a never-ending task. We never did finish, for even when the fitting out was done there was always that odd persistent leak to be traced and all the routine scrubbing and cleaning — more deck dressing... more tarring...

"So you do remember," Dorothy murmured.

Of course I did. The work was hell — a heavenly hell that none but a sailor could ever hope to comprehend, but somehow or other people do things on boats they would never dream of doing ashore.

"I'd still go through with it again."

It was quite dark now. The breeze coming in from the sea was chilly. Dorothy got to her feet and started to close the windows.

"You and your old barges!"

Chapter Two

NELLIE S

The local barges belonging to Daniels Bros. (Whitstable) Ltd. had been kept busy in the corn work since the war: the little *Cereal*, the shapely, deep-sided *Lord Churchill*, *Azima* distinctive with wheelhouse and mizzen, *Savoy*, once Dover owned, the old Sandwich hoy barge *Trilby*, the two auxiliaries *Kathleen* and *Vicunia*.

They loaded in the London docks mostly, and we used to watch them from our window as they came sailing down past Warden Point on the ebb to stand in across the flats as soon as the tide served.

The huffler always went out to meet the barges whatever the weather. They made a wonderful sight running before a strong westerly under topsail and foresail and a few cloths of the main, while the tall, lanky Bill Carpenter put out in his best boat, leisurely sculling through the confused sea off the harbour entrance, pitching and tossing in the path of the oncoming barge. A few deft strokes and he would be alongside and tumbling aboard, while the mate ran aft with the headfast.

It was just such a night when John Corello brought in his *Gold Belt*. There never was a better barge, so Bill Carpenter used to declare.

"Just coming dark, it was, when he come running in from Warden. I could see him all right, but he never spotted me till the last moment.

" 'Well, I'm glad to see you,' he says. 'I never reckoned you'd be off in this lot.'

"It was a nasty ol' night and no mistake, snowing and sleeting an' all. 'Let me have her while you get the canvas off,' I says. 'Shan't be long now.' Nor we weren't! Checked her round the knuckle and we soon got her moored up under the sucker all nice and snug.

"Next day we started unloading of her and the skipper asks me down the cabin for a cup o' tea.

" 'That was a real good turn you done me coming off last night,' he says, 'I was a bit short-handed and wasn't exactly looking forward to poking in here on me own. Could you do with a bit of meat?'

" 'No need for that,' I says and nor there wasn't. I'd never had a thing off the barges all the time I'd been on the job.

" 'Take it and welcome,' he says. 'I'd like you to have it if it's any use to you.' Seems he was a vegetarian or something and he planks down a whole leg o' lamb. Yes he did! Biggest I seen since rationing began. That was lovely eating, too!

"I tell you, that little *Gold Belt*, she's the pertiest barge I ever did go aboard."

Bill Carpenter worked on the barges discharging at the grain elevator on the

16

The Barqentine *Nellie S*, from a painting by an unknown artist, dated 1883.

West Head. He tended the long, snaky sucker that nuzzled into the grain in the open hold, and was ready for a chat whenever we passed that way, while Peter and Elizabeth stood fascinated by the ever-tumbling cascade of golden grain.

The local skippers had little to say. It was almost as if they saw behind each quayside stroller the shadow of an income tax inspector. Evenings and weekends they padlocked their cabin scuttle hatches and went off home. Yet they seemed to spend so much of their time in harbour standing about in groups under the lee of a shed; apparently Whitstable bargemen always had the reputation of keeping to themselves, but the retired seamen — and there were many such in Whitstable — were far more willing to talk of the days they served in the local craft. I got to know burly, genial Bill Etheridge who went to Dover to bring away the *Savoy* when Daniel's bought her from Crundall's in the early 'twenties. And Ted Smith, more often known as Teddy Dreadnought after Goldsmiths' coasting barge *Dreadnought* in which he sailed as mate and skipper for over twenty years. He was always glad of company when he kept bad weather watch in the Coastguard's hut on the Pier Head.

Most of the old-timers, though, were in the sailing colliers, like William George Joiner, whose first command was the brigantine *Matilda Calder* that drove ashore on West Beach, Whitstable, during the great gale and flood of November 29th, 1897. Traces of the channel they had to dig to get her off were still discernable. He had been in the salvage work, fishing, dredging, yachting and the local colliers. He even went Master for a short while in 1918 of the big boomy barge *Alice Watts*.

17

There was Alf Revell, too, whom I used to visit at his little cottage on Island Wall. He was born at Stanford, near Hythe, in 1866 and apprenticed to the brig *Woodside*, of Folkestone, but he cleared out after a year and joined the little brigantine *Rapid*, owned in Whitstable, where eventually he married and settled down. It must have been a hard life in those old sailing coasters with little enough food and plenty of work. Many, especially towards the end of their days, leaked like baskets, and even in port, as often as not, the crew had to work the cargo out.

One evening I chanced to ask Alf Revell if he was ever in barges.

"Only the once," he replied. "Time I went to Mexico."

"Mexico!" I exclaimed. "Whatever was a barge doing out there?"

"Why, that *Nellie S* was trading regularly to the West Indies and them parts."

For a few moments I was nonplussed, then suddenly it dawned on me that the *Nellie S* was one of those legendary, square-rigged, foreign-going barges that came into vogue for a short while during the last century.

"That's right," Alf went on. "She was a 500-ton, flat-bottomed barquentine-rigged barge. Mind you, that's going back a good few years. I've got my discharge here somewhere about." He began to rummage in a drawer, talking the while, and presently brought out a slip of ivory-tinged paper. "That's the one. Barquentine *Nellie S* ... Captain Francies ... and there's the year 1887. She wasn't the only one of 'em either. There was several like her knocking about that time o' day: *Esther Smeed, George Smeed* and the old *Zebrina*."

I had heard of those big, deep-sea barges, but they always carried an air of mystery. Most had finished up years ago and nobody seemed to know much about them, yet here was a man who had actually sailed in one. From an old Lloyds' Register I was able to piece together the early history of his old ship.

The *Nellie S* was built by H. H. Gann & Co. at their West Beach Yard in 1876, the largest vessel ever launched at Whitstable: length 131 feet, beam 26 feet, and carrying 520 tons on a draft of 12 feet 6 inches. Dick Perkins, a notable name in Whitstable shipbuilding, was foreman shipwright, and built her to Lloyds Special Survey after the fashion of a Thames sailing barge with flat bottom and square chine. She was flush-decked and, unlike some of the other square-rigged barges of her time, was never fitted with leeboards.

Gann & Co. kept her in the family and put her in the South American trade, for which her light draft made her particularly suitable. In 1882 the *Nellie S* was sold away from Whitstable to Thorburn Bros. of Cornhill. Her port of registry was changed from Faversham — where all Whitstable craft were registered — to London, and she came under the management of Matthews & Luff, one of the oldest firms of coasting shipbrokers in London.

The story of Alf Revell's trip to Mexico is best told in his own words.

☆ ☆ ☆ ☆

"I'd never been foreign — not deep-sea, as you might say — till Cap'n Francies, a Whitstable man himself, got talking to me.

"I'm sailing out to Mexico," he said. "Would you like to come along o' me, Alf? She's a smart barquentine, is the *Nellie S*."

I was always one to have a go at anything, you know, so I said I would, and went off up to Workington where she was loading. There was a whole lot of craft there. I looked all round but couldn't see nothing of the fine barquentine Cap'n Francies talked of.

"Where does the *Nellie S* lay, mate?" I asked a chap on the dockside, thinking she might have sailed already maybe.

"That's her," he says, and pointed down below where I stood. Dear oh dear! There she was all right — a flat thing loaded down with steel rails and scarce fourteen inches of side amidships. That didn't look much of a craft to cross the Atlantic in — not winter time, it didn't.

I dumped my bag aboard and went and saw Cap'n Francies.

"Stow your gear below, Alf," he says, but I stood where I was and shook my head. "I'm not so sure I'm shipping after all."

"Why, what's matter?" he says. He hadn't been in her long himself. I did hear he was waiting to go Master in a steel barque then building.

"I don't go much on her," I said. "She's loaded too deep to my way of thinking."

"That's a matter of opinion," says Cap'n Francies, with a snort. "Owners think she'll carry another twenty ton. That's why we haven't covered up yet."

I took a look down the hold. The rails were stowed criss-cross to keep the weight up a bit and all chocked off. There was room enough — plenty of it — but she was that deep amidships, why, you only had to lean overside and dip a bucket.

I looked at Cap'n Francies, but he slapped me on the back and told me not to worry. "I've settled all that," he said. "I've told 'em they can send along another twenty or thirty ton if they want, but they'd better send along another Master and crew same time!"

I had a walk round that night and took a look at a smart-looking steamer over on the far side of the dock. One of the officers came to the rail.

"Looking for a berth?" he asked.

"No, not really," I says. "That's my ship over there."

He swung round and took a look at the old *Nellie S*. Then he looked hard at me and shrugged his shoulders. "Please yourself," he says, "but I know which I'd sooner be aboard! We're all ready to sail and can do with another seaman."

I didn't care much for the *Nellie S* myself just then, but I thought as I wouldn't have a faint heart over it. I said I'd go, and so I would!

Seemingly Cap'n Francies squared things with his owners, for we battened down soon after. There was eight of us all told; Master, Mate, Bo'sun, two A.B.'s, two Ordinary Seamen and the Cook.

The proper wages sailing out o' Cumberland should have been three pound

19

five a month or something like that, but seeing as the rest of the crew were out o' Liverpool, that's how we come to get two pound ten. Cap'n Francies, though, he took me and the other Whitstable man aside and said he'd pay another half-a-crown. So that's what we got — two pound twelve and six a month and pound an' pint.

We towed out of Workington. And didn't we know it! The tug would have us on a long tow and instead of easing up and giving us a chance of getting it in she just slipped the lot and left us to heave it in by hand. Some job that was, with a brand new manilla tow line as stiff as buckram! Blowing hard, it was, and snowing too!

I will say that for the old *Nellie* though. She stood up to her canvas all right, and nice and easy on the helm running and reaching. Lucky we never had to round up else I wouldn't wonder but what we'd have been swept clean. Another thing, her decks were pretty tight and we never got much water down the fo'c'sle — only when she dipped her bows in and then we got a trickle as you might expect.

The weather gradually fined up as we got down south and we drifted close to the Islands. Cap'n Francies agreed to put into Monserrat so's we could post letters home before dark, but along comes a fine, fair breeze and he wouldn't stop then so we sailed on by.

He was a one for work, was Cap'n Francies. I remember one day in the tropics he was squinting up aloft and I happened to be standing by.

"Alf," he says, turning to me. "I've a mind to smarten her up a bit. D'you think you're man enough to scrape that main topm'st pole?"

That was a bit of a tall order with nothing to hold on bar the pole itself. I could see he was daring me though, so I says to myself, I'll be hanged if I'm beat. I took my knife for a scraper and a bit o' line for a bight to cock a leg through and up I shives. That didn't half want some scraping! It was painted an' all! I tell you. I got proper frizzled up in the sun. I'd have cheerfully knifed the Captain time I'd done. Mind you, he was a fine sailor and knew how to get her along.

We made Progreso just nine weeks out. We had to work the cargo out ourselves. The other chap along o' me said he couldn't manage 'em so I lifted the rails one end while he slipped the sling under. I reckon he knew what he was up to. But I was a strapping young chap in those days. By golly, though, didn't that half make your back ache!

After discharging our rails we had to sail along the coast to a place called Frontero for orders, and then we took on board great big logs of mahogany all chopped into baulks for Fowey. We finished up two tiers high on deck, away above the rail.

Coming out o' the Gulf we had a gale o' wind westerly and ran before it with only the square fores'l and lower tops'l set. We averaged eleven knots that time; Mind you, that blowed hard, with great, long following seas. Down 'ud go her bows, fores'l blanketed and hanging all limp agin the mast, while the old gal drove along with her starn cocked up on the crest of a sea and only the tops'l drawing. Then up she'd come as each roller fetched out ahead and the fores'l 'ud fill again with a noise like the crack o' doom. A wonder that didn't blow right out o' the boltropes.

Standing right aft there at the wheel was a wonderful sight. Up she'd toss, then pitch right away down. Just like a baby in a cradle, that was. She was dry, too, running — at the wheel leastways — though every so often she'd give a roll and a sea 'ud come thundering aboard by the mizzen rigging, surge along the deck and run out by the fore rigging. And all that time the great baulks o' timber we'd got chained down and the stuns'l booms lashed along the rigging 'ud creak and clank as they lifted and bumped about.

Away to the nor'ard, a hundred miles or so off Sandy Hook, a steamer drove under a big sea and got her bridge swept away. Young Cap'n Nichols, a Whitstable man, was Master in her and he was lost. When we got home his family came to see me if I could tell 'em anything about it. Of course, we never knew nothing of it at the time, though she must've bin caught in the same storm.

One day, after the worst had blown itself out, it happened to be my trick at the wheel and as she lifted to the swell I caught sight of something away down to leeward. It was a sail of some sort and flags, too. I sung out to the Captain who bided his time and put the glass on her.

"She's in trouble," he said, so I let her run off while they shortened sail, then hove her to.

She was a wooden, three masted barque laying deep in the water and very sluggish. A boat put off from her and fetched some of the crew across. Then three of us dropped into the boat to pull back when we saw the rest on 'em get their long boat over and wave us back. There were eighteen on 'em all told, and a dog.

She was a British barque called the *John Banfield*, three weeks out from Rotterdam, with 500 tons of old iron and 5,000 empty oil drums when she sprang a leak. It must've been the drums that kep' her afloat, I reckon.

Running into the Channel, it come on to blow hard again. We'd taken soundings and found shelly bottom at eighty fathoms, but it was that thick with driving rain we never raised the Lizard till we were close in under the land. That ol' thing was going along, you know, with all that canvas on her. The way the weather was, Cap'n Francies was glad enough to pick up a pilot off Plymouth Breakwater and put in there. There were plenty of riding lights but we got well in amongst the ships before we anchored. We never did make Fowey, for we shifted up into the Cattewater and put the cargo out there.

I left the *Nellie S* in Plymouth, but I did hear Cap'n Francies took his wife out next trip and went away out to some place where he got be-nipped for six months and had to take Mrs. Francies up country, it being such a sickly place.

As for me, I went back coasting and joined the little 111-ton schooner *Emma*...

☆　☆　☆　☆

21

Alf Revel in 1948, on Reeves Beach, Whitstable with the sea wall behind.

The *Nellie S* continued to be owned by Thorburn Bros. and managed by Matthews & Luff until she was sold in 1896 to R. P. de Magalhaes, of Bahia. She traded under the Brazilian flag until 1905 when, on passage from Rio de Janeiro to Rio Grande in ballast, she got ashore and was totally lost to the south of the Rio Grande Bar.

A little while later I was in the office of Daniels Bros., the Whitstable barge owners, chatting with Harry Blaxland in his room overlooking the Harbour, when I was admiring a model of their coasting barge *H.K.D.* lost during the war.

"There's another model over here in the corner," he said. "I don't suppose she's of much interest to you though."

It was an old, flush-deck steamer belonging to the last century, the sort of model one of the crew might have made from scraps of wood and nails.

"*Propitious*," I read, with a quick glance, more out of politeness than any-thing. "I wondered what happened to her."

Harry shook his head. "I can't tell you much about her. All I know a relation of mine was supposed to have been washed off her bridge and drowned."

I looked at the model with quickened interest.

"How long ago was that?" I asked.

"Oh, it was well before my time. Fifty or sixty years ago I should think."

"His name wouldn't have been Nichols, by any chance?"

Harry turned round in astonishment. "However did you know that?" he demanded.

"Why, for the simple reason I've just had the story of that very same storm in 1887 from a man who was sailing home from Mexico in a barquentine-rigged barge called the *Nellie S.*"

"Well, that's really remarkable," Harry declared, then after a few moments reflection: "You know, they're wonderful craft, sailing barges. I've had to do with them for a good few years and I've just given up being surprised at the things they get up to."

Chapter Three

WHITSTABLE HARBOUR

We were all taking a keen interest in the barges by the end of August 1948. The big bay windows of "The Nore" overlooked the harbour entrance and as soon as I came back from London each evening the children hurried to tell me of the barges they had seen come in during the day.

"Daddy, daddy," Peter exclaimed one day, rushing to open the door. "We had barges to-day."

"That's good," I said. "How many?"

"Lots and lots. Didn't we, Lil?"

"Two," said Elizabeth, with all the superiority of an eight year old.

"That's right, Daddy. Two whole barges! We seed them in the harbour."

"What were their names?"

This stumped them both. Peter looked at Elizabeth, but she screwed up her nose and turned to Dorothy. "They had funny names," she said. "What were they, Mummy?"

"*Centaur* and *Hydrogen*."

Peter nodded. "M'm. What Mummy said."

After supper I walked round the harbour. Both barges had come in light to load English wheat for London. The *Centaur* flew the gold and purple bob of Francis & Gilders Ltd., of Colchester, a fine, big 150-tonner built by Cann at Harwick in 1895. The skipper had a voice like a fog horn and suffered no inhibitions.

" 'Ewson's the name," he boomed. "H silent as in rhubarb."

Once he had been skipper of the little *Teetotaller*.

"Used to bring fats away from the Sheppey Glue Works. The smell knocked you back a bit at first, but time you'd done a couple o' freights you got used to that.

"We come away from Queenborough one time with barrels stacked on deck. Blowing out o' Sheerness we met a smart-looking yacht a-coming in and a chap sings out:'You're a bloody fine one, you are. Call yourself *Teetotaller*, with a freight o' beer an' all!' "

Bob roared with laughter. He had an insatiable thirst and must have told this story against himself many times in congenial surroundings with great effect. Latterly he had been mate in the *Will Everard* and only recently taken over *Centaur* when Arthur Keeble retired.

"Light barge, the *Centaur's* not what you might call stiff, but one good thing she does keep going. We did Colchester Gravesend the other day in seven hours with the wind no'west. Done a freight every ten days on the average since I took her. We've kept running to Stambridge Mills pretty regular, but this last time we

Whitstable Harbour about 1900.   (Douglas West)

done a freight to Hooker's up at Chatham and went round to London light. Blowed if we don't get orders then to come away down here after Kentish wheat. Proper ol' run around we've had, but we're first on turn and they reckon they'll have us loaded tomorrow."

Just astern of the *Centaur* lay Sully's big auxiliary *Hydrogen* with nobody aboard. It was a pity. I would have liked a chat with Charlie Webb, for it was June 1941 when I last came across the *Hydrogen* tied up for the night off Bona Light, Loch Ness, on her way through the Caledonian Canal to the Clyde, where she worked for the rest of the war. Indeed, she had only just come off the yard and looked to be in magnificent condition for a barge built 1906.

"So she should look good," observed Bob Hewson dryly. "Government's paid for her do-up, and they're a good firm."

September 1948 was a busy month for Whitstable, and we often strolled round the harbour. The Faversham barge *James & Ann* discharged a freight of Canadian wheat under the sucker, then warped across to the Steam Packet Quay and loaded wheat from railway wagons; the sacks were cut and the golden grain poured down burnished chutes into her hold. She was bound up London River.

24

The following day the *Veravia* came in with 750 quarters of Canadian wheat. She was a beautiful sight, having just come off Goldsmith's yard at Grays with new standing rigging and freshly dressed sails. Her crew must have had a great time with the paint pot. She had a black stern frame, white plank ends, light blue badges, and her rudder top, deck winches and hawse holes both fore and aft all painted a brilliant shade of red.

There was quite a fleet of barges in the little harbour. The *Lord Churchill* lay in a quiet berth at the far end, with the shipwrights fitting a new ceiling. Built as a ketch at Littlehampton in 1888, she had unusual lines for a barge, for looking down on her from the quay there was hardly a straight plank anywhere along her sides.

Another Faversham barge, the *Pretoria*, came in with wheat and went straight under the sucker. The *Trilby* came in, too: originally she was owned at Sandwich, so the legend on her stern reads *Trilby, Sandwich*, and underneath, *Port of Dover*.

Most of Daniels' barges were distinctive in their Kentish build, but the *Violet* had Howard, of Maldon, written all over her. She was a typical Essex stackie — beamy, flare-sided and sitting so gracefully in the water as to belie the absence of any great sheer. After most of her life working to East Mills, Colchester, she had latterly been taken over by Daniels Bros. Her skipper was tall Fred Pettitt, an Essex man whom I remembered from pre-war days.

"How's that baby of yours?" I asked.

"Baby?" he queried.

"Why, yes. The one you had aboard *Violet* before the war."

Fred chuckled. "I thought I recognized you," he said as a slow smile spread across his face. "You had the little *June* and passed us that time we come up Swin with me wheeling the pram up and down the deck. There's not much of a babe about him these days. He's twelve now!"

On Saturday, September 18th, 1948, we watched two barges sail into Whitstable; Cremer's *Edith*, with wheelhouse and mizzen and lofty gear reminiscent of old-time boomsail rig, and the *Henry*. *Veravia* had loaded her Kentish wheat and was berthed well out along the East Quay all ready to get away on the next tide. George Barker, her master, was sitting on deck when I strolled round the harbour that evening. He was a Whitstable man, born in one of the three old cottages on the Sea Wall by The Old Neptune that was washed away in the flood of 1897, but his home now was at Ramsgate. During the war he had Samuel West's big auxiliary *Lady Gwynfred*, working on the Clyde and on the West coast of Scotland as far north as the Outer Hebrides.

"And you came from her into *Veravia*, I suppose."

"No, no. I had Goldsmith's motor, the *Goldeve*, till she went to Pollock's at Faversham to be re-powered. I've not been in this one above ten weeks."

"She looks pretty good."

"Just had six weeks do-up at Grays. New standing rigging an' all."

Veravia was quite a different type of barge from the usual run of Whitstable

Whitstable Harbour with *Edith* and *Lord Churchill*.

barges. Built as the *Alarm* by Alfred White at Sittingbourne in 1898 and rebuilt 1925 by Shrubsall at East Greenwich, she had the look of a thoroughbred coaster, with her formidable sheer and wide, unencumbered decks. She took 180 tons to sea on a draft of 7-ft. 1-in. and carried 750 quarters under deck.

"She wants a tidy lot of trimming in the cupboards," George Barker declared and motioned to the small stack right aft. "There's room for another fifteen to sixteen quarters forward on account of her being so fined up aft."

He asked if I had seen Abbie Anderson's *Major* on the slip, as indeed I had. She was a real old-fashioned barge that had come off Government service and lay on the flats pending a decision as to what was to be done with her. During a north-west blow she parted her moorings and drove up athwart the slip. She had to be jacked up at each end and launching ways built under her to get her off, eventually to be hauled up on the self-same slip and extensively re-built, including the complete sheathing of sides and bottom.

The *Major* was built at Harwich in 1897 and spent most of her earlier years in the coasting and cross-channel work. She had the typical small hatches and high rails that were almost bulwarks of a true channel-banger. She, too, was a magnificent barge, though smaller by thirty tons than *Veravia*.

"I had a good look over to-day," said George Barker. "They're making a proper job of her. Putting in a motor, too. Reckon she'd made a good barge, don't you? Anyway, I've spoken for her."

From what I remembered the *Major*'s aft cupboard was so large that she carried a special trimming hatch just forward of the cabin bulkhead. It would be no picnic shovelling grain in *Major*'s hold, but I kept my counsel.

Further up the harbour lay Henry & Lecquire's *Henry*, which I had come across for the first time only a few weeks before running down Swin with sprit well off, making the best of a fair wind. And now as she lay outside the *Trilby* I suddenly realized that here was just the sort of barge we were looking for. *Trilby* was a 115-tonner, yet *Henry* looked quite small by comparison, in spite of a generous beam and hatch coamings some two feet high. But it was her general appearance of well-being that struck me most.

She looked good, with her blue sprit, light blue decks, black rail with gold streak, white quarterboards and bow capping, and olive-green badges both fore and aft on which were carved and painted the owner's blue-white-blue flag.

But there was more to it than just paint. From the appearance of her woodwork and gear she might easily have come straight from the builders, yet I knew from the Mercantile Navy List that she had been built at Grays away back in 1904. She was certainly well looked after.

George Battershall sat on the hatch top, a short, burly man of about seventy. He had a white moustache and wore a cap tilted well forward over his eyes. He watched me for a while as I stood on the quay mentally appraising his barge.

"Reckon she'd suit you all right," he said.

I started in surprise. "I was just admiring her. I saw you under way in the Swin a few weeks back."

"That's right. I know you. You took a photo of us from *Mirosa*. What's more you sung out you'd send us one." Then turning his head away as if talking to somebody at his side: "You never did, though."

"I'm sorry about that," I explained, "but it didn't come out."

George tossed his head and snorted. "That was the time we had timber for Maldon and I didn't go much on it. Getting too old to go climbing about over a stack these days. One thing about wheat, this one'll load her 450 quarters under hatches."

"Is that all she goes?" I asked in some surprise.

"That's all. When the Government finished with her the gov'nor sent her away down to Sittingbourne and had her coamings raised. She carries 450 quarters under hatches now, but she's still only a 100-tonner. That's where they made a big mistake. They should've rose on her. Got the beam for it, too."

"She's fresh off the yard then?"

"Had a twelve month on Sittingbourne Shipbuilding and only come off February 'forty-five. They put in a new keelson and a couple of steel chine keelsons, too. Dunno what they didn't do, what with new stem and windlass bitts, and doubling her all over sides and bottom. Must've cost a mint of money — over three thousand, so I heard."

"No wonder she looks so good," I said, then added ruefully. "Not much chance of getting hold of a barge like her."

27

The last two horses kept for working the grain trucks along the rails to the turntable.

Cole & Lecquire were old-established corn factors at Grays. *Henry* was their last remaining barge and when they had no cargo of their own Francis & Gilders, the Colchester barge-owners, found work for her on the market. Latterly she had been running to Colchester where a handy barge came into her own working under the low bridges up to East Mills.

"I haven't had her for long," George told me. "Only since January. Arthur Bannister — Billy, we used to call him — he was skipper of her from the time she was built right up to the war.

"No, that's the one I came out of," he went on, nodding towards *Veravia*'s towering quarters. "There's a barge if you like."

George Battershall had been in Shrubsall's big coasting barges for nearly twenty years and was more at home down Channel than in the East Anglian work.

"That's probably why I can't seem to settle aboard this barge," he concluded. "I thought she'd be that much lighter, with me turned seventy. I always had to help get *Veravia*'s anchor, but there's one thing about *Henry*. I can stay aft and leave the mate to do the work."

I was becoming more and more convinced that a 100-ton barge was our ideal. The smaller barges like *June* had practically all gone, for they were no longer an economic proposition; even *Henry* was small by postwar standards. *Violet*

Henry during her working life, in the docks.

carried 110 tons, but she looked much larger by reason of her fine lines and lofty gear. And then I remembered the little *Cereal*. She had not been in the harbour recently, and the next time I met Harry Blaxland, of Daniels Bros., I enquired her thinking she might have gone on the yard.

"Didn't you know?" he said. "We sold her for a yacht during the summer. That's why we wanted *Violet* back this side and bought out Francis & Gilders' half share."

He noticed my surprise and went on to explain: "There was nothing really wrong with the *Cereal*, except she'd been a bit unlucky with crew recently. The trouble is you can't do much with a little barge these days, not that you can really blame the chaps clearing out if they can't get a decent living. No, we had a pretty reasonable offer for her from somebody who wanted a small barge, and rather than let her lay about I thought we'd let her go and cast around for something bigger. You weren't interested in her yourself?"

"In a way. You see, we're toying with the idea of going back afloat again."

A look of dismay crept across Harry's face. "Surely you're not thinking of giving up that lovely little house of yours on the Sea Wall?"

I tried to be non-committal. "It all depends if we can find the right barge. The family seems quite keen. I must say I miss the old *June* days."

Harry nodded, and smiled understandingly.

29

George Blake and Bill aboard *P.A.M.*

Chapter Four

LONDON RIVER

Meeting George Blake unexpectedly in the City at the corner of Leadenhall Street one fine morning in October 1948 was just like a sudden whiff of Sea Reach. Unlike the barge skippers of pre-war days who often frequented the ship-brokers' offices around about Water Lane and Lower Thames Street soberly dressed in shore-going blue serge, George wore a sports coat of Harris Tweed, with a flamboyant shirt and tie that failed to match.

Bare-headed, with his shock of fair hair all awry and his ruddy-hued face wreathed in smiles, he brought up all standing in the middle of the pavement oblivious to passers by, stuck out a great paw of a hand and gave me a greeting in imitation of his father, the inimitable Tubby: " 'Ow are yer?"

"George!" I exclaimed. "Whatever brings you here?"

"I thought it was time we had a settlement so I've been to see the gov'nor to get squared up."

"Is your barge up at Maidstone then?" I asked, for I knew the *P.A.M.* usually loaded Kentish ragstone there for the Essex seawalls.

"No, we're round here in the docks with cement. Reckon they'll have us out a-dinner time. Why don't you come round to the Medway with us? We'll be locking out about two o'clock."

"It's not quite as easy as all that," I said with a smile. "We have to work for a living up here in the City, you know."

"Get away with you!" George flung out his arms as if declaiming against the hurrying throng of City workers. "People up here don't know what work is. I reckon they'd get along without you this afternoon. Come and do a bit o' barging for a change."

"M'm. It's an idea. Could you put me ashore at Gravesend if I managed to get the time off?"

"Drop you anywhere you like." Then, raising a hand in valediction, he added: "All right, then. You're shipped!"

☆ ☆ ☆ ☆

After an early lunch I made my way by bus to the Victoria Dock, a great colourful waterway gleaming in the sunshine, with cargo liners berthed on either hand in orderly array, so completely different from the higgledy-piggledy Surrey Commercial Docks, chaotic with timber laden craft as it had been twelve months before when I joined *P.A.M.* for a week at the height of the timber season.

The Victoria Dock has a sedate, almost staid atmosphere, as befits a Royal Dock. *P.A.M.* lay outside the Royal Mail *Beresina* loading on the West Indies

31

General Jackson.

berth. As I clambered down the rope ladder George came on deck in an open-neck shirt, clasping a mug of tea in his hand.

"Have you had grub?" he demanded, and when I nodded, he sang out down the hatch for a cup, which Bill, the mate, clad in his usual singlet and peaked cap, passed up with a wide grin.

George and I sat on the main horse watching the last of the cement being lifted out of the main hold by shore cranes for transhipment to Kingston.

P.A.M. was a husky 130-tonner built at Rochester in 1901 and one of the few remaining barges carrying Kentish ragstone to the lonely sea wall berths on Essex Creeks and Rivers. Re-built at Limehouse after stranding across a gutway during the war, she had been given an auxiliary engine which had proved a mixed blessing.

"We've had it sorted out again recently," said George. "Touch wood, it's going fairly well just now."

"How did you come to be loading cement?" I asked.

"Well, we'd been running pretty regular with stone, but this time word came down to Rochester they'd run short and we'd have to wait a day or two. 'May as well take a run to London and see the Gov'nor,' I said to Bill, but he didn't go much on the idea of kicking around on the buoy. 'Reckon the London and Rochester might find us a freight round to London. Why don't you go and see 'em?'

"That's what I did. Went and had a word with Mr Hayhow and he sent us up to Halling to load cement right away so as to catch a boat in the docks. I reckon it was a rush job, for that cement came aboard so hot I had to go and see the foreman about it else they'd have had all the guts out of our linings."

Outside *P.A.M.* lay the Trading Company's own *Marie May*, a 200-ton auxiliary built 1920 and the last to be launched from Albert Hutson's Maidstone yard. She, too, had brought cement from Halling. Jack Pettit came to the side and sat on the quarter rail. During the war *Marie May* was working on the Clyde and her sails were stowed down below, nailed up in the fore cupboard and while the other auxiliaries had theirs blown out, *Marie May* re-rigged when she came off service and was still carrying the same suit to that very day.

Presently the stevedores, white with cement, clambered out of *P.A.M*'s hold. "All out, skipper."

George got to his feet. "They're finished, Bill," he sang out down the hatch. "If you nip aboard the steamer and get the mate's receipt I'll start her up."

The stevedores were already working on *Marie May*'s cement as we motored out astern. Alongside the Blue Funnel liner *Ulysses* on the far side of the dock lay another sailorman, the big, steel, Clyde-built *Thistle*. A year ago I had seen her towing up the Medway with her steel sprit buckled above the sling. She had been caught out in a violent thunderstorm and although her skipper reckoned she had been struck by lightning, there was no sign of burning, so her owners were unable to claim insurance money.

Ahead of *Thistle* lay the Colchester barge *Lady Helen* flying the attractive gold-and-purple bob of Francis & Gilders.

"She'll be after Australian wheat, I reckon," said George, as we hung about waiting for the bridge to swing so that we could pass through into the Albert Dock.

"She's a nice little barge," I said.

"What her? She's not all that small. Goes about the same as us, I'd say. It's the *Thistle* that makes her look small." George broke off and drew back to quizz me intently. "Here, what's all this in aid of? You're showing a lot of interest in barges all of a sudden. Don't tell me you're going afloat again."

"No, no," I replied hurriedly. "We haven't got that far yet, but we might if we could find the right barge at the right price. And that's not likely."

"There you are, Bill. What did I say? I knew there was something in the wind. You'd better buy our firm's *Water Lily* — the one Bill Kirby used to have. They're supposed to have spent over six thousand quid doing her up at Pin Mill. Got a sixty-six' horse Kelvin and passed Board of Trade. Gov'nor's talking of letting her go for seventy-five hundred."

I smiled at George and shook my head. "Apart from the price, she's too big for our purpose."

"That *Water Lily* won't go more'n 160 tons, not with a motor in."

"Much too big for a yacht barge," I protested. "We'd never manage her ourselves."

George ran his fingers through his hair. "Well, I don't reckon you'll find much these days anything like the size of your little old *June*. I can't recall any, can you, Bill?"

"Only the Kent River Catchment Board's *Llandudno* what's working stone for the seawalls same as us. I don't reckon they'd sell her either."

"We wouldn't want anything quite as small as *June*," I said slowly. "No, my idea is a 100-tonner, and I'm beginning to think a handy corn barge would just about do us."

"Why a corn barge?" asked Bill, leaning with hands folded against the front of the wheelhouse.

"Because most of them are shapely craft with good high hatch coamings, and they're tight and haven't been knocked about by grabs."

"Some of 'em aren't all that good," said Bill out of the corner of his mouth. "You get grain down the bilges and that stinks the barge out. Rare job getting rid of it, too."

The bridge was clear of traffic and began to swing. Working through from the Albert Docks was Cremer's *Nellie*, with the mate on shore running away the light dolly wire.

"What about her?" George demanded as we made our way slowly past.

"More like the size," I replied.

"What about *Sara*? There's a flier for you," said Bill, pointing to a barge alongside the ss *Charlbury*. She was deep-loaded and her stern high in the air. There was nothing prepossessing about her; she was rather drab in fact, with a line of scum along her side, and except for her fine lines aft it was hard to identify her as the most successful racer of recent years.

"She's getting a bit rough now," Bill added. "Everard's don't spend the money on their barges like they used to. There's not the advertisement in 'em for one thing."

There was a whole cluster of craft at the far end of the Albert Dock by the Tidal Basin, and we had to wait our turn to lock out into the river. With all the jostling it was surprising how little damage resulted. The swim-headed lighters were the worst; they rode up over a barge's rail and defied all attempts to ward off with a fender.

Astrild, one of Goldsmith's ironpots, was right in the jumble.

"Look at him. He's at it again," Bill muttered as a young chap leaped aboard a passing motor barge and snatched a turn. "He's a holy terror, is Slim," Bill grinned as the *Astrild* was drawn rapidly into the vortex.

Presently came our turn to lock through, and out in Gallions Reach we found the lightest of easterly breezes. George left the sails stowed and we motored down river on the first of the ebb, coming up with *General Jackson* turning down Barking Reach under mainsail, topsail, mizzen and staysail.

"Is that more your style?" George demanded. "She's one of Eldred Watkins' old Ipswich corn barges. Francis & Gilders bought her just before the war."

She was a nice looking barge with pleasing lines. "What does she go," I asked.

Howlett's *Nellie* in the 'Graveyard' at Gravesend.

"About 125 tons."

"Too big," I said shaking my head.

George grinned and leaned his elbows on the front of the wheel box. "You ain't half particular — not that they'd let her go in a hurry. A handy barge like that's too useful for the East Mills work up at Colchester."

The tall, fair-haired, young skipper of the *General Jackson* greeted us by raising a hand in time-honoured fashion, and as he came about we noticed a pretty, dark-complexioned woman sitting on the cabin top.

"That's the way to go barging," said Bill, with a chuckle. "Take your wife with you same as Stan Yeates there."

"You don't see much of it nowadays," George remarked quietly. "My mother though, she sailed as mate along o' dad for years. What's more, she had both me and Charlie and brought us up aboard right up to the time we had to go to school. It comes hard on a woman though when she's got children to see to as well."

There were barges lying at anchor off Erith, big barges — all of them — waiting for orders, no doubt. In the old days they mostly brought up at Woolwich, where it was handier for the City. Starvation Buoys, they used to call them. Some continued to use them but there was always the chance of touching the ground at low water if there was a bunch of craft moored up together. Latterly the barge skipper kept in touch with his London office by telephone and it was an easy sail on the flood from Erith to any of the docks where a barge usually loaded.

Everard's Yard at Greenhithe had turned over from sailing barges to motor coasters. Apart from a couple of hulks the only barge on the buoy was the 300-ton, mule-rigged *Will Everard*, still sailed by Jim Uglow, who ran away from school time after time until his parents at last left him to his own devices.

There were more barges at Grays. Some lay on Goldsmith's hard and others were at anchor, ironpots mostly, although there was one wooden barge whose freshly tarred sides glistened in the sun.

"Reckon that's *Viper*," said George, but from the other side of the river it was difficult to make out her name. "She's supposed to be for sale, so I heard."

"She looks quite handy," I remarked. "I wonder what they want for her."

George looked at Bill and they both laughed. "She's not exactly small. Goes over two hundred ton in the river. Hasn't got much side but she's a good twenty-two foot beam. There's talk of Goldsmiths selling out all their barges. I wouldn't be surprised either, but I don't reckon their ironpots would be much use to you — not for a yacht barge, anyway."

Another of Goldsmith's big wooden barges was under way in Northfleet Hope: the 180-ton *Thetis*. She had been in Whitstable a short while back with wheat, a great lump of a barge built by Alfred White Senior in 1897, with an eye to carrying a good cargo rather than speed or beauty, yet silhouetted now against the autumn sunset, she took on an air of fairylike grace. It was almost her swan song, for I knew she was being offered at a knockdown price.

So we came to Gravesend. There were more sailing barges than I had expected, but I realized only too well how completely the smaller river barges had disappeared. There was no longer the work in cement, chalk, bricks, coke and rough stuff. It was mostly dock work that kept the sailormen busy, transhipment cargoes to the Kentish and East Anglian outports.

There was the usual cluster of barges off the Ship & Lobster just below Gravesend, and as we rounded up to edge in towards the shore, I could see they were Woods' powder barges, each with a green rail and bright red wale. They were smart, well kept craft and their spars shone in the late afternoon sunshine.

"*Orwell, Gipping, Dreadnought* — why, that's Teddy Dreadnought's old barge," I exclaimed, but George and Bill belonged to a new generation of bargemen and knew her only as one of Goldsmiths' old 'uns.

There were others there too, but the barge that took my eye was the little 95-ton *Ardeer*, baby of the fleet. The last time I had seen her was in the 1938 Barge Match, yet here she was looking every bit as smart.

36

Thetis in St. Clements Reach.

"Just like a yacht," I murmured.

"They keep 'em up well, those powder barges," said George. "I will say that for them. And so they should with their own yard just above the Ship and Lobster. There's usually one or other of them having a do-up. Another thing, most of the time they're just dodging about between here and Holehaven where the liners take on explosives, and it isn't often they're deep-loaded."

"I don't go much on the powder work," Bill remarked, as he hove the boat alongside to put me ashore. "Mustn't leave the barge unattended all the time there's powder aboard. I had enough of that lark up in Stangate during the war."

A red flag flew from *Ardeer*'s mizzen sprit, and as we passed in the boat on our way ashore a face appeared in the cabin hatch.

"Reckon they should look after their barges," Bill went on. "They're weekly men and don't have much else to do."

For a few moments I stood on the river bank outside the Ship & Lobster while Bill sculled back to the *P.A.M.*, which was soon under way again motoring down Gravesend Reach. They would be round in the Medway on the night tide. A motor in a barge was something more than just a modern craze for speed, for with it a man could make a decent living. This was especially so with the *P.A.M.*, for she would lower her gear at Rochester and motor all the way up the Medway to load her stone at Maidstone, thereby saving at least £10 for towage.

As I walked along the wall past the new, war-built slipway and across the lock gates of the Gravesend Canal Basin, where *June* was converted for us away back in 1933, I reflected on the changing nature of barging. A few, like the powder barges, would continue to sail so long as the Port of London Authority's regulations remained in force, but commercially the sailorman was on the way out.

37

Strood.

Chapter Five

THE ROCHESTER BARGES

I was never very conversant with the London River; my real home was the Medway, where I learned my sailing in company with the river barges. Although the Blue Circle Fleet belonging to the Associated Portland Cement Manufacturers had largely been dispersed by the middle 'thirties, Eastwood's little brickies still worked to Lower Halstow and Otterham Quay right up to the war; Solly Brice's blue-railed barges were busy in the mudwork, cement, coal, ballast and anything else that offered; Albert Hutson still looked after the Maidstone work, and there were any number of barges with the red bob and white crescent moon of the London & Rochester Trading Company.

But now the river was quite empty by comparison, and the sight of a barge's red sails showing above the saltings was something of a novelty in the late 'forties when speed had become the keynote. Barges bearing famous names such as *Vigilant* and *Phoenician* were bereft of their lofty gear and fitted with a bit of a wheelhouse and a motor in the stripped out cabin; they and many others had become a pitiable travesty of former days.

I shall never forget the feeling of revulsion at seeing the Rochester *Surrey* after the war sneaking along with a surreptitious air as if ashamed of the lump of stinking metal down below that had made her an undistinguished, humdrum, motor barge, whereas but a few years before I had thrilled to watch her threshing to windward in the Lower Hope, fighting it out with the famous *Veronica*. That was in the last pre-war Thames Barge Match. She was a thing of beauty then, exciting everybody's admiration, but as a full powered motor barge only those few in whom the name evoked a memory of the past would deign a second glance.

It was the sailing barges of the London & Rochester Trading Company I missed most. They were old friends and showed us many a kindness whenever we fetched up together on the buoys at Rochester or Strood, where it was nothing unusual to see a dozen or more swinging to a single buoy off the Oil & Cake Mills.

During the latter part of 1948, when I was puzzling over the virtual disappearance of the Medway sailormen, I made the acquaintance of Mr E. A. Gill, octogenarian and Joint Managing Director of The London & Rochester Trading Company, someone I had long admired as an outstanding personality in the world of barges. He had designed, built and operated barges all his life, and his father before him, for it was in 1858 that George William Gill, ship surveyor, built a patent slip at Chatham Intra, where Doust's Yard now stands. Trading under the name of Gill & Sons, they found plenty of work on the collier brigs and all manner of sailing craft. In addition they built yachts and mahogany

Veravia bearing away round Chatham Point.

paddle-steamers, and barges for the local privately-owned cement works, of which there were over forty in the Medway district, among them, Lee Son and Co., whose *Renown, Monarch* and *Blackfriars* were the first three spritsail barges home in the Thames Barge Match of 1867.

At that time, too, many of the local tradespeople had shares in barges. So keen was the rivalry occasioned by the Barge Matches that in 1875 two men actually challenged each other to a race though neither owned a barge. James Boulden had the *Gundulph* built by G. W. Curel at Strood and named her after his public house close by Rochester Bridge. Sam Burford, who kept the Gibraltar near Chatham Station, had the *Challenger* built by Gill & Sons. The *Gundulph* was first home but was disqualified for hitting the mark boat on the finishing line. *Challenger* easily won the second race loaded. Burford signalized his victory by having the *Conqueror* built, also by Gill & Sons; she and the *Challenger* repeatedly raced against each other in the Barge Matches until his *British Lion* eclipsed them both. Built 1879 at Gill's Chatham Yard, the *British Lion* is credited with a passage of 23 hours from Portsmouth to the Medway.

George William Gill died 1880 but the sons, of whom E. A. Gill was the youngest, carried on the business, and to cope with the growing barge work,

40

Bridge Yard was opened the same year on the site of what later became Lynch's scrap yard. When Curel died 1900 Gill & Sons took over both of his yards at Strood. The Lower Yard carried on with building and repairing, but the building sheds of the Upper Yard were relegated for use as sail loft and store.

Meantime Gill & Sons had acquired a fleet of barges mainly by building for their own account when times were slack, but they also took old barges in part exchange for new, mostly of the small river class, for which there was never any lack of employment.

Then in 1900 came the formation of The London & Rochester Barge Company, incorporating building yards and craft owned by Gill & Sons, while Stewart Bros. & Spencer, the Oil Seed crushers at Strood, afterwards merged in the British Oil and Cake Mills, brought ten barges to the company, including the well known racers of the 'eighties, *Godwit* and *Whimbrel*, also the 100-ton *Louise* specially built for their Dunkirk trade.

Nine barges belonging to T. W. Brooks, of Tovil, also came to the firm, all — except for the 120-ton *Herbert* — Surrey Canal barges such as the *Alfred, Albert* built Rochester 1871, *Edward, Tovil* and *Edmund*, trading to South Bermondsey and conforming to the canal limitations of 17 ft. 9 in. beam.

The yards turned out about eight barges each year, among them the *Centaur*, built 1899 in six weeks at the Chatham Yard and winning the Medway Barge Match the day after her launch. There is a magnificent model of *Centaur* in the Trading Company's head office at Canal Road, Strood.

The London & Rochester Barge Company was now looking after the Medway freightage requirements of the British Oil & Cake Mills, and when George Mason's Ipswich works were taken over they extended their trading operations as far as that port.

During the 1914/18 war many of the barges traded with coal and pitch to North France, but the only war casualty was their iron barge *John Evelyn*, hit by an incendiary bomb in the docks and sustaining damage to the tune of £350.

By 1924 there were sixty barges, numerous lighters and a few motor barges. It was then that the style of The London & Rochester Trading Co. Ltd. was adopted, as brickfields had been acquired at Lower Rainham, bringing more barge work. Several of Groom's Harwich barges were taken over the same year, including the *Alderman* and several older barges since broken up — *New Trader, Aline, Eastwood* and the old *Sextus* that was found to have no fewer than seven skins.

The *Cabby* was launched from the Lower Yard in 1928, the last sea-going wooden barge ever to be built. She raced the same year in the Coasting Class and later had an auxiliary engine installed. During the month of June 1947 she loaded four freights of coal away from Boston for the South.

In 1929 came amalgamation with the Maidstone owner, Albert Hutson, bringing to the company twenty sailormen, including the *Albert*, winner of the 1910 Medway Match, *Mousmé, Rosmé* and yet another famous racer — the *Surrey*.

41

In 1932 seven barges of the Owen Parry Colchester branch of the British Oil & Cake Mills were taken over, including the *King, Sirdar* and the well known *Queen*, winner of the Bowsprit Class in the 1935 and 1936 Medway Matches.

The fleet reached its peak during the early 'thirties, totalling some 120 sailing barges. Indeed, The London & Rochester Trading Company at that time was reputed to be the largest single purchaser of sail canvas in the world. At the outbreak of war in 1939 the Trading Company owned 160 craft — barges, motor barges, lighters and motor coasters. The Government requisitioned 108, mostly for mine watching and powder work, and thirteen lighters were converted to Landing Craft for the Normandy invasion. Of Covington's barges taken over, *Sam Weller* finished her days in the powder work; *Chieftain* was towed under by a powerful Government tug and was lost in the Barrow Deep. Only the *Thistle* was still trading in the summer of 1948.

Two barges took part in the Dunkirk evacuation; the *Pudge* was in tow with two others when the tug put up a magnetic mine, and she remained afloat to pick up survivors, while *Thyra* brought off 250 soldiers from the beaches.

Ten auxiliaries went to work on the Clyde, where both the *Knowles* and *Alderman* were marine casualties. *Enchantress* was lost in the blitz on the London docks when Rank's Mill fell on top of her. *Rosmé* was mined just above the Maplin Spit, while a German FW 190 brought down in the Medway accounted for the *Wouldham Court, Herbert* and *Kingfisher* as they lay together on the lower mooring off Strood Dock.

But far more barges were lost through lack of attention on Government service than through enemy action. Laying to their moorings year after year, sails gradually blew out, while bottoms grew more and more foul and eventually picked up the worm. It was only by comparison with barges trading throughout the war that Maurice Gill, then Chairman of the company, was able to prove at the coming-off survey that worm was not endemic in barges cleaned off from time to time and allowed to dry out. As a result of the depredations made by the worm, coupled with the shortage of skilled shipwrights and the difficulty of replacing gear, the Company's fleet of sailing barges dwindled. Some were broken up for their ironwork and bottom planking, as were the *Aline* and *U.V.W.* by Dutchy Day when I visited Whitewall Creek towards the end of 1948.

Out on the mudflats, moored up alongside each other in the middle of the creek, with their spars still standing, lay a great concourse of barges whose names evoked memories of better days: *Dorothea, Maysie, Mayor, Dawn, Foxhound, Fred, Raven, Greta, Sir Richard* and *Gleaner*. These were some of the barges that had come off Government service in bad repair, but not so far gone that they could not be put back into service should room be found on the yard. It was unlikely though, that many would sail again.

In the immediate postwar years The London & Rochester Trading Company mustered seven auxiliary barges, *Cabby, Marie May, Pudge, Thyra, Alan, Scone* and *Vera*. Of the sailormen, they were reduced to a mere handful: *Sirdar, Thistle, Federation, East Anglia, The Brownie, George & Eliza, Queen* and *Squawk*.

On the buoy at Strood, June 1938: *Whimbrel, The Brownie, King, Westall, William Cleverley, Sunrise, Foxhound, George & Eliza, Victa, Maysie,* and *Quarry.* (Ray Crayshay)

There was the *Arrow*, too, built by Gill & Sons in 1897 as the result of collaboration in design between E. A. Gill and W. L. Wyllie, the marine artist. She had a long, shallow hull, with a fined-up run after the fashion of the popular Gillingham sailing punt in which Mr. and Mrs. Wyllie were particularly interested. But the *Arrow* never achieved the success in the Barge Matches her somewhat revolutionary lines appeared to suggest. 'Schoolmaster' West, who trained so many youngsters, had her for many years and we came across him when we lay for weather in *June* under Shotley. During the war *Arrow* acted as a tender to the mine-watching flotilla in the estuary. She was all right until deep-loaded with a freight of coal after coming off service, when she all but sank. Eventually she was chartered to the Thames Barge Sailing Club at a nominal figure for weekend cruising.

Imperial had also been trading under sail since the war until her skipper removed the middle tie beam whilst loading logs in the Surrey Commercial Docks; she strained and opened up so badly that she went on the yard for repairs

43

and conversion to a full-powered motor barge, a fate that was liable to befall any barge needing more than the normal refit. Whereas a sailorman might be two or three days on the trip round from London to Maidstone and incur a towage bill of £10 or more, the motor barge needs but a couple of tides and requires no tug. It is not surprising that sailormen dropped out of the Maidstone work.

Yet even the motor barges have their troubles and the 140-ton *Albert*, built at Maidstone in 1906 by Albert Hutson & Co., came to grief on the night of October 15th 1948. I remember her best one lovely summer morning sailing up Short Reach, half-shrouded in mist. She had been a fast barge in her time, with an impressive racing record both before and after the war. Common to all the Maidstone barges, she emerged from her wartime powder work as a full powered motor barge and was on passage from the docks with seventy tons of coir yarn and mats when she stranded athwart the wreck of the pilot cutter *River Thames* on the Grain Spit during a heavy rain squall. *Albert* broke up during the easterly gales and was eventually dispersed.

Another casualty was the *East Anglia*, built at the Lower Yard in 1908 to the special requirements of the Colchester East Mills work. She was designed with moderate sheer and low windlass bit heads to carry 130 tons on an easy draft especially for working up through the bridges and was on time charter to Messrs. E. Marriage & Son Ltd. right up to 1926. *East Anglia* was actually on passage to East Mills when she fouled the anchored auxiliary barge *Glenway* off Yantlet at about 5.30 a.m. December 10 1948. They started to apologize but the skipper of *Glenway* told them to watch out as she looked to be sinking. Presumably *Glenway*'s anchor chain must have cut through her chine for she turned right over and sank. They raised her the following Monday and placed her ashore at Rosherville just above Gravesend, but Maurice Gill told me at the time it was extremely doubtful whether she would be worth repairing.

I had learned enough to know the way things had gone with sailing barges since the war. The London & Rochester Trading Company had plenty of other irons in the fire; fruit growing had followed bricks and they were expanding their fleet of handy motor coasters. The 350-ton *Crescence* preserved the link with the sailorman's familiar red bob and the white crescent moon after the Latin *crescere*. Thereafter the motor coasters run through the alphabet, each ending with the suffix - *ence*. Painted a distinctive golden-brown, *Dominence*, *Eminence, Faience* and *Gardience* were only the forerunners of a considerable fleet of attractive modern coasting vessels.

Strangely enough, even as late as the winter 1948/9 there was still plenty of work about for sailing barges to and from the docks, where a sailorman was well able to stand the risk of demurrage. It was then that rumour had it that The London & Rochester Trading Company was about to buy up Goldsmith's fleet of ironpots. I asked Mr Gill if there was any substance in it, but hard of hearing at the best of times, he failed somehow or other to take in my question and adroitly steered the conversation away from the subject.

For all that, I thought I detected a twinkle in his eye.

44

Chapter Six

OTTERHAM AND LOWER HALSTOW

I had learned enough of the Rochester barges to get a fair idea of what to expect in the little village outports at Otterham Quay and Lower Halstow which I had known for twenty years as the haunt of Eastwood's handy little brickies, mostly named after birds, counties and the Greek alphabet.

One Sunday morning early in January 1949 I walked from Gillingham along the sea wall past Grange and the remains of the old Otterham barge *Dick Turpin* that came with dung one high tide setting her chine on the edge of the quay and so damaged herself as to finish up there; on past Bloor's farm wharf where we berthed *June* for our wedding reception away back in 1933. It was unused in those days and overgrown with grass but Shaw's of Kent (Rainham) Ltd. had somewhat incongruously established a ship breaking yard there, with the *Virocca*, reputedly about the best of Goldsmiths' ironpots, to carry away their scrap.

Just beyond lay the Rainham Cement works, derelict these thirty years in spite of its modern appearance and white, cement-encrusted walls and window sills. Goldsmiths' barges used to trade here, sailing up Half Acre Creek towards Motney Hill, and as soon as the tide served standing in over the flats where a barrel on a pole served as a mark on one of the muddy saltings.

But there was stark tragedy lurking even in these sheltered waters for in 1925 Goldsmiths' *Haughty Belle* and *Gloria* came in deep-loaded from Stoke Mud-hole and brought up at the back of the hill. That night it came on to blow hard and next morning one of Knight's tugs was the first to see the mast and sprit of the *Gloria* under Oakham Ness, where she had dragged anchor and sunk. Both skipper and mate were drowned. Possibly a hatch cloth had lifted and she had swamped down, for the *Gloria* was as flat as a stick. So was the *Haughty Belle*, for she was hogged all out of shape since her racing days but she came through and her crew knew nothing of the sinking of the *Gloria*.

From Lower Rainham I struck out across the brickfields to Otterham Creek where the *Crouch Belle* lay hulked, broad in the beam, flush-decked and incredibly square ended; the only barge built at Hullbridge in living memory. She must have carried a wonderful stack in her time; although her trading days were finished the hull looked to be in fair condition.

Another old-timer being broken up was Storr's *Kent*, well known to my old friend Josh Francis of the Colchester barge-owning firm of Francis & Gilders Ltd. He wrote:

> "Messrs. Storr's bobs were exactly like ours, Orange and Purple. I copied this when I commenced barge owning as the colours appealed to me. You may not be aware that I was Skipper of two of Storr's barges, *Bessie Taylor*

and *Kent* for a few years, and left the latter barge to go Skipper of their tug *Medway.*

Old Gerrard Storr was a dear old chap to work for, but usually expected almost impossible things to be done, and if not done, he was not such a dear old chap. It was a busy life in those barges, but we had two men besides the Skipper — all of us weekly (not on the share). I well remember the last seven weeks I had the *Kent* when we did fourteen freights; unloading general cargo for a wholesale grocer at Maidstone on Monday, loaded Hops on Tuesday, up to West Kent Wharf, Hop Exchange, above London Bridge, and unload ready to load General cargo on Saturday. When one considers it was gear flat down both in London and on the Medway, it was hard work and not much sleep.

We just could not help doing those fourteen freights as winds were so favourable to us *and* if we were not at Rochester to tow to Maidstone Sunday afternoon or early Monday morning's tide, one of Storr's tugs ran down from Chatham as far as Sheerness, if required, to get us alongside Albion Wharf for six o'clock start for unloading."

A little higher up lay the Sittingbourne barge *Maria* owned by Andrews and Ellis and discharging ballast. This was the only sign of activity on the water; although Eastwood's brickfields beyond the road was still working with soil brought from Bobbing on the Sheerness Road barges were no longer required. Indeed Eastwood's barge yard at Otterham Quay was offered for sale by auction in July 1946, together with a vast accumulation of gear of all description. The Catalogue, comprising 353 lots, is a fascinating document. Here are a few taken at random:

Lot   34 Approx. ½-cwt. of cowhair.
Lot   59 Tree nail mute and 3-in. reemer.
Lot 125 New 11½-in. steel mast case with winch and handles complete.
Lot 183 Four leeboard crabs and one brail crab.
Lot 207 Thirteen runner plates, nine 12-in. rudder head bands, and twenty-six iron dogs.
Lot 261 Fifteen vang chains with blocks attached, three runner chains with hooks, bar for funnel bending.
Lot 306 Three sprit spars each 51-ft. long (10-in. middle diameter).

Lots 1 to 6 comprised the sailing barges *Bedford, Cheshire, Mid Kent, Iota, Alpha* and *Theta* but failed to reach their reserve, although the 95-ton *Iota* was subsequently bought by Geoffrey Dutson for conversion to a yacht.

A crowd of barges lay against the sea wall; *Alpha* was hulked and so was the *Scud* which I had last seen before the war sailing up to Conyer; *Gamma, Coot* and *Heron* were obviously finished; *Kappa* had been sold but never taken away. She must have fetched away thousands of tons of sand from the Leigh foreshore in her time, and now she lay sunk; so too were *Mid Kent* and *Theta*, though *Theta* still had her spars on board. Some of the barges had a small deck house aft

46

Lower Halstow.

from mine-watching days. And others were too far gone to identify. They had all been handy barges carrying their thirty-five to forty thousand bricks from the Kentish brickfields to the London depots. And now road transport direct to the building sites had superseded them. The war had only hastened the inevitable.

Only the *Cumberland* still floated at the quay; she had been stripped of all her gear and there was talk of her towing away to Chiswick for a house-boat.

Otterham Creek in the old days was a busy place. A. J. Knight owned the Rainham brick fields along the south bank and a fleet of over thirty barges, some of them real old-timers like the *Providence* built Faversham 1826, and the *Caroline* built Aylesford 1825, but they also had barges from their own Acorn Yard at Rochester; the *Dawn* built 1896; *Twilight* and *Morning* 1898; *Afternoon* 1901; *Evening* 1903. Knight sold out to The London & Rochester Trading Company in 1924 who continued to work the brick field for a few years until the top soil gave out.

Traces of the cement works still stood on the opposite bank although derelict and overgrown. Bowker & Kings' *The Diamond* and *The Monarch* brought in the coke, and Wakeley Brothers of Rainham supplied the chalk, piped from the chalk hole near Bloor Lane. They had two barges of their own built by Gill in the early 'nineties named *Norrab* and *Noclaf*, backslang versions of Barron's Falcon Cement Works. *Noclaf* was sold away but *Norrab* still worked to Otterham right up to the First World War.

There were several small local owners in those early days. Thomas (Rummy) Dennis had the *Rainham*. George (Bounce) Clarke had the *Stanley* as well as the public house The Three Sisters. Jimmy Hubbard owned a small brick field above the cement works and used Otterham Quay for loading his Milton-built *William*

Stone and the delightfully named trio: *Honest Boy, Dick Turpin* and *Little Linnet*, all built by Shrubsall in the creek at Overshore where the Hulk of the *Mid Kent* lies.

The *Honest Girl* and the *Honest Boy* were built alongside each other in 1873, the latter for Charlie Eltham, another small brickmaker at Otterham. *Honest Girl* was sold away to Covington's, but her brother got mixed up with firing practice off Shoebury and finished up with a shell through the side.

Horace Shrubsall built for local owners on Wakeley's land at Overshore from the 'sixties until the turn of the century. The Wakeley family took most of them for their own work; *Kate Emily* 1867; the stumpy *Melody* 1879; the little tiller-steering *Richmond* 1876, which was Arthur Hawke's first barge and loaded many a stack from Reculver Beach and Herne Bay; *Unity* 1897; *Macklands* 1899; named after William Wakeley's house at Rainham. *Utility* was their last barge and the only one Wakeley built themselves at Overshore. Bob Barnes stayed on as foreman shipwright after the yard was sold to the Gravesend barge owners Samuel West and built the little stumpy *Nell Gwynn* in 1907. She was the last of the Otterham-built barges; Samuel West tried several times to slip their *Undaunted* for repairs but found the ways too steep and eventually moved away.

Wakeley Bros. were big people when barges were in their heyday. Not only did they own three brickfields at Overshore and red brick and tile works at Twinney, but were also hay and straw and general farm merchants. At one time they owned or had on charter over forty barges, many of them running bricks to Durham Wharf, Chelsea, and Honduras Wharf, Bankside, where the brothers conducted a vast brick selling agency covering the whole of London. Percy Wakeley's *Gertrude May* was coasting down to Great Yarmouth and beyond; others were working to the farms on the Medway Creeks and all round the Isle of Sheppey and the North Kent coast as far as Margate.

Wakeley's brick making finished up at the end of the First War, but there were a few barges still flying their red, white and blue bob until 1939, and although coming to the end of their working life they were always smartly turned out; royal blue rails with gilt streak and scrollwork, green transom, varnished sprit and any amount of graining. Their *Utility* was the last. She came off mine-spotting very much the worse for wear and never worked again.

Wakeley Bros. (Rainham) Ltd. still had considerable farming connections. Their store at Rainham had timber worked into it from the old barge building sheds at Overshore, and Arthur Hawkes who had been in nearly every one of Wakeleys' barges during his sixty-seven years with the firm had vivid recollections of the old days when barges turned away up Otterham Creek, where now all is mud with but a narrow, winding gut.

Somewhat saddened, I tramped over the hill and through the village of Upchurch, resisting the lure of the little-used tracks to Ham Green and Twinney, and presently arrived at Lower Halstow, where the old church stands at the head of the creek, with the fresh water stream from which generations of bargemen

Westmorland at Lower Halstow with *First Attempt* beyond.

have filled their water breakers and run the risk of typhus. Eastwoods' brickfields were working at Lower Halstow but there was nothing like the great line of barges berthed alongside the quay as in the days before the war.

The *Northampton* lay there with hatches uncovered, and mast and sprit flat on deck. Her paintwork was still good and at first glance there seemed to be little wrong with her. But the starboard rail was splintered amidships; then I remembered she had sunk in May 1947 off Jenningtree Point in the Thames. Coal-laden at the time, she had apparently pricked herself on her own anchor and leaked down, while the rail was probably damaged by the wires of the P.L.A. wreck lifting lighter. She was brought back to Lower Halstow and had lain there ever since, with no chance of ever fitting out again.

Just ahead of her was Eastwood's last remaining fully-rigged barge, the 100-ton *Westmoreland*, built by Alfred White at Conyer in 1900, and a regular entry in the Barge Matches. She was still well kept up and painted after the traditional Eastwoods' fashion of royal blue rails with yellow streak, green stern with white tuck, brown quarter boards, rudder head and plank ends picked out in red. She was no longer loading bricks away from Lower Halstow, but brought in an occasional freight of coal or coke, or Leigh sand which was no longer dug with the traditional fly tool against a 5/- licence from the Salvation Army, but by the new-fangled dredger *Prittlewell*. Eastwoods retained the *Westmoreland* more out of sentiment than for any other reason, for they had little work to warrant a barge, and the skipper filled in his time in the brick fields.

But there was one other barge working out of Lower Halstow, the *Durham*, also from White's Yard at Conyer, and rigged out with a small half-sprit and mizzen. She only made a passage of a few hundred yards out on the flats to load her mud for brick making, a messy job yet one that once gave employment to a whole fleet of barges.

Eastwoods started brick making here in the 'eighties, buying up John Wood's business together with a small barge yard and a few barges. Eastwoods had been largely lime and cement merchants; now they wanted a fleet of barges for their bricks, and brought Ambrose Letley from Curel's at Strood to build for them. *Grebe* was his first in 1890, built in the open, half way along the wharf, and launched down temporary ways laid on a drawdock long since gone. He built a whole succession of sharp-bowed little barges named after birds; *Lapwing*, *Landrail*, *Kestrel* and so on. His trade mark took the form of a single riband right across the stern, with the name on one side of the stern post and port of registry on the other, and in each of the two swallow-tail flies was carved a six-pointed star.

Ambrose Letley gave up in 1898. Alex Styles, then in his early twenties, was offered the job of foreman shipwright, but after a short spell, during which he was subjected to criticism by the ship's husband, he told the manager that he preferred to go back to his tools. The job was advertised and Archie White came from Conyer where, with brother Alfred, he had been turning out barges for Eastwoods cheaper than Ambrose could build at Halstow. So it was that Ambrose Letley framed up the *Theta*, Alex Styles sheered up the frames and did the wales and top, while Archie White finished her off and launched her in 1898.

The White family — Alfred White Senior and his son Ernie at Sittingbourne, and his two sons Alfred and Archie at Conyer — had a name for building a good sound barge, full-ended but nicely lined up aft to a shallow stern frame, giving a good cargo carrier with a surprising turn of speed as with the famous *Sara*. Archie White built five county class barges at Halstow, rather larger than most of the birds, then his wife, who was a London girl, began to find Halstow lonely, and persuaded him to accept a seven year's agreement to build for Goldsmiths at Grays. Once again Alex Styles took over the yard, finished off the pretty little *Devon* and built the *Norfolk*.

Meantime Archie White had taken a number of the local shipwrights with him to Grays, where he eventually built the *Henry* for Cole & Lecquire. Faced with the impossibility of getting more men locally Eastwoods took over Shrubsall's yard at the head of Milton Creek, Sittingbourne, and Alex Styles went on to build a whole sequence of county class barges, inclining towards White's shape of hull, but conforming to certain of Ambrose Letley's well tried methods of construction. By 1907 Eastwoods had a fleet of some fifty barges. They finished building at Sittingbourne with the *Hereford* and *Wiltshire* but presently found the need of another yard to maintain their craft. At first they considered moving to Conyer but Alex Styles would have nothing to do with it, for he had a young family at school. Eastwoods then turned towards Halstow again until Alex Styles bethought of Eastwoods' own piece of freehold land behind the houses at the head of Otterham Creek and found he could manage to work in a

Otterham Creek: *Theta* and *Curlew*.

couple of sheds. So it was in 1912 Eastwoods' barge yard opened up at Otterham. No barges were built there but many were hauled out for major repairs, and Alex Styles was kept busy right down to his retirement in 1940. His last job was to prepare the catalogue for the Auction Sale after the war.

He built barges in their heyday, handy little workaday craft whose chief attraction lay in their absolute fitness for their job. They had to be kept flat to comply with the restrictions imposed by the Regent and Surrey Canals, yet somehow he contrived to give them shape and individuality. The pity of it is that so few survived the war. Just beyond the point at Lower Halstow, though, I found four derelict hulls; the Letley-built *Whaup*; the White-built *O.L.S.*; Conyer-built *Surrey*; and the *Devon*, prettiest little barge of them all, laid down by Archie White and finished off by Alex Styles. She would have made a lovely little yacht, but it was not to be. She was too far gone — finished. To anyone, though, who knows something of their story, those four old barges were the epitome of local barge history.

Lower Halstow was quiet in 1949 and very little used. Barges no longer brought in the foul-smelling London household rubbish, commonly known as "rough stuff", to smoulder and breed rats. The great mounds were covered in grass and the atmosphere was pleasant and salubrious. Yet I missed the dozen or more barges that were usually to be found there before the war when Eastwoods still had a fleet of some thirty brickies, each with EASTWOODS BRICK MAKERS painted on her sails.

Eastwoods had brick fields, too, at Conyer, off the East Swale, where our own little barge *June* finished up. The dock at the head of the creek served the Teynham works and the *Bedford* loaded the last freight of bricks late 1939, since when the narrow, winding gut has so silted up that it is doubtful whether a

51

loaded barge could poke up that far. The larger and more modern works lay below the village and used Butterfly Wharf at the mouth of Conyer Creek. But sailing barges were gone from there, too. The *Kestrel* was having a new stem piece fitted but her gear had been placed ashore and she was destined to end her days in the mudwork, which entailed so short a trip that sails were superfluous.

The only other craft at Butterfly Wharf was the Milton-owned motor barge *Victory*... and the derelict *Band of Hope* whose rotting hull shewed no fewer than four skins.

Conyer Creek had become a haven for converted barges. At the head of the dock that once served the Beehive Cement Works as well as the Teynham brick fields, *Waveney* and *Mermaid* had their permanent moorings, complete with gardens and all shore amenities. They were probably the best of the pre-war conversions.

Waveney came from Paul's Ipswich fleet of grain barges and was fitted out as a most comfortable yacht and home by Anderson, Rigden and Perkins at Whitstable in 1933. *Mermaid* was the famous Maldon barge which Billy Austin sailed for many years. She used to work to James Lasts's own wharf at Heybridge with cement and chalk from above bridges in the Medway, as well as with flints from Gillingham, Hoo and Oare. She was sold just before the war for £240 and George Gates made a yacht of her at White's old yard behind The Ship at Conyer.

Dear old George was the ideal man for the job. Not only had he been apprenticed to Alfred White and helped to build the *Joy* and *Annie Byford* in 1914, the last barges ever launched at Conyer, but he had the true craftsman's artistic soul and his ingenuity knew no bounds. Working with Eileen Flint, the owner's wife, who was an interior decorator, he made a wonderful job of the *Mermaid*.

In *June*'s old berth astern of *Mermaid* lay the *Henry & Jabez*. She was one of Wills & Packham's old barges, named after the partners Henry Packham and Jabez Wills and sank after colliding with the Queenborough light. She was a post-war conversion, with *June*'s skylights and companion hatch built in her cabin top. *June* herself lay a complete wreck in a backwater, stripped of all gear and everything useful. That much I knew, but was amazed to find a barge could fall to pieces in so short a time. There was a great hole in her bows which may or may not have been made intentionally, but what really apalled me was the state of her timber tops. The covering boards were far from perfect when we had her; underneath though, there was hardly a sound frame the whole length of her sides. As a demonstration of the cumulative effects of deck leaks and sheer old age, it was most convincing, and the impact on me was such that I came away profoundly thankful we had decided against fitting out *June* at the end of the war. Without the slightest doubt we would have broken our hearts.

Quite close to the wreck of *June* was the partly converted Faversham barge *John & Mary*, whose owner, D. H. Clark, better known as Nobby, was busily engaged in fitting out Colonel McFee's *Harold* and making a colourful job in red and green. There were other barges in the creek. The *Pall Mall* had spent most of the war water-logged in the S.W. India Dock, but B. F. W. Bessemer, who bought her for £1,000, was fitting her out again. Then there was the *George* that formerly belonged to Colonal Bingham; the *Colne* that was sunk in collision at Blackwall in 1939; and the Maldon *Sunbeam*, all three stripped down and turned into houseboats.

Just below White's old yard was the little *Glasgow*, of much the same size as *June*, and converted at the beginning of the war. Bunny Thorpe was fitting her out with the aid of *June*'s old spars and a mainsail bought for £40 from Whitstable's *Thomas & Frances*.

Yet another barge was the *Golden Fleece* from Francis & Gilders' fleet. Mr. and Mrs Barras had been living on board for some time and their timber licence had just come through. The owner was not a young man, nevertheless he went mate in *Cambria* to get used to the ways of a barge until he broke a leg in Ipswich Dock. With an inventor's fertile brain, he was tackling the conversion in a cheerful, practical manner.

At that time early in 1949, barges were still enjoying a considerable vogue as yachts and homes. It was interesting to see so many of all types and sizes lying in the creek, but I was not enamoured of any of them. Perhaps it was seeing *June* as a wreck that made me sceptical of pre-war conversions, for most of them were getting on in years and had suffered much the same wartime neglect. Mere age is no criterion, but any wooden barge needs decks to be dressed from time to time and the sides cleaned off and tarred to keep the weather out. As for those converted since the war, very few would stand a really thorough survey; they had either come off Government service very much the worse for wear, or else worked out and barely worth all the time and money required to make a yacht of them.

I was becoming more and more convinced that we had to search for our own barge in the dry trades, and that meant paying a full price for anything really good.

"But we'd never afford it, surely," Dorothy declared when I got back that night. "I don't know what trading barges go for these days, but if *Glasgow* is worth £2,400..."

"Well," I said. "The more we spend on the barge, the less we'll have to pay for the conversion. A thousand pounds for the barge and another thousand pounds for the conversion, that's my idea."

Dorothy was still sceptical. "Didn't I hear they wanted three thousand for *Pall Mall*?"

I nodded. "But you see we wouldn't want an engine for one thing, and if we start off with the right barge we shouldn't need to line out the hold or raise the coamings. I still think we'd manage it, even at to-day's prices. We'd have the galley lockers and dresser all built in, and bunks and wardrobes and dressing tables, too. As for the rest — " I paused to look around our land-based lounge — "Well, all this lot came out of *June*'s saloon — tables, chairs, carpet and so on. If it suited one barge, surely it would do for any other."

Dorothy was not altogether convinced. "M'm," she said non-committedly. "We'll see."

53

Chapter Seven

LADY OF THE LEA

By now the children were taking a lively interest in my wanderings and when I announced one Saturday that I was going to Sittingbourne and would like sandwiches Elizabeth decided to come too.

"But you don't want to look at a lot of old barges," I said.

"Yes, I do," she protested. "I like barges and we're going to live on one, aren't we, Peter? Besides," she added, with all the irrelevance of her sex: "I like picnics."

So we took the train together to Sittingbourne and walked across the waste ground past the head of Milton Creek, where Alex Styles followed on with Shrubsall's Yard and built for Eastwoods. It was low tide. There were a few derelict barges against the near bank, so old that no one remembers their names, and the creek itself was all mud of a particularly noisome type that made Elizabeth screw up her nose.

"What a pong!" she exclaimed.

"I don't think that's very ladylike," I said.

"And I don't think that's very nice mud, either," she replied.

As a lover of the East Coast creeks and saltings, I do not dislike mud in the normal way, for a barge is never so happy as when she sits in a soft mud berth, but Milton Creek certainly smells. Indeed if it were not for the barging associations the creek would be a most unpleasant spot, lined with derelict brick fields and cement works and great dumps of rat-ridden garbage. Mercifully, nature has hidden the worst with scrub and vegetation, but there was no disguising the foulness of the mud. Not only did it turn white paint yellow, but it was even too much for ship's worm, as I saw for myself with the *Five Sisters* that spent the war as an ammunition barge in Stangate Creek and picked up the worm in her bottom. She lay in Milton Creek for six months before Tom Larkin had her surveyed by Harry Beale who pronounced the worm to be dead, which I could hardly credit until I saw the barge for myself hauled out on Perkin's slip at Whitstable.

I explained all this to Elizabeth. She had seen worm in old bits of timber washed up on the beach from time to time, which I had split up for firewood. There is nothing more loathsome and revolting than a ship worm, and even Elizabeth took a more kindly view of mud that could wipe out such a creature.

Time was when the creek was full of barges. Smeed, Dean and Co. alone had over one hundred at the turn of the century; Charles Burley, Wills & Packham and Charles Wood each owned another forty, all working in the cement and brick and kindred trades. They had their own yards, and there were many others besides. Now, the sole local owners were Andrews and Ellis, who owned half-a-

Lady of the Lea at Crown Quay, Sittingbourne.

dozen barges between them, while George Andrews had an interest in the barge yard of the Sittingbourne Ship Building Co. Ltd., which incorporated the building sheds of Wills & Packham, the biggest of its kind on the coast. They no longer built barges, but undertook major repair work. Cole & Lecquire's little *Henry* was rebuilt there towards the end of the war; Sully's *Trilby* was lengthened, widened and 'rose-upon' to emerge as a full-powered motor vessel; and the well known racing barge *Phoenician* was repaired after being blitzed and well nigh destroyed at Felixstowe.

Shrubsall's *Verona* lay at Sittingbourne eighteen months re-building after coming off Government service, and I saw her in the Spring of 1948 newly fitted out with bowsprit and a complete new suit of sails, waiting for a slant out of Milton Creek. She went away to the Colne for a freight of sand to see how she behaved before going back into the dry trades but she made more water than the pumps could cope with and her crew had to put her on the mud at Brightling-sea and again at Burnham. She took up after that, and Francis & Gilders, who worked Shrubsall's barges on a percentage basis, soon had her back in their own grain work.

And now *Verona* was on the yard again with damage sustained in the docks. As if that was not enough, on the trip round, she got athwart Kingsferry Bridge and the repair bill was likely to amount to some two thousand pounds, so it was said. She was a lovely looking barge, built at Shrubsall's own yard at East Greenwich in 1904 with an eye to racing.

The London & Rochester Trading Co.'s *King* was having a 44 h.p. Kelvin Diesel installed, and hauled out in Wills & Packham's old shed was the *Vicunia*, jointly owned by Daniels Bros. and George Andrews & Son. She had been trading as an auxiliary since 1940, and Elizabeth, who had seen her in Whitstable Harbour from time to time, was intrigued at finding her under cover.

"What about her mast?" she asked. "It'll stick up through the roof."

"I'm afraid there won't be a mast any more," I replied. "You see they're putting two engines in and turning her into a motor barge."

"What, no sails?" she exclaimed scornfully. "I don't think much of that!"

Neither did I and it was the *Verona* on the blocks that took my fancy, for she was still without a motor. A barge re-built, as she was, with sides and bottom doubled and new keelsons would be good for another twenty years at least. In the old days it was nothing to 'put a barge in a box', and some acquired several skins in the course of a lifetime. But to-day, it was an expensive business running into two or three thousand pounds and only a trading barge of some 150 tons was worth the expense.

Lying on the flats off the yard was a miscellaneous collection of old craft: Horlock's *Dorothy* and Stone's *Klondyke* and most interesting of all, the hulk of the *Arcades*, built here at Sittingbourne as the *Olive Mary* in 1921 by Wills & Packham. She was sunk in collision with a Buckie drifter in 1936 whilst towing into Gorleston laden with linseed cake, whereupon Alfred Sully bought out the other owners and had her re-built as an auxiliary. She was trading right through the war, but on passage from Colchester to Ridham Dock with a stack of straw June 1947 she suddenly went on fire. And now she lay off the yard where she was built, with enough of her still remaining to give some idea of what a magnificent composite barge she must have been.

There was talk of repairing her at one time, and Alfred Sully was reputed to have asked George Andrews, his partner in the barge, whether it was possible to re-build. George Andrews said The Sittingbourne Ship Building Company would do the job for £7,000 the half share.

"That they won't!" replied old Alfred. At least that is what a barge skipper told me, and *Arcades* still lay on the flats.

As we walked through the gates of the barge yard to Crown Quay, I remarked to Elizabeth: "You remember the *Thomas & Frances*?"

This was the little barge that lay in Whitstable Harbour for use as a block-ship in case of emergency, an 80-ton barge with unusually high hatch coamings.

"I remember," said Elizabeth. "The one in the corner those boys used to play on."

I nodded. "Well, she was built here in 1878."

"Was she?" Elizabeth made a face and looked around the deserted, grass-grown wharf which must have been a very different place when Spencelaugh was building and millions upon millions of bricks were shipped away from here.

"Did you see her then?" she added.

I shook my head. "I'm not quite so old as that, but Grandpa was a little boy then."

"Was he? That *must* have been a long, long time ago." Then her face lit up. "I know. Let's have our lunch."

I sat on a log and brought out the sandwiches. There was a barge lying alongside the quay. As it was low water I could only see her gear and Elizabeth skipped off to read the name.

"It's *Flower* something or other," she said. "She's a funny old barge. You come and see."

"*Flower of Essex!*" I exclaimed. "So that's where she's got to."

Aloft, her gear looked quite normal and she had a steel sprit which was quite a feature in some of the more modern barges. On deck, though, she looked incredibly bare. Her hatches were wide open and there was no signs of covers or cloths. Booms, oars and hitchers had gone — cabin scuttle hatch and skylight — everything moveable had disappeared.

"She does look a bit funny, doesn't she, Daddy?"

"Yes," I said. "But you see that's what happens when a barge gets sunk. Come over here and sit down and I'll tell you her story while we have lunch."

The *Flower of Essex* when I knew her, belonged to Cranfield, the Ipswich Millers, but Frank Mumford, of Stanford-le-Hope had bought her since the war and got a man from Woolwich to take her away with him as mate. She loaded coir yarn and bone meal in Tilbury Dock and sailed for Maidstone. It came on to blow and she got ashore on the Nore Sands. The two men made flares of spare clothing, but their signals were not seen and eventually they had to take to the boat. The *Flower of Essex* was raised two days later and brought into Queenborough, where she discharged what was left of her cargo. That much I knew, also that she had been sold by underwriters for £150. And here she was at Sittingbourne looking in remarkably good condition for such a knock-down price.

Elizabeth had been listening attentively. "So nobody was drowned, then?"

"No. The two men got ashore in the boat at Minster and trudged across the flats and up the cliffs."

"Goody. Goody. May I have some more cake, please?"

A little later, when we had finished our lunch and drunk the sweet, sickly-looking cherryade that was Elizabeth's especial favourite at that time, she suddenly demanded: "Now tell me a story about that barge over there."

"All right," I agreed. "Let's go and have a look at her."

But when we got to the lower end of the quay where she lay, I had to admit defeat. She was the most unusual, narrow-beamed stumpy barge called the *Lady of the Lea*, with tiller steering and mizzen stepped on the rudder post — in short, a real old-timer and a complete reversal to the sort of craft in vogue two hundred years ago.

"There's a bottle of milk on board. And there's a ladder, too. Do you think we could go down?"

"No, no, " I said hurriedly. "You can't do that, Elizabeth. Besides, the cabin is shut up so I doubt if there's anybody aboard."

57

Headsheets on *Lady of the Lea* with William Aslett, her owner, and Andrew's *Victoria* beyond.

As we stood there, a man with a shopping basket came across the wharf.

"Here he comes," Elizabeth whispered, her hand clutching at mine. "Ask him, Daddy."

He was clean-shaven, bespectacled and obviously a good natured, friendly individual, but I had no need to speak for he paused at the top of the ladder and smiled across at us.

"I don't suppose you've seen many like this before," he said.

"No, indeed. I thought I knew most of them," I replied, "but I must confess the *Lady of the Lea* is new to me, although I have the feeling I did hear something about her before the war. Is she yours?"

"Why, yes. I've just bought her. Would you like to come down and have a look round?"

Elizabeth's hand tugged at mine. "D'you think I could come?" she whispered. There was no need to ask, for the owner flashed her a smile and beckoned from the ladder.

Lady of the Lea was a lovely little barge, coming from Hyam & Olivers' yard at Rotherhithe in 1931. Little had been seen of her, for she was built to the order of the War Department to carry arms and ammunition between Waltham Abbey and Woolwich Arsenal. As such, she was not registered, but would probably gross about 30 tons and carry some 65 tons of cargo. Rather shallow-sided, with a tucked-up stern and very little sheer, four men were reputed to have built her at a cost of £1,500. Her bottom was of British Columbian pine without a single knot; chines were of elm and sides of oak. The knees in her hold were brass and she was copper-fastened throughout. No wonder she was dubbed locally the wonder barge of Rotherhithe.

Originally, the *Lady of the Lea* was fitted with a compartment in the main hold for the stowage of TNT but the bulkheads had been dismantled. She was in wonderful condition down below and the arrangements for ventilating behind the lining were the most elaborate I had ever seen in a barge. With only 4-ft. 6-in. side amidships, the problem of obtaining reasonable headroom had been overcome in the cabin by extending the top out to the sides, quite a common practice in the old days, with the effect, as it were, of a raised poop.

William Aslett, her owner, first came across *Lady of the Lea* while serving as mate aboard the well known Mistley barge *Redoubtable.* Lying at anchor off the docks one day, he and the skipper were in the hold unshipping the middle tie beam when another craft bumped alongside. That in itself was nothing unusual; presently a pleasant-faced young chap appeared at the hatchway.

"Just hanging on to you for a bit, skipper, if you don't mind."

"That's all right. What you got in?"

"Cordite!" came the unexpected reply.

The *Lady of the Lea* was quite dwarfed as she lay alongside the *Redoubtable,* but William Aslett liked the look of her, and when she was offered for sale by the Small Craft Disposal Board after the war, he bought her and sailed round to Sittingbourne, where he had a job with a firm of road contractors.

Having taken us through the barge, we were invited down to the comfortable little cuddy aft. There was a kettle singing on the stove and we were soon seated with a pot of tea between us. Nor was Elizabeth overlooked. A bag of toffees was placed on the table. Elizabeth took one and was bidden to fill her pocket.

Elizabeth looked at me with a predatory gleam in her eye, but I shook my head.

William Aslett was no stranger to the sea, for he sailed in the small, copper-bottomed, Fowey schooner *Isabella,* and was cook in the *Little Pet,* both engaged in the Newfoundland cod and salt trade. He served, too, in the old schooner-rigged barge *Belmont,* owned by the Whitstable Shipping Company, originally two-masted and later given a third because she was so heavy on her crew. He had fond memories of the *Belmont,* for the Cornish mate, William Honeyball, taught him to knot and splice. "He'd been bo'sun in the *Thermopylae* at one time and a most extraordinary man, for he never wore socks, but had them tattooed on both feet from the knees down."

He also went mate in a number of spritsail barges: the *P.A.M., British Lion* and the Sittingbourne mule-rigged coaster *S.D.,* built and owned as the initials implied, by Smeed Dean, and familiarly known as the Sudden Death. Sailing past Dover once, they were almost cut down by the German ss *Vaterland* (later to become the White Star liner *Majestic*). Forced to take to the boat, they were all but swamped before they pulled back aboard.

Another of William Aslett's ships was the *Evelyn,* of Port Madoc, the last of

Lady of the Lea. William Aslett at the tiller.

the British trading brigs. And now he was master and owner of the diminutive, stump-rigged *Lady of the Lea,* the very last of the sailing barges — for no more have been built since 1931. He had ordered a new mainsail and planned to install an auxiliary engine so as to take her away trading if suitable employment could be found. If not — well, he was happy enough jogging along, for he was a man of many parts — violinist, poet and song writer, with a philosophy that would stand him in good stead whatever befell. Above all, he had a wonderful way with children.

On the way home late that afternoon, Elizabeth snuggled close in the train. After a while, just as I thought she had gone to sleep, she murmured: "I do hope we go to live on a barge, don't you, Daddy?"

She was silent for a while, then she said softly: "I did like that *Lady* barge." Rummaging in her pocket, she brought out a bag of toffees. "And wasn't he a nice man to give me these?"

It reminded me of Elizabeth's epitaph to a dear old aunt of mine: "You know, Mummy, she *was* good. Whenever I asked her to read to me she always did."

It is a pleasing and enviable way to be remembered in this world of 'Don't bother me now' and 'Haven't the time.'

60

Chapter Eight

FAVERSHAM AND OARE

Faversham Creek has always been a favourite haunt of mine. Sometimes we sailed up the coast from Whitstable in *June*'s old boat but more often than not I used to walk there by way of the Graveney and Nagden Marshes, rarely meeting a living soul on that lonely, wholly fascinating stretch of sea wall bordering Whitstable Bay and the East Swale.

Faversham, with its slender church spire and delicate stonework tracery rising above the tree tops, is one of those mediaeval ports whose trade has largely fallen away over the years, but there are plenty of reminders of more prosperous days, and Abbey Street has well-proportioned houses and an air of spaciousness vaguely reminiscent of Buckler's Hard on the Beaulieu River. The old wool warehouse still stood though the inscription was so worn as to be hardly decipherable; on the quayside was another magnificent red-brick and timbered warehouse still in use, and an ancient weather-boarded sail loft whose sign board had been left untouched so long that the peeling paint bore traces of no less than three owners.

Overseas trade languished years ago and the little basin at the head of the creek where collier brigs and ketches once discharged their North Country coal no longer had but the occasional barge with corn from the docks or coal transshipped at Erith for the local gasworks. Faversham and Sittingbourne grew up side by side as barge centres, but the men were always poles apart just like the Kent and Essex bargemen. It used to be said by the Sittingbourne bargemen that you could never knock on the wrong door in Faversham, the sort of scandalous remark that was hardly calculated to promote good feeling.

Barges used to turn up Faversham Creek as far as the shepherd's black timbered cottage on the borders of Nagden Marshes. This was the house we rather fancied after the war and known to bargemen as Nagden Palace. If a barge got that far the old wooden paddle tug *Pioneer* would tow her to Faversham for half the standard rate of 2½d per ton light.

Horsford, Gillett, Dan, Cremer, Goldfinch, Seager and Anderson; these were the big barge-owning families and they had some hundred and fifty barges between them at the turn of the century, serving the cement works, gun powder factories, ballast pits, brickfields, pot and tile works, as well as the coal, corn and timber merchants.

At one time, too, John Horsford owned the Conyer-built *Lord Nelson*, one of the few Faversham craft to take part in the annual Barge Matches after they were revived in 1927. She might well have won had not Horsford insisted on his nephew sailing her instead of Vic Fields, the regular skipper. Vic was a hunchback and a dry old customer, but he could certainly sail a barge. Horseford's barges did a lot of brick work up river to Kingston and Hampton Court, and when Vic had the *Four Sisters* he towed up country from Woolwich with a 7-lb. tin of boiled sweets invariably by his side on the cabin top.

Horsford's skippers were generally considered a rum lot of the rough and ready type, but Charles Cremer was a staunch Congregationalist which was reflected in the names of his earlier barges: *Providence, Gratitutde, Diligent* and *Ebenezer*. His men were expected to attend chapel if they were home for the weekend, and woe betide any of them overheard using bad language. Whether they were equally circumspect in London was another matter, although that fine bargeman, Harry Simmons, master of Cremer's *Swift*, could never be dubbed a hypocrite, for he refused to sail on a Sunday, and no matter wherever he happened to be at midnight Saturday down went his anchor and it was not hove up until midnight Sunday. There were times when it landed him in a packet of trouble.

Osborn Dan was barge owner and land owner. He had a small brick and tile works at Uplees on the East Swale just outside Faversham Creek, where he built the sailing barge *Uplees* in 1897, a most unusual-looking craft with a stern like a Chinese junk, so that she appeared to be perpetually on the point of sinking by the head. Then he took over a meadow at the head of the creek next to the Co-op yard, where he built a number of fine barges, including the *Baden Powell* and the 150-ton *Cecil Rhodes*. Osborn Dan owned the boomy *Lord Beaconsfield* and over twenty barges. He shipped bricks from Dan's Dock, Uplees, as well as stone, sand and flints from Bulldog Wharf in Oare Creek, but like so many of the local owners, he did not work all his barges himself but hired them out to the big brick makers like Chambers & Co. and Court & Pryer.

George Knox Anderson, of the Faversham Cement Works which stood just below the timber yard, named his barges after rivers: *Forth, Humber, Severn, Thames* and *Tyne*. Mrs Emma Seager had a fleet of eight barges, but the name of Seager is best known as the maker of winches, pumps, mast cases and all manner of barge ironwork. The Gillett family, first Thomas and then Walter, were wharfingers and barge owners, mostly in the dry goods work between London and Faversham. They had the old Faversham-built *Ella, Brick, Two Brothers* and *Surprise*, also the Curel-built *Maltster* and more latterly the ex-A.P.C.M. *Harold Margetts*. She was the last of Gillett's barges, a famous racer in her day, for with Jack Waterhouse as skipper, she led the whole fleet home in the 1927 Thames Barge Match. I had seen the *Harold Margetts* at the Oare barge yard after coming off Government service and she looked very rough, but this was before she went for a yacht and took on a new lease of life on the Broads.

In 1866 a number of shipwrights got together to build a barge on Elgar's Wharf at the head of the creek by the gasworks. Nobody thought they would manage it, but they kept on saying: "Why not?" And that was how she was christened: *Whynot*.

Most of the Faversham barges were built on the western foreshore known as The Brents, just below the basin. One of the best known was the 250-ton schooner *Goldfinch*, later cut down to a ketch and sailed out to British Guiana in 1930 to finish her days trading on the Demerara coast. The Goldfinch family were not only the biggest of the Faversham builders but John and George both owned barges in their time.

Although by the turn of the century the collier brigs no longer traded to Faversham, there were still a dozen or so large barges owned there. Charles Marshall had the ketches *Ellen*, built Sunderland 1860, and the *Kate*, built Ipswich 1867, also the schooners *Lucy Richmond*, built by Robertson at Ipswich in 1875 and the three-masted *Ellen Smeed*, built by Smeed Dean in 1872.

But Faversham with its narrow, winding gut of a creek was really a port for spritsail barges. Apart from the big owners, Whittle, the timber merchant, owned the *Atlas* jointly with Charles Cremer, while Stapleton Payn, the corn merchant, had the shapely little *Orion*, sold later to William Green of Brantham Mills and subsequently renamed *Gold Belt*. She finished her trading days with John Corello but Tom Harding made a very smart yacht of her later.

It is curious how often some of the Faversham barges changed hands among the local owners. The *Esther*, built Faversham 1900 by Alfred White Junior for Mrs Emma Seager, passed to John Horsford during the First War and subsequently to the Cremer family, together with *James & Ann*. These two, with the *Ethel*, *Nellie*, *Edith* and *Pretoria*, comprised Cremer's post-war fleet trading under the style of The Faversham Freightage Company in corn, coal for the gasworks and the occasional freight of timber. But the Faversham barges had gone; their demise is the same old story of worked out brick fields, *anno domini* and the competition of the internal combustion engine.

Possibly the most intriguing of all the Faversham barges was the 26-ft. *Little Jim*, specially built for Ike Dane to run beer across to Harty on the Isle of Sheppey for a wage of £2 a week. She was later sold to Jessie Rowden of Whitstable who had an engine installed and used her for dredging oysters for George Tabor.

When I walked to Faversham one Saturday morning early in 1949, *Pretoria* lay in the basin alongside the gasworks, the only barge in the creek. I crossed by the basin swing-bridge and skirted The Brents where shipwrights working for Goldfinch and White once plied adze and saw on well-seasoned Kentish oak. But Pollock's were building lighters and tugs and motor coasters just below where Perry & Company had their brick fields, and the air was rent with the hideous racket of drilling and riveting and all the trappings of an up-to-date steel ship building yard.

I was on my way to Hollowshore — 'Ollyshore to bargemen — to see the *James & Ann* on Cremer's yard at the mouth of Oare Creek, some two miles below Faversham. She had sunk off Leysdown earlier in the month, dropping down on the ebb from Bellamy's Wharf, Deptford, with 466 quarters of maize for Faversham, and hitting a submerged object out beyond the range buoys and quietly settling on the bottom. We could see her clearly from our windows at The Nore some four miles across the bay, with sails furled and decks just awash at low water. For two days it blew hard from the north-west, then the Queenborough-owned motor barge *C.I.V.* went out with powerful pumps and managed

63

Ethel in Oare Creek.

to get her further up the flats. The hole was temporarily patched and we watched her tow into the Swale with topsail set.

The maize was sodden but more or less intact, and having been condemned by the Ministry of Food was transhipped into the *C.I.V.* to be taken to Barking Creek for the manufacture of gin. Meanwhile the *James & Ann* went on the yard while they decided what to do with her.

The actual damage was not extensive. She had probably fouled the engine of a sunken aircraft for there was still a piece of aluminium jammed in the hole in the starboard bow just abaft the stem. On deck she looked incredibly naked. Most of the hatch covers had gone. So, too, had cabin scuttle and skylight; spars and everything moveable had disappeared. The foresail and the tack of the mainsail were in shreds and bleached by the seas; oil and ochre had been washed out. It was thought that if Cremer's were to do anything with her they would make a proper job by opening up her hatchways like the rest of their barges in the grab work.

The barge yard was a picturesque jumble of wooden buildings dominated by the red-roofed, tarred and weather-boarded building shed stockaded all around by a tall wooden fence. They built three barges here: the *Bertie* and *Nellie* in 1901 and the *Pretoria* the following year. Nobody lived on the premises, and the only other house within half a mile was The Shipwright's Arms just beyond the

64

yard, a pleasant wooden building, buff-painted, with tiled roof and a verandah overlooking Faversham Creek, where the withies marked the gutway winding away down to the East Swale and Shell Ness beyond on the far Sheppey shore. This verandah was the Coastguards' lookout for some years when their old hulk, the *Cadmus*, was withdrawn from her station at the mouth of the creek.

Time was, when fifty barges were working out of Oare Creek and at Christmas, when bargemen always aimed to be at home, they lay at the wharves three and four deep. There was no room for a barge to tack in the creek, and if the wind happened to be foul they would try to get a good start, then put a man ashore with a track line. Sometimes they would have to drop their gear but they always seemed to manage one way or another.

There was no longer any trade in or out of the creek and Bill Gregory had only one shipwright working alongside him on the yard, and a venerable blacksmith who came in once or twice a week. Yet they still looked after Cremer's barges, working the old-fashioned saw pit and thinking nothing of cutting out a new stem piece entirely by hand.

Lou Wood, one-time master of Cremer's *Ethel*, whose passion for cleanliness ran to scrubbed and white-washed coal lockers, had the little motor tug. He recalled the wild goings-on at The Shipwright's Arms when drinks were to be had at all times of the night or day, and how warning was given by lookouts at the approach of the police, until one Saturday night two constables hid in the barge yard and pounced on the assembled company early the following morning. Those were the days when whole fleets of barges lay weather-bound in the East Swale and their crews sailed many a mile in the bar of The Shipwright's Arms.

Many an Essexman came into Oare Creek in the old days to load flints at Ham Wharf for the Essex roads. It was here, too, that thousands of tons of rough stuff were brought down from London to be burned to ashes for brick making. And at the head of the creek, close by the village of Oare, Cremer's and Horsford's and Wood's barges took away bricks as well as flints, but the trade faded away with the working out of the topsoil. The loading berths were still there close up by the road but they have long since mudded up.

One of the last regular traders up Oare Creek was Wakeley's *Fanny*. Tubby Blake used to bring sludge from Beckton for the farms and invariably took back a jar of home-brewed cider.

"That was the strongest cider I ever come acrorst," he declared. "The chaps up at Beckton, they used to come down aboard for a mugful till one day one on' 'em fell off his bike going home to dinner. That finished that lark. The gaffer clamped down on cider after that."

It was very seldom that a barge visited these waters in post war days except to go on the yard, yet that winter's day I was intrigued to see a barge's sprit and topmast standing up above the sea wall at Ham Wharf a short distance up Oare Creek. The sun was setting over the village; there was a crispness in the air that betokened frost later, and a clarity of atmosphere that so becomes the East Coast creeks and low-lying countryside.

65

Harold Margetts on Cremer's Yard, Oare Creek, with the Shipwrights Arms beyond.

What a glorious spot, I thought, to moor a barge, with a good mud berth and a bare two miles across the fields to Faversham. Others apparently had the same idea for the barge was no trader but the yacht barge *Iota*, formerly one of Eastwood's little brickies that had failed to find a buyer at the Otterham sale but subsequently purchased by Geoffrey Dutson and converted to a yacht by The Whitewall Barge Company. The hatchways had been decked in and skylights fitted; there were portlights in the hatch coamings and a companion hatchway just abaft the mast. Right aft was a sunken wheelhouse and the mizzen had been removed after the usual trading barge practice for auxiliaries, but she was still painted in Eastwood's traditional colours: royal blue rail, green stern frame and deck fittings. *Iota* was something more than a house boat; she was a yacht, too, and all gear appeared to be in excellent order.

Geoffrey was working on the foredeck touching up the windlass. Presently he looked up and recognized me although we had met only once before.

"Hullo," he exclaimed. "I didn't know you were there. Coming aboard?"

"I'd very much like to," I replied, "only I don't want to stop the work."

"That's all right. I'm just knocking off anyway." He dabbed away at the ironwork for a few more minutes. "It's getting a bit late for painting and I'll have to cover up soon to keep the frost out. You know, the trouble is to find time for all the odd jobs at weekends.

"She looks very well," I said with an appreciative glance along the deck.

Geoffrey smiled. "There's one thing about a barge. You do get results, not like a garden where you have to wait a couple of months or more."

Iota still retained her spritsail rig: except for her mizzen, her gear was unchanged from trading days. They piped water from a spring outside The Shipwright's Arms; otherwise they were quite independent of the shore for there were two generating sets abaft the wheelhouse, one to charge batteries for refrigerator, pumps and lights and the other for such luxuries as carpet sweeper, electric iron and deck hose.

"You manage all right on your own?" I asked.

"Oh, yes. We got as far as Southwold last summer. There's Grace and myself and Jo; she's old enough to give a hand if we need it. Of course, we've got an auxiliary. You know you really do need one for getting in and out of a place like this. Even so, we got stuck across the creek a short while back. Dried out, too."

"Whatever happened? Did she strain badly?"

"No. In spite of the fact we've got no keelson." My horrified expression made Geoffrey laugh. "Yes I know it's all against the rules, but I really don't see why a keelson's necessary. After all, we're box-shape and it's not as if we're going to load a cargo again. I'm damned if I can stomach an iron girder running down the middle of the saloon, so we cut off the top flange level with the ceiling."

I was still unconvinced. "M'm. I'm afraid I'm old fashioned. But you're like Dorothy. She's got a phobia about keelsons too."

Geoffrey gave me a searching glance. "You're not thinking of going afloat again by any chance?" he demanded, whereupon I had to smile and confess we were toying with the idea.

"Well! Well! Well!" he exclaimed and called to his wife. "D'you hear that, Grace? The Bennetts are going afloat again."

"It's not quite as definite as all that," I protested, as Grace appeared at the companion hatch. "There are all sorts of snags and Dorothy hasn't really come round to it yet, although she says she wouldn't mind if we could find the right barge and the right place to keep her in."

"What's wrong with Oare Creek?" Grace demanded. "There's plenty of room and it only costs ten quid a year. You send her along to me. I'll talk to her."

"I'm not so sure about that," I replied ruefully. "I hear you've cut out your keelson."

"I'd jolly well think so, too. You don't imagine I'd stand for a thing like that, do you?" said Grace. "Did Geoffrey tell you how we stranded across the creek though? My God, was I scared! Aren't you coming down; It's cold up here."

Below deck the accommodation was truly delightful and the layout just about perfect for a handy-sized barge. The main beams in way of the mast case being too low for full standing headroom, cabins had been grouped fore and aft to avoid ducking as much as possible. In the fore hold were two sleeping cabins; amidships, where headroom was least, there were airing cupboard and fresh water tanks carrying about a thousand gallons. The living accommodation was in the main hold; bathroom to port at the foot of the companion ladder; galley to starboard giving access to the saloon with its built-in dinette, fitted carpet, cedar panelling, well-polished brasswork and an all-pervading air of sumptuousness. At the aft end of the main hold was a spare bed cabin.

The accommodation was based on the standard Whitewall Barge Company's layout, and vastly improved to my mind, by the elimination of passage ways. Our little *June* had a beam of but fifteen feet, but here was *Iota*, handy barge of 90 tons, with an extra two feet beam that made it possible to plan quite large cabins side by side. I could visualize great possibilities in a barge like *Iota*.

"We won't show you the engine rooms", said Geoffrey. "I know you've no use for such things, but it's tucked away on the port side there behind the curtain."

"Then there's the original stern cabin," I remarked, steadfastly refusing to be drawn on the question of an engine.

"There isn't much left of that, I'm afraid. The wheelhouse takes up most of it, but we can sleep a couple up there if we want. A wheelhouse is just a matter of choice, of course. Have you any ideas where to go for the barge conversion?"

"I had Paglesham in mind," I replied slowly. "Frank Shuttlewood has a soft spot for barges — and his wife, too. His father built them — and grandfather — so I'm told."

Geoffrey nodded. "I'm all for getting hold of somebody who's really interested."

"Me, too," added Grace. "That's more than half the battle."

"It's time that's the real trouble," I said. "We'd have to sell our house first to get the money for the barge, then we'd have nowhere to live. Frank only has one man and a boy and I'm afraid they'd take too long even supposing he took it on. But that's the sort of yard I had in mind."

"What about the yard here?" Grace asked. "It's marvellous what Bill Gregory and his mate get through, isn't it, Geoffrey?"

But Geoffrey shook his head. "You'd never talk him into it. They've got their hands pretty full looking after their own barges. We've had a few jobs done there but if one of their own barges comes on the yard they drop everything else like hot cakes. What about the Whitstable yard?"

It was my turn to shake my head. The previous winter the *Five Sisters* had come to Whitstable and was hauled out at Perkins' slip for conversion on a cost plus basis. We got to know Tom Larkin and his wife, and watched progress with great interest. They particularly wanted the barge by Christmas but the more they urged the job along the bigger was the eventual bill for overtime and in the end it cost nearly twice as much as they had expected. "No," I said. "We'd have to try and get somebody to work to an estimate."

"Well," said Geoffrey. "I don't know, but you might find it worth while getting the Whitewall people to give you a quote. They've done about twenty barges since John Briant started up. You'll find them all right if you know what you want and don't keep changing your mind like some of them do."

68

I nodded agreement. "Well, I must say *Iota*'s a good advertisement for them. They've made a lovely job down below here."

Grace, with arms folded, was leaning against the galley door. "You'd have to stand over them," she said. "We did and that's why we got what we asked for."

"Things are getting easier, too," Geoffrey added. "They were really up against it with some of the earlier barges, but there's more timber about now and there shouldn't be the same hold-up getting materials and fittings. They're shifting out of Whitewall Creek down to Hoo very shortly and starting up the Marina Club so you might find a berth there, too."

☆ ☆ ☆ ☆

I had always tramped over the fields from Faversham whenever I visited Hollow Shore before. Taking Dorothy and the children to see *Iota* I thought it best to go to the village of Oare at the head of the creek and walk down the sea wall. Possibly there is an easier way but the path we took led over a broken down wooden bridge which Dorothy found rather trying although the children made light of it.

"Of course, this isn't the usual way," I said hurriedly.

"I should jolly well think not," she replied warmly. "Whatever made you bring us?"

"Just that there happens to be a bus. I thought it might be more convenient than walking across the fields."

Dorothy shook her head despairingly and picked her way gingerly across a narrow beam. Then we pushed on along the rough and muddy track that skirted a little wood and the dock that once belonged to John Hall's Powder Mills, with the aptly named barges: *Black Boy* and *Guy Fawkes*. We came out on the sea wall within sight of *Iota* and the marshland stretching away to the East Swale where the white Ferry Inn beyond stood out against the green hillside on the far Sheppey shore.

It was a lovely part where *Iota* lay — remote and lonely, of course, but that was part of its charm. We were given a warm welcome on board. Grace took Dorothy below. The companion ladder was too steep for Peter and he had to be lifted down, but Elizabeth was in her element. She scampered through the cabins and came up on deck, where I got so engrossed with Geoffrey's account of how he bought *Atlas*'s sprit from the barge yard for £15 and the ease with which Bill Gregory parbuckled it aboard, that I completely forgot the children. Then suddenly there was Dorothy in the hatchway absolutely horrified.

"For heaven's sake grab hold of Peter!"

I swung round. Unbeknown to Geoffrey or myself Peter had climbed the companion ladder and was cheerfully walking over the cabin skylight. It was a mercy that the glass had not broken.

"I thought he was down below with you," I said mildly, as I led him out of danger.

69

Sara shows her weather chine.

"So he was. Then I looked up and saw him walking over my head. It's just as I said. You can't take your eye off the children for a moment. That's the sort of thing I mean," she added, pointing aft where Elizabeth was performing somersaults in the mizzen rigging. "It's all very well for you to laugh, but I can't settle to anything if I'm worrying about the children all the time."

That evening in the bus on our way home to Whitstable, Peter lay asleep in Dorothy's arms and Elizabeth snuggled up against me in the seat behind. I thought she was asleep, too, for her eyes were shut, but her lips moved and I bent my head to catch a whisper: "We *are* going to live on a barge, aren't we, Daddy?"

Dorothy turned her head. "What did she say?"

"Only asking if we really are going afloat," I replied, whereupon Dorothy pursed her lips and shook her head.

"It's hopeless. You realize that yourself, don't you?"

It was no time to argue. All the way home we sat buried in thought.

70

Chapter Nine

BUYING A BARGE

For over a week Dorothy and I tacitly avoided the subject of barges until one day we were hurrying to catch a bus when Elizabeth darted across the busy road before we could stop her. She dodged through the slow moving traffic on the near side. A great lorry thundered by on the crown of the road going the other way. Dorothy and I stood petrified on the edge of the pavement. There was a screeching of brakes and it seemed an eternity before the road cleared and we saw Elizabeth standing in the middle of the road.

We were both very quiet for the rest of the day. That evening we sat by the fire and Dorothy herself broached the subject again.

"I think we may as well go ahead with a barge."

I looked up enquiringly.

"Yes, I know," she continued, "but after this morning I can't help thinking the roads are more dangerous than living afloat."

I relaxed in the armchair and stretched my legs luxuriously. "That's fine. At least we'll make sure there aren't any skylights to worry about. I never did like the things. For light we'll have ports in the coamings and lifting hatches instead."

"Another thing," Dorothy broke in. "Oare Creek is too far out. We'll have to fall back on the Medway, I expect. The first thing is to find a barge though."

I had been in touch with the brokers ever since the war and kept an eye on prices. At first there was hardly a decent barge to be had. There were plenty for sale — of a sort — either straight from Government service or else pretty well worked out, at prices ranging from four hundred to a thousand pounds. Few of them were really suitable for yachts. The better class barges seldom came on the market; at first there was good money to be earned in East Anglian work. But recently the top had come off and there was barely enough work for all the barges that had been rebuilt or converted to motor. Cranfield, the Ipswich millers, had recently sold their 160-ton *Colonia* for £1,150 and she was trading under Francis and Gilders' flag. It was possible they might also let the *Petrel* or the *Spinaway C* go for about the same figure. They were both built at Ipswich by Orvis & Fuller in the 'nineties. They had a lovely sheer, sitting the water beautifully; their lines were rather finer than most of the Thames and Medway barges and were more akin to coasting schooners with the bottoms cut off.

Roger Finch knew them well.

"... Both barges were in Ipswich Dock recently, and I had a good look at them. Both would make fine yachts. The trouble of head-room hardly occurs because *Petrel* draws nearly seven feet and *Spinaway* over six feet. This should nearly give you head-room under decks and as both have eighteen

Henry   (Les Arnold, from the Tony Farnham Collection)

inch coamings little or no raising would be required. *Petrel* is the bigger barge and would go anywhere; she has rather a narrow beam for her size with a resulting tendency to 'go over'. But Ken Horner, her skipper, assured me she went so far and then nothing would push her any further. She had a new stem this winter, but is older than *Spinaway* and might be a bit 'seedy'. Her cabin is a little gem and it would be a pity to strip it, anyway, all her skippers have been decent chaps and kept it very well. She has had a new staysail and is a bowsprit barge. *Spinaway* has no bowsprit. In my opinion it boils down to *Petrel* bigger but older, *Spinaway C* slightly smaller but probably (not certainly) sounder. Pincher Bloyce of the *Remercie* said *Spinaway C* and I'd back his word any time.

"The pair of them have been in the flour and grain trade for the last twenty-five years at least and *Spinaway C* ever since she was built. Ceilings and Linings, as far as I could judge, were in excellent condition. Both often lie for a week loaded in the dock and so must be pretty tight. You would certainly find either of them rather a contrast to *June*, more thorough bred but probably more likely to have little ways of their own."

Actually *Petrel*, carrying 125 tons to sea or some 580 quarters, was the smaller barge in spite of her depth of side. Either of them rigged out with bowsprit jib would make a yacht to glory in, but their size was the trouble. They were really too big for us to handle by ourselves with any confidence.

The brokers had nothing else to suggest. *Petrel* was on her way to London. Would I care to see her? Still I hesitated. Meantime I had written to Josh Francis, my old barge owner friend at Colchester who was a contemporary on the Medway with my grandfather many years ago. Knowing Francis & Gilders had recently bought *Colonia* and the difficulties they were experiencing with crews, I wondered if one of their smaller barges might be coming up for sale.

The reply I had from Josh drove from my mind all thoughts of *Petrel* and *Spinaway C*.

"...The little *Henry* (100 tons) belonging to Mr. Fisher of Cole & Lecquire, she is I think in really first class condition but *too small* for trading purposes. I think the main reason for selling is that the Fisher family are thinking of selling out and emigrating to Canada..."

"What do you think of that?" I demanded, tossing the letter across the table to Dorothy. "There's the barge for us."

"*Henry*," she repeated. "What do we know about the *Henry*?"

"Why, she was in Whitstable harbour a few months back. Surely you recollect the little barge with the blue-white-blue bob we admired so much? George Battershall had her. You know, the skipper who remembered us from the old *June* days."

"M'm. I see what you mean. Sounds interesting."

"I should jolly well think so too! Why she's the finest little barge afloat —" I broke off, for Dorothy was laughing at me. "All right, but I'm certain she's just the very thing we're looking for."

73

"What makes you so keen then?"

"Because she's the right size to start with. We always did say a 100-tonner was our ideal. Then she's been rebuilt, which makes her good for another twenty years at least. We wouldn't have to build up the hatch coamings as she's already had them done, so we'd save on that. And down below, the linings and ceilings are as good as new so there'd be no need for panelling anywhere."

"But you don't know what they're asking. They'll probably want an enormous price."

"Maybe, but I'm only going by the letter Josh sent. He wouldn't mention her if he didn't think she'd suit our pocket."

Apparently Cole & Lecquire, an old-fashioned firm of corn factors and seed merchants at Pier Wharf, Grays, wrote first of all to Josh Francis when they thought of selling *Henry* because they looked to his firm for work when they had none of their own. But Francis & Gilders already had one of their own craft laid up for want of a crew and in any case a 450-quarter barge was considered too small to be economic.

Dorothy was quite right though. Cole & Lecquires' reply to my request for particulars came as a cold douche.

"... As Mr. Francis has told you, *Henry* is for sale. Full particulars are not available here at the moment but she has a carrying capacity of 100 tons. She is the usual Thames topsail sailing barge with full gear and in perfect condition as she was completely re-built at Sittingbourne in 1944.

"We are hoping that she may be sold into the yacht market for conversion and we are asking £2,000 or near offer as she is to-day, knowing that she will pass any survey with flying colours. If you would care to see the craft, if you will let us know, we will try to arrange a suitable time and place..."

There was no need for them to arrange an inspection, for *Henry* at £2,000 was quite beyond us. I was bitterly disappointed and wrote back right away that we were keen on the barge for we had already seen her in Whitstable harbour, and acknowledging that she was probably worth all the money they were asking, but £1,000 was our absolute limit however good she might be.

For the next few days we covertly watched the post, secretly hoping for a miracle. A week went by, then another, and still no sign. It was now getting on for the end of February 1949, and the weather was particularly trying. After a succession of south-westerly gales the wind suddenly flew into the north-west and continued to blow with ever increasing force. Our house, The Nore, situated on the seaward side of the sea wall, was wide open to the north-west and at night we lay awake listening to the wind shrieking across the flats and beating against the large bay windows until it seemed that no ordinary glass could possibly withstand such ferocity.

The tides were coming up to Springs. Luckily *June*'s boat was not laid up for the winter on our private strip of beach but was in Perkins' yard for repairs, but the big seas at high water came thundering up the beach uncomfortably close to the house itself. The basement had been living quarters at one time but we used the big room opening on to the beach as a playroom for the children, and the rest comprised workshop, coal cellar and pantry. It was just as well that Dorothy had insisted on making the kitchen on the ground floor, for on the last day of February she came on the telephone to me in London after lunch.

"We're all right," she said. "But it's going to be a very high tide and it's blowing worse than ever."

"Is the water seeping in down below then?" I asked, for once or twice in the past there had been water over the concrete basement floor at Springs.

"It's coming over the top of the wall," she replied.

"Oh Lord! Is it very deep?"

"About half way up the stairs. Gosh! Hold on ... I expect you heard that big wave. It washed a great big mast up the beach and I thought for a moment it was coming right through the lounge window."

I was silent for a few moments. There was so little I could do sixty miles away. "You don't think you ought to get away out of it?" I asked. "Tide's got another half an hour to go yet."

"Er — no, I don't think so. The police are standing by on the Sea Wall. Pacey and I cleared out the pantry early on and brought the carpet out of the playroom. We piled the rest of the stuff on the shelves."

It was some consolation, at least, to know that Mrs. Pace, our daily help, was with them. She was a staunch friend, completely imperturbable and invariably cheerful whatever happened.

"What about the children?"

"Oh, they're not worried. I had to meet Elizabeth from school and carried her up the alley where the water was sloshing about. Pacey's with Elizabeth and Peter and they're having a high old time from the noise. No, we're all right. I only 'phoned in case you were worrying. See you to-night. Bye."

The tide had gone when I got home but it was still blowing great guns and there was every prospect of a wild night. The basement was half full of water but the level had dropped a few inches; apparently the foundations had been constructed with the possibility of floods in mind and the water was able to find its way out. Moreover, the ground floor of the house was a good three feet above the level of the Sea Wall. The houses on the landward side, however, were low-lying and many of them along West Beach had their furniture floating about in the garden. Our house must have withstood similar assaults from the sea from time to time over the last fifty years, and that night we took what comfort we could as we watched the boiling, white-crested waste of water that was Whitstable Bay. It was a terrifying scene, yet not without its beauty — just such a night when the brigantine *Matilda Calder* washed up the beach in November 1897.

Next morning we were able to take stock. Our breakwater had clean gone, with our strip of private beach and little rock garden alongside the wall. But I saw little of the aftermath, for I went down with jaundice. Dorothy and Mrs. Pace had the job of clearing up the shambles in the basement when the flood subsided while I lay in bed the colour of a Chinaman, and the children peered round the door from time to time with awe and wonderment on their faces.

About the middle of March, just as I was beginning to take an interest in things again, I heard from the barge brokers that *Petrel* had been sold subject to survey, but they had just received instructions to sell *May Flower*, built 1888, about 80-ft. by 19-ft., new keelson 1947, price £850. I knew the *May Flower*. She was Maldon-owned and I had often seen her trading to Green Bros.' Mill. But a 120-tonner was bigger than I wanted. Another thing, I seemed to remember John Moyes, her young skipper, cheerfully assert in good round Essex speech that one good bump on the Buxey and he reckoned the "owd girl's starn frame'll drop clean out." There was probably some structural weakness aft. Of course, it may have been nothing serious and I was turning over in my mind whether it was worth while having a look at her myself when, quite out of the blue, on the last day of March, came another letter from Sam Fisher of Cole & Lecquire Ltd.

He was sailing for Canada the following week. *Henry* was still unsold and it seemed as if he would have to drop his price. Was I still interested? If so, perhaps I would care to meet him in London the following Monday.

So there was a chance still. Dorothy and I looked at each other without a word. We were determined not to bolster ourselves with false hopes this time. Far better to take a realistic — even pessimistic — view of things. Nevertheless, I would have to know where we stood on the cost of conversion, so I wrote off to the Whitewall Barge Company for a rough estimate.

John Briant's reply came by return of post.

"... A conversion to our standard plan, let's deal with coach roofs first, suggest 1½-in. T & G boarding laid on existing coamings, using existing hatch cover beams; these would be cleaned off and planed up. Roof covered with cotton duck canvas 10 oz. glued to boarding, roof painted before and after canvas is laid, three coats to finish. Dead lights in roofs in place of skylights, sliding hatch and companion ladder, bulkheads to standard plan of 1/8-in. Hardboard laid on both sides of 2 by 1½-in. studding, 2 by 3-in. for grounds where necessary to give rigidity to main bulkheads. 500 gallons water in two 250 gal. tanks under mast case beams, 50 gal. header tank, Kentigern No. 91 W.C. 5-ft. panelled bath and wash basin in bathroom, all plumbing in copper pipes with exception of service from storage tanks to header tank, existing linings sanded off not covered in. Crane (or similar) boiler stove in fo'c'sle 1¼-in. piping for heating round ship. Rayburn in galley for water heating and cooking. I should say we could do this for £1,050 (one thousand and fifty pounds) including bunks, wardrobes and small dressing tables in the sleeping cabins..."

So far, so good. It did not completely cover our requirements, for there was no mention of wiring for shore electricity, but it was obvious we could not afford any more than £1,000 for the barge. I wrote again to Josh Francis for advice.

"You remember I wrote to you a little while ago about possible barges for conversion, well I heard from Fisher of Cole & Lecquire and he wanted £2,000 for the little *Henry*. I told him I was interested but couldn't run to his price. Then Nicoll & Ashton wrote to say Cranfield's were prepared to sell *Petrel*. I'd already made some enquiries through an Ipswich friend who gave me the low down on both her and *Spinaway C*, but almost immediately I went down with jaundice so had to let things slide. Since then I've had *May Flower* mentioned at £850, but I hear through the bush telegraph that her stern is not all it should be, although she had a fair bit done to her a couple of years back. Would you recommend her? Being in the flour trade she'd suit my purpose well enough.

"Yesterday, though, I had another letter from Fisher telling me he was prepared to drop his price and asking to meet me in London on Monday with a view to talking things over. I know she's a splendid little barge and I've heard nothing but good from any of my barge friends. Obviously, I cannot afford to pay anything like £2,000. My idea was £1,000, not because she wasn't worth more, but £1,000 is about my limit. I would be very glad if you'd drop me a line in confidence as to your opinion and whether an offer of £1,000 subject to survey would be reasonable. Fisher tells me she's at Colchester now having her mainsail repaired. If you'd prefer it, I could give you a ring Tuesday evening... I'm hoping you'll not find me too much of a nuisance, but I'd very much value your advice regarding *Henry*. She's the barge for us, I'm pretty sure."

The reply I had was just the impartial, reasoned view I wanted:

"... From your point of view *Henry* is, I agree, just the type of craft to suit you, but from a carrier's point of view the value is no more than £500 to £600. From my experience, the 100-tonners are a liability rather than an asset. They cost practically the same for upkeep and insurance as a much larger craft — and the crew problem is worsened. Again, for working down Swin winter months, they are not so comfortable to get a passage when loaded as the larger ones. I'm not trying to put you off buying her, but the Owner must appreciate the position as I do, nevertheless. I agree that he may tap the yacht fraternity and get a bite. However, I would suggest that you stick to your *highest* offer of £1,000 — and not a penny more, and of course a lesser amount if possible.

"I feel sure no trading firm will come to anything near the £1,000. If he does contact me on the matter I shall be quite truthful about it and give my opinion of her value for trading at £500 to £600...

"Whatever you do *don't* touch *May Flower*. Her top was so bad three years ago that she had to have the decks sheathed. No flour is carried in this barge."

Thus armed I met Sam Fisher in London as arranged. He was a man of about my own age, and we took to each other immediately. It was obvious that he was extremely fond of the barge in which he had often sailed with Arthur Bannister who had been skipper from the time she was launched in 1904 right up to the last war. *Henry* was named after Henry Cole, who, with Sam's grandfather, Samuel Lecquire, carried on the business of corn merchants founded by William and Henry Landfield at Pier Wharf, Grays.

At one time Cole & Lecquire had a number of barges, but *Henry* was their favourite, always well looked after, and employed most of the time in the firm's own corn work. She was a family barge in every respect with the younger members of the family often going away for a sailing holiday. As a consequence, when *Henry* came off mine watching at Swanscombe in 1943 very much the worse for wear, Cole & Lecquire decided to have her rebuilt and sent her away down to Sittingbourne, where they spent the £500 they had from the Government and some £3,000 besides. To all intents and purposes she was a new barge.

Sam Fisher offered to send on the repair accounts. "You'll see that £2,000 isn't exorbitant really," he said. "Not when you consider what she had done; new keelsons, new inwales and stem and doubled all over. The whole lot was to Board of Trade requirements. Anyway, I'd take £1,750."

I shook my head. "It's out of the question so far as we're concerned."

Sam Fisher pulled a face. "You know, we spent far more on the barge than we should have done, but it was a case of either making a proper job of her or letting her go. Of course, while we had plenty of our own work, it was all right, but grain's controlled and there's no sign of it coming free again. That's the reason I decided to sell up and take the family fruit farming in British Columbia. Getting the store flooded out as we did at the end of February didn't help the sale, either."

We were on common ground there. It was more than possible the flooding would affect our sale as well.

I smiled sadly. "Sorry, not a chance. Even at £1,000 we'd have to sell our house at Whitstable to finance the deal."

"Don't let that worry you. I wouldn't mind waiting for the completion. How long would you want?"

"I should think a couple of months would give us time to sell. The summer's coming on and that's when a house like ours would be most likely to fetch its price."

Sam pulled out his pocket diary and flicked over the pages. "What about completion by midsummer's day? That would give you just over two months."

His suggestion was very fair, but there was still the question of the price. We just could not run to £1,500. Besides, as I pointed out, a little barge like *Henry* really was not worth anything like that for trading.

Sam Fisher pursed his lips for a few moments, then broke into a smile. "I'll tell you what. I'll leave *Henry* with you at £1,250 while you go and have a look at her. No, no. Don't say anything now. When you've been aboard you'll realize what a lovely yacht she'll make."

78

Henry freshly tarred and still with the grey rails.

I was about to protest, but he held out his hand. "No, please. All I ask is for you to see her. She'll pass any survey, I know. I don't mind who you send along."

I had to laugh. It seemed churlish to stand out further. "All right," I said. "I'll do as you say so long as it's understood I'm not committing myself in any way. There's one thing though, it wouldn't do to lay *Henry* up until June. You know how it is with a barge. Her decks would open up and gear go to pieces in no time."

"What do you suggest, then?"

"Well, the best thing would be to let her carry on even if we did come to terms or at least to keep a crew on board."

"Sounds reasonable to me. I'll agree to that." He glanced at his watch, rose, and stretched out his hand. "I do hope very much you'll take *Henry*. It's not much use being sentimental about it, but I'm very fond of that barge of ours. I've had some good times aboard, that's why I'd like to think of her as a yacht."

"We'd like it, too," I began, then broke off and we both laughed.

"All right," said Sam, holding out his hand. "I know. Anyhow, I'm off to Canada tomorrow, but I'll leave everything with my solicitor at Grays."

And that was how things rested. It was a pleasant way of doing business.

Chapter Ten

HENRY AT GRAYS

As soon as word came through that *Henry* had sailed from Colchester I went down to Grays and called at the skipper's house. George Battershall himself opened the door, a short, burly figure in blue serge suit and thick grey jersey.

I apologized for disturbing him, for he seemed somewhat sleepy-eyed. "Perhaps I've come a bit too early," I ventured, particularly anxious not to start off on the wrong foot.

"I was just having a nap after dinner," he explained. "Don't matter. I'm awake now."

We set off down the High Street. I was not at all sure that he had recognized me. Of course I knew him from the time *Henry* came into Whitstable; it was hardly to be expected that he should remember every quayside stroller who stopped to stare and chatter.

But George only snorted when I asked him. "Of course I know you. I remember you up at Maldon before the war with your wife. And that dog o' yours that got in the mud."

I laughed. That was nothing unusual for our black and tan terrier Chimp who used to spend so much of his time paddling up and down the river bed after flounders.

"I saw you in Whitstable last year. I know quite a bit about you one way or another. Read your books, too. Only wish I could write half as well."

"Well," I said, somewhat startled and more than a little embarrassed. "I suppose I could say the same about sailing a barge."

"What have you got to worry about? Used to sail the *June* before the war, didn't you? Once you've got it, you never lose it."

We came down past the market place and over the brow of the hill, where barge topmasts showed over the roof tops, then turned to the left past Goldsmiths' barge yard to Cole & Lecquires' premises. There was a fine old Georgian house on the left of the entrance, with a large balcony overlooking the Thames. Sam Fisher and his father had lived there, and Old Samuel Lecquire, his grandfather, before them, but it stood empty now. We went straight down the yard past the granary to the jetty, where *Henry* lay.

The mate, a tall youngster, had just washed, and was donning a yellow shirt.

"Where are you off to, all dolled up?" demanded the skipper.

"J-j-just g-going ashore," came the reply.

"Well, you can lend a hand with these hatches before you go."

The mate promptly stripped off his shirt again, and while he and the skipper

80

uncovered fore and aft I took a quick look round on deck. *Henry* was a thorough-bred. There was no doubt about it; she looked really good with rail, deck and gear all in first class condition. Indeed, at first glance, the barge seemed newly built. She had a teak, brass-bound wheel with gratings on either side, and a compass with iron corrector balls, big ship fashion. The setting booms lay on the hatch top and the spare lines were neatly coiled down. The hatch coamings themselves were unusually high for a small sailing barge — some 24-in. amidships.

The skipper joined me.

"She never used to have 'em high like that, you know. Right up to the war she was in the river work to the docks and back with an occasional freight to Maidstone for the Maltsters. After coming off mine watching she went to Sittingbourne and that's where she got her coamings. With eighteen-foot beam, they'd have done better to have rose on her instead. Same as now, she can manage 450 quarters under hatches, but she's still only a 100-ton barge and that's what you get paid freight on."

We went down the ladder into the hold. Linings and ceilings seemed absolutely new, and the half beams under the side decks completely untouched by grabs. The hatch carlines were of oak. I noticed one had a shake; the rest were perfect. Another thing, the keelson was an unobtrusive, H-shaped girder with either side blocked out with wooden filling pieces — quite unlike the ubiquitous baulk of pitch pine in the older barges and bisecting the hold.

"She had that put in at Sittingbourne — steel chine keelsons too. Of course I wasn't in her then, but she had a pretty good do-up by all accounts."

The mate was still hanging about on deck and I volunteered to help cover up so as not to hold him up.

"All right," said the skipper. "You can clear off."

I took a few measurements. The keelson stood a bare six inches above the ceiling. There was at least seven feet headroom under the hatches. The worst place was in way of the mast case, where there was but 4-ft. 9-in. headroom under the main beams, rising with the sheer of the barge to full standing headroom in the fore cupboard. *Henry* was ideal for conversion. The generous beam and full ends would enable us to have a central bulkhead at either end with cabins side by side, which we could not manage with *June*. And the steel keelsons, too, took practically no room at all in the hold. There was, however, a massive oak tie beam across the main hatch at deck level. This would have to be removed, or else have a door frame worked into it as we did with *June*.

Back on deck, we took a quick look at the gear. The blue sprit seemed enormous. It was at least a foot in diameter, and I wondered that a handy barge should carry such a massive spar.

"That's hollow," said George with a chuckle.

A hollow sprit! I had heard of hollow steel sprits. Both *Flower of Essex* and *Colonia* had them, and so did some of Horlock's and Everard's barges, but I had never heard of a barge carrying a hollow wooden sprit before.

81

Henry at Grays, with George Battershall on the hatch top and showing the white tuck in the stern frame.

"Well, that one's hollow all right," and the skipper gave it a smart tap with the brail winch handle. "Of course, the heel's solid. Got a plug each end to form the joggle. You can hear the difference easy enough."

I looked at the sprit somewhat dubiously. "What's your opinion of it?"

"All right. Gybes over nice and easy and only half the weight of pine. I wouldn't want to swop that."

We strolled forward. Windlass bitts were new and so was the windlass itself.

"Must've been put into her at Sittingbourne."

"What about the stayfall?"

"Brand new. Just rove a new one. Nothing wrong with the other till it jumped the sheave as we rigged and got pinched. Thought it was a bit heavy. Never noticed why till we're hove up."

"And the sails?"

"Not bad. We've just come off the yard up at Colchester on account of the sails. The tug never came down for us, so I turned her up from Wivenhoe to Rowhedge and it's a long time since that's been done with a loaded barge, so you can tell she's pretty handy. Just above Rowhedge, though, one of Everard's motor coasters got aground and we fell athwart her. Bent the davits and tore the mains'l. I put the davits ashore. The mains'l had to have some new cloths. Got it back on board and blowed if it didn't catch up on the mizzen stayfall cleat and got torn soon as we started to heave up. Mains'l's the poorest, but that'll go for a few years yet. One thing, her sails do fit her. Putwain made them for her time she went on the yard at Sittingbourne."

The mate had locked the fo'c'sle when he went ashore, but the skipper had a key and opened up. "That's something they went wrong on," he said. "This fo'c'sle hatch should've been over to port instead of starboard. Makes it awkward fleeting the chain same as it is."

I dropped below into as good a little fo'c'sle as ever I had seen. It was lined with grained and varnished matchboarding, with a bunk on either side and racks over. There was a table to port against the bulkhead, and a full length cupboard to starboard. Set between the windlass bitts was the coal galley range. Lamps had a special bin to port; stayfall, rowing irons and sundry wire gear stowed opposite. Deadlights set in the deckhead helped to give light.

"The mate lives forrard then?"

"Yes. This one only shipped at Colchester last freight. I asked him whether he'd live aft, but he reckoned he'd sooner be on his own. Thought he wouldn't have so much work to do, I shouldn't wonder. Mate always has lived forrard on this barge, even when Arthur Bannister had her."

We went aft to see the skipper's cabin.

"It's a bit upset," George declared. "We had mice come aboard with the last freight o' wheat we done for East Mills. I'd sooner have rats than mice, I would."

The cabin was handsome and well fitted. There was the usual glass-panelled door with brass guard rods at the foot of the ladder, grained and varnished woodwork, drawers and lockers right aft in the Yarmouth Roads, and large cupboard bunks on either side. The horseshoe lockers beneath had dark blue fitted cushions. Set in the recess against the forward bulkhead was a blackleaded stove with the time-honoured, brass-bound mantleshelf complete with mirror, the whole swinging open to reveal the stove chimney. In the corner on the starboard side was a built-in wash basin, which the skipper displayed with a vaguely apologetic air.

"Sam Fisher had that put in," he explained. That was for when he came away

83

in the barge. It's got a tank up under the deckhead though there's never been water in so long as I've been in her. Couldn't get the deck plug out for one thing."

There was an all pervading smell of mice and much torn paper in evidence.

"Traps aren't much good. Poison don't seem to touch 'em neither. "We'll have to have her fumigated before we take her away again"

The mice rather spoilt the general effect though it was easy enough to visualize the cabin in winter with a fire going and the swinging lamp over the table shining on the gleaming brasswork.

"She's a good little barge," said George as we sat chatting on the hatch top, "It's her size that's against her. We're weekly ourselves — five quid for me and the mate gets three pound ten — with a bonus every freight, but you couldn't make a living out of her, not on shares. I think it's her being so small that I never felt properly settled."

"Were you never in the river barges, then?" I asked, for I knew he had spent many years in the channel work, and had actually come into *Henry* from the 180-ton *Veravia*. "Or did you start straight away in the coasters?"

"No, I started on the river at thirteen, then went under Goldsmith as mate in the *Richard*."

I had heard of the *Richard*, built Chiswick 1833, and it was popularly supposed that the Goldsmith family fortunes were founded on her.

"I don't know about that," said George shortly. "Reckon they made more out of what she never loaded. Then there was their *Mary*. First barge I went Master of fifty-two years ago — all but a month. She was a hard-headed little old barge. Turn up anywhere, she would. Couldn't help yourself. Same as Oare Creek, just bore up till you couldn't hold her any longer, then dodged clear o' the tiller and she'd put herself about."

We finished on deck. George locked up the cabin hatch and I followed him up the ladder on to the jetty. On the far side lay Goldsmith's *Goldrune*, a husky-looking motor vessel with deckhouse aft.

"That was one o' mine," said George.

"Do you mean the *Goldrune*?"

"She was the sailing barge *Runic* time I had her in the first war and loaded two hundred and eighty tons. There was no motor in her then, more's the pity, else we wouldn't have had to anchor fourteen times same as we did one trip to Antwerp. Of course, it wasn't always like that. Another time, we had in 150 tons of scrap and 70 tons of waste paper. Mustered early one morning in the Gore and we were in the Scheldt that night.

"That's another of mine," he added, pointing across to the far side of Goldsmith's yard where a number of barge hulks lay on the foreshore. "I had that *Trojan* before the *Runic*. I'm told she got washed up Southend Beach a short while back, so that's her finished, I shouldn't wonder."

"Were you ever in the boomies?" I asked.

"Only the once. That's when I went in for ship-owning and bought the *Harold* in 1924."

"*Harold*," I repeated. "Surely, she was pretty fast, wasn't she?"

"She'd get along all right. Leastways, she'd go to wind'rd all right loaded. Sailed best trimmed six or seven inches by the head. But she wasn't all that wonderful running. Nor she wasn't on the wind after we carried away a leeboard off Nieuport when all I could get was an eighteen foot one instead of twenty foot same as she'd had."

"How did you make out with her?" I asked.

George Battershall shook his head. "She cost too much to run. Not that I skimped her. Might have done better if I had. Lost her March 1928 off the Humber. Underwriters didn't go much on it, I can tell you. She hadn't been insured with them all that long, 'cos she'd always been in the Harwich Club until they gave up the First Class barges. That's how I come to go in Shrubsall's."

A bargeman has a hard, exacting life, especially in the coasting work. Not only must he be tough and strong, but able to stand up to long spells at the wheel. The astounding thing is that so many carry on well into their seventies. It was so with George Battershall, but at the age of seventy-two he was beginning to feel his years. "Felt it more this last twelve month then all the time I've been to sea. I'm packing up and coming ashore."

"I'm sorry about that," I replied and explained how matters stood with Sam Fisher, and how he had agreed to keep *Henry* working until I was ready. "Mind you, though, we haven't agreed on the price yet. Twelve hundred and fifty is more than I can afford."

The skipper's face was a study of conflicting emotions. "Of course," I added. "She's well worth it for anybody who's after a small barge."

"And that's not many," George added, turning his head to look fixedly down river. "Not these days. No money in 'em."

"It's the survey that's holding us up," I went on. "When do you think Goldsmith's will manage to get her on the blocks?"

"Why, as soon as they get *her* out," he replied, nodding towards the *Asphodel* laying alongside the Quay with her gear lowered and sails all over the deck. She was one of their old Deptford-built ironpots and had sunk off Whitstable, ballast-laden, whilst on passage from the Colne on the night of the great gale when we were flooded out at The Nore. Her crew had been taken off by the Southend lifeboat, and after lying submerged for several weeks, she had been raised and brought to Grays.

"They're talking of shifting her out of her berth Monday day tide. Then they've got to get the blocks down for *Henry*. I reckon it'll be Tuesday if there's water, otherwise Wednesday. Who's doing the survey?"

"Percy Shrubsall," I replied.

"Can't teach him much about a barge." George was silent for a few moments, then volunteered: "If you should come to terms with them over *Henry*, I'll hang on till June, if that's what you want."

It was indeed just what I hoped for. I came away with *Henry*'s cargo book in my pocket to study at leisure.

85

Chapter Eleven

SURVEY ON *HENRY*

"Good morning, Skipper,"

George Battershall looked up from his perch on the hatch top and nodded.

" 'Morning," he replied. "Thought you were coming along at half-past eight."

"So I was until the Surveyor said ten o'clock would be early enough. He reckoned we shall have a good two hours before there's water round her."

I walked across the gang plank and sat down beside him. The blocks *Henry* rested on were great baulks of timber forming a portable grid to enable the bottom to be inspected — one forward, one amidships and one aft.

"Sooner she comes off the better. She's all right but she don't like these blocks all the same. Have you spoken to Percy Shrubsall? Saw his car turn in the gate just now. I expect he's having a word with them in the office first."

We sat and chatted for a few minutes while the young mate made a few desultory passes with a broom at the barge's side. Presently he rested on his broom and looked up.

"Finished?" asked the skipper.

"Y-yes. She's p-pretty clean now."

"Did you leave some water in her, skipper?" I enquired, for the surveyor had asked that the bilges should not be drained so that he might see if she leaked in the bottom.

"She may have a drop in her, but I haven't touched the pumps, not for three months, and she's got no plug."

A short, sturdy figure was coming across the wharf. He had a pair of sea boots in one hand and a light hammer in the other, something after the style of an old-fashioned toffee hammer.

"That's Mr Shrubsall," said the skipper and I went ashore to greet him, standing on the edge of the wharf while I explained what I had in mind for *Henry*, and how she was reputed to have had £3,000 spent on her at the end of the war.

The surveyor nodded. "Of course she's not worth anything like that on today's market. A 100-tonner is too small for trading these days unless there's special work calling for a little barge. Are you thinking of sailing her yourselves— you and your wife?

I nodded. "The children will have to lend a hand soon. Both of us are ten years older than when we sailed before the war!"

The surveyor laughed. "Aren't we all? That goes for barges, too! I've never done a complete survey on *Henry* but I've known her a long time and she was always well kept up. When I saw her down at Sittingbourne at the end of the war they were certainly doing a lot of work on her.

" 'Morning, captain," he sang out as he unlaced his shoes and wriggled his feet into sea boots. "Got a ladder handy?"

George acknowledged the greeting and pointed to the end of the gangway where a short ladder stood propped against the barge's side.

"She seems a nice little barge, captain."

"Well, she's never cost the Club much. You know that."

We went overside; it was fairly hard though we found patches of soft, squelchy mud here and there as we made our way forward.

"Now," said the surveyor, as we stood under *Henry*'s bows. "Let's see what we can make of her." He lifted the hammer and gave a series of smart blows. "Hullo, what's that?" he exclaimed as his eyes lit on a small copper tingle covering a couple of plank ends.

The skipper was standing on deck with the yard foreman who had just come aboard. "The chap who had her before me put that on."

"What for?"

"Thought she leaked or something."

"A bit of refastening and caulking would have done the job and have looked a darned sight better. Can't have that."

Tap, tap, tap ...

The hammer stopped and the surveyor stood back to look at a series of scores in the starboard bow just above the chine.

"That's queer," he murmured as he brought out a penknife and jabbed at the jagged planking, half an inch deep in places. "What happened here, Captain?"

The skipper shook his head. "Never noticed it till last week."

Meantime the yard foreman had climbed down the ladder and joined us. Ernie Carter knew *Henry* well. He and the surveyor deliberated together, measuring between the scores and prodding with their knives. Eventually they decided that they were cuts from some boat's propeller.

"It's only the sheathing," the surveyor explained. "You could have most of the scores trimmed off, with a small graving piece, perhaps, fitted to the chine side trunking."

Away he went again, with his little hammer pausing every now and then for a second tap.

"Hear that?" he demanded, hitting first one plank then another, so that even my untrained ear detected a slight difference in the sound.

"Is there trouble?" I asked somewhat anxiously.

"No. Just that the sheathing hasn't quite taken up. Could do with a little extra fastening here ... and here," and he defined the area by tapping all round again.

He paused when he came to the leeboard. "You've got an outsize in leeboards, Captain."

"You're right. Never had 'em right down on account of them being so big and heavy. Same as in the docks, we're always getting into trouble with lighters riding up over 'em. You can see the ironwork's a bit bent."

87

The leeboards were of rather an unusual, elliptical shape with a sharp leading edge after the style of *Phoenician*'s racing leeboards, a speciality apparently of the Sittingbourne yard.

Right along the starboard side of the barge went the surveyor, tapping all the time, reaching up for the wale, bending to examine the chine, even calling for a plank to lie full length under the bottom. Then under the starboard run, just where the flat bottom planking curved up to the stern, he paused and took out his knife again, pressing on the small blade until any moment it seemed likely to snap closed on his fingers.

"That's queer," he exclaimed. "Just you take a look. There's adze marks on that slight hollow in the planking and I can't make out why."

He beckoned to the foreman, who also stretched full length on the plank, though there seemed little enough to look at — just a few scalloped marks of an adze.

The surveyor considered it carefully. "It's all right," he assured me, "I can't find any trouble there, but it's been faired off for some reason or other."

He probed and tapped again, then looked up from his plank. "D'you know what I think? That original planking must have been a bit proud and they didn't notice it until they got this plank on. What would you have done if she'd been on the yard here?"

The foreman grinned. "Had it trimmed off, I reckon."

"That's just it. You'd probably tell off the nearest chap to fair it with an adze. Like as not it was some apprentice who made too good a job of it."

Some barges, especially those built with an eye to racing, have a fine run starting well forward, but *Henry* had very full ends, though George Battershall averred she could get along pretty well — to windward, at least.

The surveyor stood back to look at her. "She can't draw much."

"One foot nine forrard and two foot four aft," I said. "That's right, isn't it, skipper?"

"That's right. Light barge, she's a bit boxy, and that's why they put on another couple of inches along the foot of the rudder."

"Must be awkward. What happens when you take the ground on a hard bottom?" I asked.

"Rudder gets hung up sometimes. Makes a rare ol' noise when it drops in the middle of the night, I can tell you. You wonder what the devil's up."

Meantime the surveyor was tapping away at the lower gudgeon iron fastenings on the rudder. "These bolts are slack. Sooner they're renewed the better. And what's happened to this skeg? Got a bit chewed up, hasn't it?"

He was closely examining the aft keel or deadwood which normally protrudes beyond the stern post to prevent lines from getting foul of the rudder. The skipper had told me he got athwart *Cambria*'s chain not long back and this was the result.

"I don't suppose there's much to be done with the skeg. Better fit a heel plate, I suppose," and the foreman nodded.

On the block at Grays, with Percy Shrubsall.

There was less to pick on along the port side; the top plank of the leeboard had been set in by craft in the docks, and some of the anchor chafing plating was worn and ought to be renewed.

"So far so good," said the surveyor, as we clambered up the ladder in our muddy seaboots. "Nothing much to worry about there."

My shoes lay close handy, but the surveyor's were on shore.

"I'd better watch out or I'll have the skipper swearing at me," he said with a grin, as he padded along the deck in his stockinged feet.

"You've never heard me swear at you yet," came the reply, a reference to the many years he had been with Percy Shrubsall as Master in the coasting barges, and with his father before him.

I laughed. "You notice he says you never *heard* him."

There was a twinkle in the skipper's eye as he turned to gaze steadfastly down river. "No more he hasn't — yet!"

The surveyor sat for a few minutes writing in his notebook. "All right. We'll have a quick look down the cabin, captain, then the hold, if you wouldn't mind having a few covers off."

There was little to remark on in cabin and fo'c'sle. The surveyor peered into odd corners and probed here and there with his knife, but in the hold he tapped and prodded all along the lining and inwale on either side. Once he bade me listen and looked at me expectantly. But I had nothing to say and could only stand by while he deliberated.

"I'd like to drill to make sure," he said at last. "I wouldn't, though, unless the owner were here." More taps. "But I think it's all right."

It took a little while getting used to the dim light of the 52-foot hold with only three of its covers removed. The three great beams in way of the mast case caught the surveyor's attention. All three were scarphed on the starboard side.

The surveyor seemed quite sad. "Fancy doing a thing like that."

"It must have been when she was rebuilt," I said. "D'you think they could have been short of timber at the tail end of the war?"

"Not so short they couldn't have made a job of it if they'd wanted. Doesn't make sense scarphing new to old when they'd everything in their favour with inwales down and her all opened up."

He brought out a torch and examined the scarphs carefully to make sure they had a good lodging.

"Mind you, they're all right for the job you have in mind. What's more, the barge has been carrying cargoes without any sign of working. I wouldn't recommend you to put in new beams now the inwales and iron knees have been refitted. That would be a pretty big job. All the same they're not as strong as they would have been. What's more, these scarphs would certainly detract from the value of the barge if ever you came to sell her."

"Then that might serve to get the price down, maybe?"

"Yes, indeed, and a very strong point, too." Then, as an afterthought: "Looks to me as if owners might have decided they were spending too much money and were drawing in their horns a bit."

Before we left I gave the surveyor a rough idea of the layout we proposed for cabin accommodation in the hold.

"What about this chap?" he demanded, pointing to the tie beam across the middle of the main hold, chest high.

When we converted *June* before the war this had been worked into a stout door frame, but here the beam bisected the proposed saloon.

"I suppose we could cut it out," I said. "After all we'd not be loading cargo again."

The surveyor pursed his lips. "I'm all for keeping it in some form or other. Maybe you could work in a web frame on the coamings to pick up a good stout beam under the coach roof. Probably be all right without it, but if you sat on a bad berth some time or other it might make all the difference whether or not she'd stand up to it.

"And what about this keelson?" he went on. "You're not taking that out?"

I had no such intention, but proposed having a filling piece on either side of the six-inch-high keelson so there would be no more than a slight bump in the middle of the carpet.

"That should be all right, I suppose, but I'd never advise cutting out a keelson.

Even a light barge whips in a seaway. I remember the *Imperial* we had built at our yard some years back. We took her out for tuning up before the Barge Match and the foreman shipwright went below when we were jumping about a bit and could hardly believe his eyes.

"He called my father down to look at the keelson, which was a great baulk of pitch pine in *Imperial*. Even that was whipping! Gives you an idea when I tell you they stood a batten up on edge against the main beam and it jumped 2¾-inches!"

On deck there was little fault to find; gunwales, rigging chocks, rails, hatch coamings and covers were all in good condition. Then followed inspection of standing rigging and all the gear; deck winches, worm steering, windlass and anchor chain.

"What are the sails like, Captain?" he asked, testing a seam of the foresail.

"Not bad. One thing, they do fit her. We're just off the yard after getting the mains'l seen to. That's the worst sail though it should last another couple o' years."

Finally we came to the sprit, the most distinctive feature of a sailing barge. The surveyor eyed it up and down.

"That's hollow," volunteered the skipper.

"Just what I was wondering," and he gave it a smart tap.

"That's a thing I'd like your advice about," I said somewhat apprehensively. "Do you think it's all right — a hollow wooden sprit?"

But the surveyor had no qualms. "Why, yes. I do. After all, yachts have hollow spars. In fact, if I were having a new spreet for one of my barges that's what I'd go for — provided I could get good, seasoned timber. Look at the weight it saves aloft ... Hold on though. I don't like the look of this."

All the while he was talking he had been exploring the heel of the sprit with his knife. Apart from the usual score where the sprit rubbed against the mast, there was a nasty jagged place.

"Looks as if that's been done by the lower jackstay bolt on the mast when the spreet's squared right off to port. That's a pity." More probing and tapping. "Can't make out how far the plug runs up. The end's solid, you see, and if it comes up this far, then it won't matter; we could trim it off and have a small graving piece fitted. Wonderful what can be done with the new glues these days."

The skipper was peering at it. "I don't remember the spreet ever fouling the jack-stay," he said. "Never had her squared off that far since I've been in her."

"D'you happen to know how long the plug is?"

The skipper shook his head. "The spreet was shipped from here, so I gathered. Yard ought to know," but the foreman was unable to help, though he reckoned the damaged part could be trimmed off easily enough.

"The gov'nor bought a couple down at Cowes. Come out of the big yachts time they turned over to Park Avenue booms. I know I had the job of cutting them down about ten feet and fitting new plugs, but how long that plug is I just can't remember."

"You don't remember which yacht *Henry*'s spreet came from," I asked.

Ernie Carter shook his head and murmured: " 'J' Class, I fancy."

"Was it *Britannia*?"

"Could have been."

But the surveyor was more interested in the damage. "It's probably nothing serious. The best thing would be to have a good look at it when the gear's down."

Time was getting on. I glanced at my watch; it was gone half-past-two and I had a train to catch.

The surveyor walked across the yard with me to the gate before returning on board to complete the survey.

"Well," I said. "What do you think?"

"She's a good little barge — as good as any you'll find of her size."

"And the price?"

"You say they're asking £1,250 and you're after the best barge you can get for £1,000. Well, you'll have to reckon on a bit of shipwright work. Depends how much you decide to have done, but that shouldn't amount to much — say £50. Then there's the possibility of a new spreet which would cost sixty quid, and maybe a mains'l in a year or two. And there's the scarphed beams. I'll be letting you have a full report as soon as I can, but you've got an idea of the most important points. Why not make an offer ...?"

☆ ☆ ☆ ☆

I had a reply from Sam Fisher's solicitors by return of post:

"... Owners are not willing to accept your offer of £700, but if you care to increase it to £950, being half way between their price and your offer, we think an offer of this amount would receive favourable consideration ..."

Perhaps I should have stood firm at £700, but I came up another hundred pounds, provided the barge was fumigated. And instead of keeping her trading over the next five weeks, I suggested she lay on Goldsmiths' yard while I arranged for essential repairs to be carried out.

My proposal soon brought a reply.

"... May we suggest that you telephone us when we will endeavour to conclude a bargain with you ..."

We did. I bought *Henry* for £800.

Chapter Twelve

ON THE YARD AT GRAYS

Henry had been shifted off the blocks to Cole & Lecquires' Jetty when I took Dorothy and Elizabeth aboard for the first time. It was drizzling as we left Whitstable after an early breakfast and although the sun broke through on the Ferry from Gravesend to Tilbury, there was a nip in the air and I was glad to find the skipper had lit the fire.

"I was just going to give the cabin a birthday when my son brought your letter down, so I thought I'd better leave it."

"Birthday?" Elizabeth whispered. "What does he mean by giving a birthday?"

"He's going to give it a scrub."

"Well, I hope he doesn't give me a birthday, too!"

She quickly slipped down the ladder and demanded to be told where her cabin was to be. One of the hatches was off and I pointed below. She leaned over the coaming to peer into the hold, then drew back and screwed up her nose. *Henry* had already been fumigated. There were warning notices plastered over the hatch tops and traces of brown sticky paper where scuttle hatches, pumps and ventilators had been sealed. I thought perhaps it was the gas Elizabeth found repugnant, but the skipper shook his head.

"I've aired through down below," he said, "but it's the limber boards that's up and letting out the stink from the old wheat down the bilges."

"Just the job for the mate," I suggested.

"He's gorn. Cleared out this week and shipped in the *Scot*."

"That's a pity. What about the mice? I hope they've gone, too."

"Haven't seen any about — only dead ones. Plenty o' them in the cabin."

Leaving Dorothy and Elizabeth on board I walked round to Goldsmiths' office to show the survey report to Ernie Carter, the foreman shipwright, and discussed the work to be done. There was nothing very serious:

"Trim off scoring on fore end of chine trunking, also the upper scoring on starboard bow.

Remove metal plating on both port and starboard bow plank ends, caulk and refasten stem plank ends and make good anchor chafing plating in way.

Remove and renew bolt fastenings of lower rudder gudgeon iron.

Make and fit a new heel plate to after keel.

Trim scoring on upper plank of starboard leeboard, and tiebolt after end.

Remove and renew broken stern fashion moulding."

The sprit we decided to leave until I came down again, but Ernie Carter promised to let me have an estimate for the rest of the work early the following week.

Dorothy seemed quite favourably impressed with *Henry*, though I would have preferred a more propitious day for her first visit. Luckily Elizabeth had forgotten about the smell, and back at Whitstable when she and Peter were put to bed that night, we heard her describing with a great wealth of detail the skipper's cabin that was to become their playroom. We never had any real doubts about the children's reaction to living aboard a barge, but it was encouraging to see their enthusiasm.

Goldsmiths' estimate came to £28, including the lowering of the gear for inspection of the sprit, and I gave instructions for the work to be put in hand. The following Friday, when I went down from the City after lunch, I found *Henry* already on the yard and lying just off the quay where the blocks had been. The skipper had the boat alongside and ferried me across. He was a bit taciturn and I thought he might have missed his afternoon nap, but realized later he had taken the sprit episode seriously to heart.

"Won't take long to get the gear down," he said, as we cast off topmast forestay and unshipped the dolly winch. "Better ship the wheel guard before we forget, same as at Colchester when we slit the mains'l on the mizzen stayfall cleat."

The gear came down easily enough. It was the same procedure as with *June*, the only difference being in the gear for striking the topmast. In *June* we used a rope tackle, whereas *Henry* had a chain leading from an eye bolt in the deck to a single block on the tail of the wire heel rope, thence to the metal-welped barrel of the mast case, round which it was surged. For sending the topmast aloft, three turns of the chain and it could be safely left to its own devices, leaving both hands free to heave away on the winch handle. The usual thing was to let the chain run off the barrel into a bucket beneath.

The sprit fell away from the mast as it came to rest on the hatch top, and I brought Ernie Carter aboard to make his inspection.

For a few minutes he probed with his knife, then looked up and smiled. "Plenty of strength there. That may be hollow, but there's a two-inch wall all round, don't forget." He took his time: "Just wants trimming off, that's all. Besides, I've never heard of a spreet going at the heel, have you, George?"

The skipper looked up solemnly. "Only the once, and that was your *Carina*. Spreet went right through her deck. I only know 'cos we had the job of taking her a new one!"

"Might as well leave the gear down," said the foreman. "We'll get this done tomorrow."

"Then we'll leave the heaving up to you," I laughed, and the other two joined in. "That's fair seeing we lowered down."

" 'Tain't the lowering down," said the skipper. "It's the other I object to."

"But the gear's pretty light," I persisted. "Your mate told me he's rigged *Henry* himself."

The skipper looked up scornfully. "What him? With three other bargemen on the handles more like!"

Ernie Carter laughed again. He was very easy going. "That's all right. My chaps'll give a hand."

Meantime the skipper was cutting away the old blue-white-blue bob from its frame. "I knew they had some new ones in the office. No use to them any more. Better put one up while we can get at it nice and easy. There's four more down below."

I took the new bob and frame to Goldsmiths' sailmaker as I had no needle and thread, leaving the skipper casting around for something to serve as a truck on the spindle end.

The bob was duly rigged and George produced a smart, rounded truck, which certainly looked the part at the time; it was months afterwards I came to suspect surrealist tendencies and discovered it to be a madly sprouting potato.

The first thing I saw when I went below and rummaged through the port bunk was a dead mouse. Then I saw something move — white wriggling things. They were maggots.

"That's a good start," I exclaimed, turning up my nose in disgust.

The skipper came over and picked up the mouse. "Must've been the flies. There's been a few about recently. I did have a go at the lockers, but I can't get into 'em properly."

"Have you a brush on board?"

The skipper produced two. One was new. "Bought that down at Whitstable last time we were there. Cost Sam ten bob. I've looked at that several times and thinking that 'ud be more use at home. Too honest, that's my trouble!"

He had already swept up a number of dead mice. "Must be pretty strong stuff, that gas. Even stopped the clock! And all the brasswork's gone black, too."

Presently we went on deck. The tide was away, and it was time for us to be gone as we had to get the boat to the head of the dock while there was still water.

The next Saturday when I went down to Grays again, I found the gear up, although the topmast was still struck. They had cut off the offending eye bolt and shortened the mainmast jackstay. The sprit, too, had been trimmed in way of the chafe and dressed.

I took off my coat and turned up my shirt sleeves. It was hot down below and there were still a few flies about. I unshipped the cabin skylight and started clearing out the port bunk, which George had used as a repository for spare gear. There was a canvas signal flag locker which was quite new; so was the boat sail. Then came sundry oilskins, bobs, foghorn and bits of clothing. There was any amount of paper and mouse dirt but no more bodies. I swept out the bunk, then tackled the small, dark locker with a sliding door situated beneath the bunk. Out came a miscellaneous collection of spun yarn, oakum, marline, tarred hemp, shackles, thimbles, nails, a hammer and other odds and ends. I sorted them out, threw away the unwanted trifles and stowed the remainder in a couple of sacks.

After that I tackled the lockers in the Yarmouth Roads. The shelves unshipped, which made things easier. I brought out from the back a well-stocked First Aid chest, a dry card compass and a set of brass stencils.

95

The table unshipped; there was a small locker underneath containing spare lamp glasses, cutlery, and a gimballed oil lamp. A large drawer above was empty, except for a bottle of ink, a couple of charts and the ship's papers wrapped in a canvas wallet. The starboard quarter locker was empty, except for a burst packet of salt and a considerable quantity of wood chips probably left by the ship-wrights at Colchester where the davit sockets were removed and holes plugged after *Henry* got foul of the Everard motor tanker. The next locker contained a teapot and a tin box for bread, while the small locker beneath contained the cleaning materials. I cleared everything out and swept through.

The skipper came aboard while I was on deck for a breather. He seemed quite glad to see me.

"Thought I'd come down and finish the decks off down aft. They're pretty dry and just crying for a lick o' paint."

We took a look at the sprit.

"You know," he said. "I've been thinking about this a lot, and I still don't reckon that was the jackstay that chafed the sprit — not while I've been in her anyway. I never had the sprit squared off that far. Too much blooming hard work getting it in!"

The skipper got out his paint and started on the quarter deck while I worked in the cabin. I pulled up the linoleum in way of the cabin companion ladder and prised up the small hatch. There was a mass of nauseating black wheat and water in the bilges. One sniff and I closed it hurriedly.

"A pity the mate didn't stay on a bit longer," I said as we climbed on deck for a breather. "He might have cleaned out these bilges."

"Not likely! He'd have been missing soon as a job showed up. They're all the same these days. The only one I've had with me any good since the war had his wife away with him. She was a worker. Good as any mate."

"It looks as if I'll have to get the yard to do the job."

"Reckon they'll say that's the crew's job. I'm not doing it though. Might've done once a time, but not now!"

Work progressed slowly aboard *Henry* during May. I was in no great hurry. Our house at Whitstable was still on our hands, but I was borrowing from my mother to enable me to complete the purchase by 11 June, when I planned to take *Henry* away sailing for a week, finishing with the Marina Club Barge Match, which I had been persuaded to enter, before starting on the conversion.

One fine sunny morning Dorothy came up to Grays to help. Elizabeth came too, and helped me fetch water from the fitter's shop for Dorothy to scrub out the cabin.

We passed the bunk boards up on deck. Meantime I found an incredible amount of gear in the fo'c'sle in spite of the fact that the skipper had told me there was not much in the way of spares on board. There were three shovels, three pinch bars and a couple of crowbars for shifting timber, a set of well-greased rigging screws neatly sewn up in sacking, stanchions and wire guard rails, deck scrubbers, mops, two black, folding, tin signal balls, spare leeboard pen-

The new crew.

nants, two mooring wires, several rope tackles, a bunch of shackles, spunyarn, marline, cotton line, chain strops and blocks of every description. And under the stove where I lit a fire to make tea were three dead mice.

Presently Elizabeth appeared at the hatch.

"Mummy wants us to buy her three cups and saucers and some more Vim and a teapot, and ... " Then after a few moments' pause the words came tumbling out: "... And please may I have some fizzy lemonade."

We went shopping in the market at the top of the hill. Elizabeth had her lemonade, and candy floss besides, and we came back aboard to find lunch laid on the hatch top. Dorothy had scrubbed right through the cabin having used three Vims and a cake of carbolic soap.

Ernie Carter came on board and had a cup of tea with us and I asked him about the bilges which still smelled badly of sour grain.

"Best thing would be to have 'em stoked out. We've an old chap on the yard who enjoys pottering about with a rake and shovel. He's been stoking out our *Esterel* up at the top of the dock. You can guess what her bilges are like after laying sunk off Clacton for five months with a freight of wheat. And I suggest we bore a hole aft so's to let a foot or two of water in to swill around, and when she's drained off a bit we'll pour in some carbolic."

97

I knew George had an aversion to plugs; they are always liable to work loose or get knocked up on a hard bottom.

"I can't talk, though," George said. "I had four in the *Clara*. Same as working the River Lea, light, we had to let in water up to the first rung of the fo'c'sle ladder so's to get her through bridges."

It was finally agreed that a plug with a graving piece fitted over the hole outside could do no harm.

While we lay on the yard, news came through that eleven of Goldsmiths' steel sailing barges — their entire fleet except for the 180-ton *Scot* and *Briton* — had been sold to The London & Rochester Trading Company. The *Asphodel*, which had sunk off Whitstable that wild February night, was among them and was refitting in the dock. Just beyond her lay the *Esterel*, without gear and looking very desolate and forlorn, surrounded by small piles of evil-smelling, stoked-out wheat. *Esterel* was going for a lighter.

I was standing on the edge of the dock when the yard manager came along. He was an engineer, for the yard was mostly concerned with motor craft since the war. Sailing barges he regarded with amused tolerance, especially yacht barges.

Did I know the *Black Swan*? Her owner was one of the richest men in the City, so it was said.

"...They dropped down river at the end of March on their way to Holland. The old gentleman came into my office and said he'd like us take a look at the gear for he thought there might be some work to be done to the sails.

" 'All right,' I said. 'You fetch her in and we'll see what we can do.'

"I didn't give it much more thought till the sailmaker came along and asked if I'd seen her canvas. They'd hung out her sails. Thin! It wasn't a case of seeing the light through. Why, you could see the whole blooming river!

"I got hold of the old chap and told him he'd better let us set the barge up with a new suit, but he wouldn't have that at all.

" 'No, no,' he said. 'They're not all that bad. We'll make do. Just you get your sailmaker to patch 'em up.'

"When they came to lower down, our chaps found dry rot in the sprit. It had gone in the usual place up by the yard tackle band.

" 'Well, well,' said the old chap, shaking his head sadly. 'That won't do. Better have it ashore if you can't repair it.'

" 'Too far gone to repair.'

" 'I thought so. Then perhaps you can find me a decent second-hand one cheap. You must have lots of them lying around in a yard like this.'

"But we hadn't — not to fit him, anyway. In the end he decided to let us make him one for sixty quid.

"Then he started on about the old one. Wanted to know what we were going to allow him on it.

" 'Nothing,' I said. 'That's no use to us.'

" 'Come, come,' said the old chap. 'What about five pounds?'

" 'No. It's not worth a penny — not to us.'

"You know he was so persistent it was terribly difficult to make him realize that spreet was as soft as a pear and we'd got too many like it littering up the yard.

" 'But surely a fifty-foot spar must be worth something,' he said. 'Can't be all that bad. Like the curate's egg, you know — good in parts!'

"You couldn't help laughing the way he came out with it. Yes, he paid all right. The money came along by return of post with a covering letter.

"We'd been a bit hard, so he thought. We really ought to have allowed something on the old spreet. But you had to hand it to him. D'you know what? Said he only did business in round figures. Damned if he hadn't knocked off the odd shillings and pence."

Several years later I met Chris Merrett who went skipper of *Black Swan* at Grays. He grinned when I told him the story of the curate's egg.

"He never did get that five quid," he said. "No, no, but when we come to get away the yard manager said he reckoned I'd be looking for something out of it, and I said I shouldn't bring the barge back on the yard again if I didn't. No, no. Old man Hoare never did get that five quid 'cos they gave it to me instead."

I knew nothing of all that as I stood chatting by the side of the poor old *Esterel*, but I did warn the yard manager not to expect the odd shillings and pence from me either, whereupon he snorted and swore nobody was going to get away with that a second time.

"... Another thing," I added, tongue in cheek. "I want an allowance too."

This was too much. He gave me a swift, searching glance, but I managed to keep a straight face. "Whatever for?" he asked.

"Why, for all that wheat you've taken out of *Henry*."

"All that what!" For a moment he thought I was serious, then grinned and shook his head. "If it's wheat you want, just help yourself from the *Esterel*."

A year or so later I told the story of the *Black Swan* to a crowd of visitors aboard *Henry*. Among them was a young sapper who owned a very fine yacht barge and his wife Barbara.

"You knew the *Black Swan*? So you knew my uncle. You see I was a Hoare before I was married."

It was a mixed gathering aboard *Henry* that night but to their eternal credit not a soul laughed. Later on I told Barbara that she really must be more careful what she said.

"But so I was a Hoare ..." Then she clapped her hands to her mouth and was covered in confusion. Poor Barbara!

While still at Grays I sold *Henry*'s 15-ft boat to Percy Shrubsall for £37.10.0 as a reserve boat for his own big barges *Gladys*, *Verona* and *Veravia*. We preferred *June*'s old boat, partly out of sentiment and partly because the smaller boat could be more comfortably carried in davits. Besides, *Henry*'s boat was rather fine forward and inclined to tow under in a seaway, so George said.

The Kelsey brothers brought *June*'s boat from Whitstable on board their

Vicunia. Alf and Horace had been together for many years before ever she had an auxiliary engine. Now she had been given a second engine and her gear taken out altogether. The barge was beautifully kept. The cabin had been given over completely to the engines and they lived in the fo'c'sle, which was light, airy and immaculately clean. On top of the black-leaded cooking stove stood a battery of gleaming Primus stoves. It was a revelation to me that bargemen who had been in sail all their lives should readily adapt themselves to these new conditions. They were as proud and as careful of their engines as any qualified engineer, detecting the slightest variation in beat that eluded me completely. Indeed, it set me wondering whether I who was gormless at anything to do with engines might yet have a spark of mechanical genius within me.

The mood passed. It was low water at Grays and I had to wade through mud to get aboard *Henry*, which lay alongside the gutted motor barge *Servic* just outside the shed where she was built forty years before.

It was my last weekend on board before we fetched the barge away. The work had been completed. The bilges were now quite sweet although some water and disinfectant had been left in to swill around. Having lit the fo'c'sle stove and fetched water I swept through the hold and squared off the cabin, finishing up by black-leading the stove and polishing the brasswork.

Very dirty and somewhat tired, I enquired of the watchman for the nearest telephone, thinking it would be just outside the gate.

"It's up at the station," came the reply.

I hesitated and looked down at my clothes. "I can't very well go up the town like this."

"The boys from the barges do."

Pocketing my pride and acting on the principle of nobody knowing me hereabouts, I trudged up the hill in my seaboots, only to find the telephone required two pennies even though I intended reversing the charge. I had to return aboard for change, then up the hill again and meeting all the good folk of Grays coming out of church clad in their Sunday best.

It was worth it though; Dorothy agreed to bring Peter as well as Elizabeth that Whit Monday morning.

We viewed with some apprehension Peter clambering up the ladder to board *Servic* and picking his way over her much-littered decks to the plank that led down to *Henry*.

Peter disdained all help. I went first, very carefully, turned and found him following me quite unconcernedly. Then he, too, turned and called to Dorothy.

"Can 'oo manage, Mummy?"

As I remarked to Dorothy, we should worry!

Chapter Thirteen

GRAYS CRAFT

Grays waterfront must have been a fascinating place in the old days when barges were in their heyday. The Goldsmith family had been sailing barge owners for a hundred years but there were others, too, whose story is all but lost in the passage of time.

Between Goldsmith's yard and Pier Wharf or Landfield's Wharf, as some of the old folk knew it, there used to be a pier where the steam hoys called and a Customs House which was later incorporated in Cole & Lecquires' premises and only pulled down in quite recent years.

The granaries and stores hardly changed at all and William McNamara, one of the new directors, came across a fascinating relic tucked away at the back of an office desk.

"Particulars and Conditions of Sale of the valuable long Leasehold Interest in the extremely eligible mercantile property known as THE PIER WHARF situated on the North Bank of the River Thames with the substantial dwelling house in the High Street, Grays, also of 10 valuable sailing barges and the goodwill of the old-established business carried on by the late Mr. Landfield; which will be sold by auction by G.B. Hilliard & Son at the Pier Wharf, Grays, on Tuesday, Sept. 25th, 1888, at four o'clock in the afternoon, by order of the Trustee ..."

Mr Lecquire, to whom application had to be made to view, was Sam Fisher's grandfather, clerk with Mr. Landfield, and it appears that Lot One included the craft which he wished to retain, for he afterwards took over the business, joining up with Henry Cole, farmer of West Tilbury.

Lot One comprised the house, grain warehouse, hay and straw warehouse, coach house, iron warehouse with carpenter's shop and paint shop, blacksmith's shop, coal yard with poultry house, cement water tank and dung and sawpits, also five sailing barges all well found and well known on the River Thames with their rigging, running gear, cloths, anchors, stores and boats.

The Major. Spritsail barge (stumpy). 41 tons reg. Built Wandsworth 1880. Master: John Alexander. This was a 100-ton barge which Alexander had for many years and she was owned in the firm right up to the 'thirties.

Emma. Spritsail barge. 37 tons reg. Built Grays 1845. Master: J. Baker. She was a swim-headed barge and Arthur Bannister (*Henry*'s first skipper) had her for a while. Then young Bill Alexander took her and she finished up about the turn of the century.

Gladiator. Spritsail barge. 35 tons reg. Master: Henry Surrey. "And as disagreeable an old man as ever stepped aboard a barge," was George Battershall's comment. She finished up during the first war.

101

Esther. Topsail barge. 39 tons reg. Master: William Taylor. This was a Ware barge built at North Hyde, Hertfordshire, 1837 and she, too, finished up during the first war.

James. Spritsail barge. Master: Alfred Coppin. She was really a lug barge or wherry carrying some 30 tons. "Alfred Coppin made his fortune out of her," said George. "It couldn't have been from the money he got, for the skipper's weekly wage was thirty bob, the mate twelve bob, and they got a hundredweight of coal a week. She was what they called a cotchelling barge loading a little bit o' corn here and a little there. Worked a lot for Randall, Maltsters, whose main place was at Barking."

Lots 2, 3, 4, 5 and 6 were sailing barges obviously to be sold away for one reason or another, and only the *Landfield* was written up as the valuable topsail barge, well found with all her rigging, running gear, cloths, anchors, stores and boat. The others were just advertised as the good barge *Good Intent* etc.

Lot Two. *Landfield*. Topsail barge. 44 tons reg. Master: Walter Wennel otherwise known as Old Bluff Wennel. The barge was built on Pier Wharf 1864 and launched sideways. She was a beamy stack barge and was bought by Underwood of Southend, passing later to William Smy, Ipswich, and derelict since the last war on Bloody Point, Shotley.

Lot Three. *Good Intent*. Topsail barge. 43 tons reg. Built Chelsea 1790. Master: Isaac Pomfrey. Sold to Tom Baldwin, landlord of The Hoy, now The Theobald's Arms. "That's the barge," declared George, "that went up through Southend Pier one time o' day." She finished up with Harwich owners.

Lot Four. *Henry*. Topsail barge. 34 tons reg. Built London 1827. Master: Cripps. Sold to Henry Curtis, Plaistow.

Lot Five. *Sarah and Ann*. Topsail barge, 45 tons reg. Built Nine Elms 1853. Sold to Henry Gozby Solly, Whitstable.

Lot Six. *Star*. Spritsail barge. 33 tons reg. Built Lambeth 1836. Master: Henry Bannister. Sold to Ambrose Ellis, Stanford-le-Hope.

A later addition to Cole & Lecquires' fleet was the *Burnham*, built by Taylor at Sittingbourne in 1864 and formerly Maldon-owned. When she eventually finished up in the late 'twenties, an old deaf chap who had once sailed her, went to live on board and eventually broke her up on the hard.

Then, of course, there was the *Rose* built by Goldsmith's in 1899, and Arthur Bannister came out of the little *Emma* to take her. But some of her timber was apparently unseasoned, for the *Rose* developed dry rot, and was eventually sold away to the South Coast for trading in the Isle of Wight.

When our *Henry* was built in 1904 her timber was specially selected, with Arthur Bannister standing by. Quite by chance, I happened to find myself seated at dinner in London alongside a stranger whose father, it transpired, had helped to build *Henry*. I knew, of course, that Archie White brought shipwrights with him when he came from Kent to manage Goldsmith's barge building yard; apparently Fred Preston was one of them, also Arthur Daniels and Jimmy Birch, who usually went by the name of Windy. Others who worked on *Henry* were

Walter Daniels, Walter Johnson and Charlie Cole. They had all gone, but I did come to meet Ernie Horncastle, apprenticed to Archie White and later becoming a successful furnisher at Grays, also Bill Hall, grocer, who carved the name on *Henry*'s stern.

I heard from Bill Hall the story of *Henry*'s first trip when a party went down river for the day. It started breezing up and the barge began to heel. Mrs. Lecquire felt ill and demanded to be put ashore.

"You're a nice one," her daughter Carrie declared and forthwith had to make a dash to the side herself.

Henry was the last barge to be built by Goldsmith's. They scrapped their own building programme in favour of the 280-ton Dutch-built ironpots *Runic, Servic, Britannic, Doric* etc. Archie White's contract was cancelled against a payment of £200 and he went to Toronto to build scows for the Canadian Government.

Through the good offices of Reg Preston I came to meet Arthur Bannister's widow, also his son Joe who was mate in *Henry* from 1909 to 1914. From them I gleaned quite a lot about *Henry* and her old skipper.

Arthur Bannister started at the age of eleven as third hand with his father in a barge belonging to Curtis of West Thurrock. He was a very particular man and Arthur told the story of young Curtis coming down to the cabin and being told in no uncertain terms that the cabin had just been scrubbed out, and that he was to go and wipe his boots.

They were ten in family; three of Arthur's brothers were drowned from the barges; one was swept overboard by the tiller; Harry was run down; the youngest one was shifting his barge in the dock with a hitcher and was lost overside.

Joe Bannister was often away with his father as a youngster, and one of his earliest recollections was of falling between the barge and the quay at Mortlake with a pot of peas in his hand. *Henry* was built as a stackie, with considerable flare to her shallow sides, sometimes lifting up to fourteen loads of straw from the front of the jetty at Grays for Limehouse or Greenhithe. Apart from Cole & Lecquires' own corn and stack work there was quite a lot of outside work from the maltings at Grays and Barking to the London Docks for shipment by the Irish packets to Guinness at Dublin: there was malt for Mortlake and an occasional freight to Maidstone. *Henry* also carried imported barley from the docks to Seabrook's brewery at Grays.

Henry was run down and badly damaged by the L.C.C. sludge steamer *Bazelgette* whilst at anchor in Long Reach during fog. Another time she drove up over her anchor off the Millwall Dock as a passenger steamer went by, pricking herself and sinking. She was in trouble, too, when a German steamer came into her whilst brought up off the London Dock, but on the whole she led an uneventful life, and Arthur Bannister saw to it she was well kept up. Young Joe was made to scrub out the coal lockers, and there was never any stinting of paint. Even the hold lining was decorated with blue above and red beneath, but graining was Arthur Bannister's great hobby and he was very clever at it by all accounts.

Henry was taken up for mine watching duties along with many other barges. She lay off Swanscombe mostly, and Bill Tester, whose Greenhithe firm was engaged in servicing the craft, told me she was looking pretty rough by the time she came off in 1943. No wonder it was a case of breaking her up or rebuilding. Cole & Lecquire decided on the latter; *Henry* was towed to Milton Creek and the Sittingbourne Ship Building Company took her in hand.

Mr. H.W. Harvey was the surveyor employed to supervise the work, and it must have been a job after his own heart, for he had a real affection for sailing barges and hated to condemn any of them. Between them they made a good job of *Henry* in spite of the scarphed beams, and Putwain, the local sailmaker, certainly produced a good-fitting suit of sails.

Jimmy Barrell, a fine old bargeman and a great character, who had come ashore out of Goldsmith's big iron-pots, stood by *Henry* for the last two months and brought her away from Sittingbourne 8 February 1945 to load English wheat at Grays for Empire Wharf, Erith. As Sam Fisher had said, she was to all intents and purposes a brand new barge — still only a 100-tonner but capable of carrying her 450 quarters under hatches, snug-loaded, as the bargemen say.

Henry was an East Anglian barge now fit for trading down Swin, and when Cole & Lecquire had no freights of their own in the river she went wherever business offered; Whitstable, Southend, Queenborough, Ridham Dock, Colchester, Felixstowe. By autumn, though, poor old Jimmy Barrell was a sick man. His heart was troubling him and he had to go ashore. Unfortunately he died before I had the chance to meet him, but he must have been a wonderful character for Sam Fisher thought the world of him.

Richard Shepherd took *Henry* away; river freights were interspersed with outside cargoes to the usual outports as well as places like Strood, Faversham, Ipswich, Heybridge Basin and Maldon. But Trunky Shepherd and Sam Fisher fell out. They had words over laying windbound in the Ness while other barges were making their passage, and it was then that George Battershall came out of *Veravia* to take *Henry* at the end of February 1948.

And now she was a yacht, and Joe Bannister and all the other good folk were keenly interested, for they had known her so well over the years.

"What was she like to sail in the old days?" I asked Joe.

"Pretty fair," he replied. "Especially light barge to wind'rd."

It was interesting that he should say that for George Battershall said much the same. Indeed George reckoned there wasn't much to touch her in the river with a fresh breeze and a strong weather-going tide. Yet those full ends seemed to belie any pretence to speed.

Joe shook his head. "I can only tell you we came away from Grays one time with 300 quarters of wheat along with Harry Pearce in *Satanita*, and beat him the length of Long Reach. That was to wind'rd and her one of Goldsmith's racers, too!"

Chapter Fourteen

FIRST TRIP

I got Nick, a pre-war sailing friend, to come away with me for a week. *Henry* had been put off to her anchor, and it was good to feel her lift to the wash of passing craft. We were in good company, for Shrubsall's *Veravia* lay just above us as well as the smaller *May Flower*, whose deep, old-fashioned stern frame was still intact and but recently painted a rather pretty shade of blue. She had a white mainsail. It was new, so the mate said, and they bent it the last time they were in Maldon. John Moyes, the skipper, was away home for the weekend.

Inshore of us was the deep-laden *Senta*, steel-built and flying the crescent moon of The London & Rochester Trading Company in place of Goldsmith's tricolor. She had rammed the lock gates of the Gravesend Canal Basin a few months earlier, but steel barges seemed easier to repair than wooden ones. With a wooden barge — and most were over 50 years old — an owner was usually apprehensive of what he was going to find once inwale and lining were stripped down, and more often than not a barge that met trouble was sold to avoid expensive rebuilding. But even iron-pots could not last for ever. *Senta* was built at Southampton in 1899, and plates that once stood up to the rough and tumble of London River were now so dented that her bows were quite corrugated between each frame.

Towards high water Cremer's *Nellie* towed out from the jetty with topsail set. Grain-laden, she had been in collision with a steamer in Tilbury Reach a few days before and beached at Cole & Lecquires' premises for temporary repairs. Now, with a rough tingle on her starboard bow and her crew busy making sail, she towed out under our stern, slipped her rope and bore away down river for Whitstable.

We, too, were bound down river in *Henry*, but I wanted to freshen up the cabin before we got away. Nick and I stripped to the waist and brought out paint pots and brushes and started painting out the two cupboard bunks.

They were done by evening and all the cabin panelling washed down. Then we relaxed on the hatch top and ate bread and cheese for supper, washed down with tea that invariably tastes so much better than a similar brew ashore.

In the peace of that summer evening, when even the spate of river traffic had quietened for a while, *Veravia* and *May Flower* lay at anchor in a golden, shimmering pool, their gear and rigging standing out stark against all the glory of the setting sun. At such moments there is magic abroad on the London River.

We camped in the hold that night. I found it hard to get to sleep. The fact was I missed my bed and as I lay awake I fell to wondering whether I was going to stand up to a life afloat once more. This hankering after the creature comforts was disturbing. Perhaps, after all, I should have listened when Dorothy reminded me we were ten years older than the old *June* days.

105

Henry.

By morning though, whatever doubts I may have harboured were gone. The old urge was still there. I turned out at six o'clock, lit the coal range in the fo'c'sle, cleaned the cabin deckhead and had the varnishing all but finished by the time Nick called me to the sort of gargantuan breakfast I could seldom face on shore.

Some time before noon we had the cabin done and I thankfully stowed away the pots and brushes and brought out the grease for sprit muzzle and collar lashing. Then I went round with the oil can — worm steering gear, leeboard winches, vang fall blocks, main brail winch, windlass and so on. At last we lay back soaking in the sun while the breeze came ... and died ... and came again in catspaws that scarcely ruffled the placid waters.

Presently the flood began to take off.

"What about it?" said Nick. "Shall I shorten in?"

I nodded, then rose and stretched luxuriously. "When you like."

We lay to a couple of shackles. Nick shipped a windlass handle and hove away. There was very little up tide now and he worked to a lively clank of the windlass pawls.

Presently he paused and straightened up, for the chain had worked over to port on the windlass barrel. I cleared away the pile of wet chain and flaked it on the headledge grating.

"All yours, Nick. Let's see you fleet it, if you remember how."

Nick grinned. "Let me see now." He slackened back a foot or so over the barrel, then gripping the chain with both hands flung it adoitly across.

In a flash the chain snubbed taut and Nick nodded appraisingly at his hands as if surprised to find them whole. I left him to shorten in while I went aft to set the mizzen and drop the leeboards.

Nick peered over the bows. "Up and down," he called.

I hauled out the topsail sheet and hoisted away. That topsail certainly set well with its diagonal crosscut seams which were seldom seen these days.

"We'll make a trip inshore to start with," I said, after a quick glance at the motor barge *Saxon* that lay outside us. "May as well get the stays'l ready for hoisting. There's not enough breeze for the fores'l."

I gave her a few cloths of the mainsail by slacking off on the main brail winch, then dragged the great mainsheet block aft to the traveller on the main horse, and moused the hook.

With the wheel hard over, up went the light staysail sheeted to windward, and Nick broke out the anchor.

"She's aweigh!"

I took the weight of the main brail, lifted the pawl, quickly unshipped the handle, and let the heavy folds of the mainsail drop out on the run, then slipped aft to overhaul the sheet.

Henry paid off slowly. I let the staysail draw; it flapped lazily and filled. Almost immediately it was time to come about.

The anchor was up now. Nick had unshipped the windlass handle and was stowing the last of the chain.

"We'll let her come," I said quietly and put the wheel hard over, wondering all the while whether she would come about for it seemed we scarcely had steerage way.

She came all right, winding under *Senta*'s stern, and we stood slowly out into the river clear of the wreck of the old training ship where the tide sets so strongly on the ebb. Then, with a breeze that flattered only to deceive, we went away on a long board on the port tack down Northfleet Reach, eventually to

Peter, Sarah Rogers and Elizabeth sitting in the hatchway.

come about again off Tilbury Jetty in such light airs that steamers coming up river shaped to pass ahead of us while yet a good mile off.

Presently though, the easterly breeze began to freshen and water gurgled along our sides. We set the foresail and beat down past Gravesend. *Henry* was sailing now, coming about and filling on each fresh tack with encouraging docility. We hardened in the mainsheet and experimented with the vangs. She sailed best with a good flow in mainsail and topsail.

Just below the ferry I made to get yet another inch or so on the mainsheet as we winded. Somehow or other the sheet got foul of the hatch cover we had purposely left off to air the hold. Turning up with one hand I made to free the parts with the other. In a flash I had my hand jammed against the hatch cover, and the mainsail full of wind.

Nick saw I was in trouble and came running aft; luckily I was able to get my hands clear with nothing more than barked knuckles and a white score across the fingers. We had to put *Henry* about again to clear the sheet. It was just another reminder to take no chances. Trimming the mainsail whilst winding in a breeze of wind with the heavy sheet block slamming to and fro across the horse calls for the deft hands of a bargeman.

It was amazing how quickly the breeze piped up out of nothing at all. Within a few minutes of drifting down past Tilbury we had a smart breeze easterly so we had to hand the cotton topmast staysail. The intention was to bring up off The Ship and Lobster just below Gravesend but we could not resist the opportunity of a punch to windward down the reach. *Henry* was sailing beautifully, with very little heel, and ate out to windward on the weather-going tide until at last we called it a day and we bore away round the Ovens Buoy to run back over the tide.

Ernest Piper, deep-loaded, came running in from sea, probably with ballast from the Colne. She held up along the Essex shore, where the tide had less strength, but we squared away on the port gybe and gradually fetched across to the Kent side. I stowed the mizzen so as to steady her. At times we were running by the lee.

"Will she hold it?" Nick called, as he came aft having stowed the forsail.

"Should do," I replied, keeping a weather eye on the bob.

After all, we were bringing up shortly by the cluster of powder barges at Denton. But the breeze was fluking and the mainsail clew was beginning to lift. We were too close to the shore to luff.

"In with the mainsheet," I shouted. "We'll have to gybe."

Suddenly, without further warning, over she came, catching Nick with the sheet in his hand. Before he could snatch a turn it was running through his fingers. He yelled as the sail slammed over and the sheet whistled out through the blocks. Then he hopped about nursing his fingers.

It might have been worse; he got off lightly with only two large blisters.

The barge looked after herself. The lee vang had been set up luckily and took the worst of the gybe. Even so there was plenty of weight in the breeze. And yet that gybe was surprisingly light. Indeed *Henry* hardly seemed to notice it.

As we came into the anchorage we got sail off with the intention of bringing up between Wood's *Asphodel*, last of the fine old Portsmouth-registered, Admiralty powder barges, lying just below the pier, and Everard's coasting barge *Greenhithe*, away out in the stream.

Nick struggled with the mainsail, for his hands were painful. The sail was heavy and the brails jammed against the backstays and runners.

"Let go your anchor, Nick," I shouted, and dashed forward to drop the topsail headstick.

A few fathoms of chain ran out, then silence.

"She won't pull the chain out," said Nick.

"Never mind. Give her plenty," for I felt sure the anchor was not yet on the bottom.

I picked up the dip bucket and threw water over the barrel. The chain went with a run and Nick leaped back. Of course I should have warned him. Luckily he still had his fingers.

With a shackle and half out *Henry* tended to sheer about as she drove up over the tide. We were almost past caring — Nick and I — as we sat for a while on the cabin top nursing our wounds. Nick's fingers were blistered and my knuckles raw and bleeding. It was our first day's barge sailing for ten years; all in all, *Henry* had let us off lightly, for in the space of a few hours we had relearned the hard way lessons both of us had off by heart before the war.

We watched *Ernest Piper* drive up through the anchorage, holding the same gybe all the way. She brought up just above The Ship and Lobster. The sun set while we ate supper on deck; this time it was *Greenhithe* silhouetted against the western sky, Everard's big steel coaster that Bob Roberts banged about the North Sea.

We had a quiet night. Again I was agreeably surprised what little noise *Henry*'s leeboards and rudder seemed to make. Or it may have been we were just too tired to notice. I suffered no more inhibitions but slept like a log.

The breeze was south-westerly by morning. *Lord Roberts* and *May*, both loaded, dropped down on the last of the ebb and brought up just above us. *May* was beautifully done up in true Ipswich fashion, her stern an epic in colour and gallant scrollwork.

I spent an hour on deck cleaning an accumulation of soot from the riding light, watching the while all the comings and goings of London's shipping. And later on, while I scrubbed the decks, *Greenhithe* got under weigh just before low water. She was bound up river and stood across to work the slacks over on the Tilbury side.

Towards noon, with most of the more immediate jobs completed, Nick and I went ashore after stores. They could let us have paraffin at the barge yard but not stockholm tar, which they no longer used. It was in short supply during the war and now they made do with cod oil and a dash of coal tar for dressing shroud lanyards.

On the blocks lay *Revival* (ex *Eldred Watkins*), whose master, Trunky Shepherd, a round-faced, jovial man, had *Henry* for a time after the war.

"I'd have stayed in her, too," he told us, "but that after Jimmy Barrell left her she'd really been promised to George Battershall who was getting on a bit and wanted something smaller than *Veravia*. That *Henry*'s a good little barge. Only trouble is she's a bit small to get a living in. Same as winter down Swin, times you can make a passage in a big powerful barge when a little 'un can't look at it.

"There's one thing you want to watch out for," he went on. "And that's the rudder. Don't cut things too fine across the sands else you'll catch out one day ... break yer arm if you're not careful. They went and put a bit on the foot of the rudder so's it sticks out now a couple of inches below the bottom. Said it would help the steering. Reckon they'd have done a sight better to fit an extra bit on the blade same as I got 'em to do with this one."

Revival was a smart looking barge, with narrow hatches and pronounced camber found in many of the older Ipswich craft. She gave the impression of being well cared for — something intangible yet none the less real.

"It's up to you how you keep 'em," Trunky declared. "Make what you like of 'em. Most owners don't worry."

I asked what he thought of our hollow sprit and whether it had anything to do with our involuntary gybe, but he had no fault to find.

"No. That spreet's all right. They usually do gybe easy with the gear all new."

"I went round with the grease pot yesterday," I said.

"There you are, then!"

110

Nearby, two shipwrights were fashioning a new topmast with adze and saw. It was to go in *Ethel Ada* that was coming in on the next tide to take *Revival's* berth, for she had carried away her topmast when the shrouds caught on a coaster's flaring bows as she towed alongside.

These barges with the red wale were owned by Successors to T.F. Wood (Gravesend) Ltd., an associated company of Imperial Chemical Industries, and engaged in the carrying of explosives to and from the anchorage at Holehaven. There were famous names among them. In addition to *Asphodel*, *Revival* and *Ethel Ada*, there was *Ardeer*, the baby of the fleet, *Dreadnought* (formerly Goldsmith's racing coaster), *Gipping* and *Orwell* (both from Paul's Ipswich fleet), and *Edith & Hilda* (once owned by Samuel West, Gravesend).

Early morning, towards tide time, the barge anchorage came to life. *Lord Roberts* got her anchor and reached slowly over the last of the flood bound for Stambridge Mills near Rochford. Then *May* hoisted her topsail and shook out her mainsail. She was away down Swin for Ipswich.

Revival came off to her anchor as we picked up friends for the trip to Leigh. It was time for us to get away, too, for the barges were already on the swing.

The weather was sultry at first and the breeze fitful. However, we had the ebb under us down the Lower Hope, where the breeze came again from the northeast and freshened. We came up with Horlock's *Millie* in Sea Reach, grain-laden no doubt, for Mistley or Ipswich. Then the breeze took off again and came in catspaws from all points of the compass. We held over towards Canvey, trimming our sails as best we could, while *Millie* soaked away down in the best of the tide and brought up with *May* and *Lord Roberts* and several other barges off Westcliff.

We rounded Leigh Buoy and presently found sufficient breeze to fetch over the last of the ebb coming down the Low Way, dropping anchor at 8 p.m. in 2½ fathoms just below the Ray. Later that night we sailed up the creek in the boat and landed our guests opposite the Crow Stone. Nick and I saw them across a couple of small rills where the bottom was quite firm and sandy. Then we returned for fear of losing the boat in the dark, and sailed back to *Henry*.

Ours was a pleasant anchorage, remote and alone, with buoys flashing and ships' lights out in the fairway; there was neither noise nor wash from passing ships; only an all pervading sense of detachment, with banks between us and the shore.

☆　☆　☆　☆

It was raining when I looked out on deck at 4 a.m. We had thought of slipping down to Whitstable on the ebb, but the bob hung lifeless, and it was only then as I turned in again that I realized my left hip was hurting, a relic of the previous night when I took a crack from a swinging backstay block. Both Nick and I were still full of aches and pains, but our hands were hardening in spite of our cuts and blisters and skinned knuckles.

111

We spent the morning working on the gear; ratlines needed new seizings and the serving on the shrouds was worn in places, and grey for the want of dressing. Towards mid-day we took the flood up Leigh Creek in the boat and landed at Bell Wharf. I searched the town for stockholm tar, but the various ship chandlers no longer stocked it. The Leigh bawleys had gone and their place taken by a new type of motor craft. Cockles still came ashore in vast quantities in time-honoured fashion, ferried in bulk in each cockler's boat and landed in baskets along a whipping plank. But there was no longer any call for stockholm tar, so I was told. True, the sailmaker had a little he could spare us, but when we called to collect he was busy on some racer's sails.

"It's a rush job," he said. "Can't you come back tomorrow?"

We could not. A fine easterly breeze had sprung up, which was too good to miss. By the time we had sailed out to *Henry* and thrown off shore clothes, it was six o'clock and almost two hours ebb. The intention was to reach up the creek under topsail while we hove up the anchor, then to come about and fetch the Leigh Buoy, setting mainsail under way. Maybe we should have shortened right in first. As it was *Henry* came driving up and grinding over the chain as soon as the topsail sheet was hauled out, and it took the two of us to break out the anchor before setting the foresail and gybing round. Then we gave her the mizzen and a few cloths of the main, but the topsail gave trouble, for the lowest hoop had got foul of the mainmast cap.

There was no time then to clear it. We needed sail on her quickly and we gave her the full mainsail, getting what we could of the sheet and hardening in as we came about with a mighty flogging of half-set canvas.

We had to make several trips to keep in the channel, for we were not sure whether there was still water enough over the sands, but once to weather of the Leigh Buoy we cleared the topsail and shook her up to trim the sheets.

May, *Lord Roberts* and *Millie* were still at anchor as we sailed past close-hauled on the port tack. Beating down Sea Reach in the sparkling sunshine with the sails properly set, *Henry* began to show her paces, jumping about in the sea-way and flinging spray over the foredeck so that Nick had to secure the fo'c'sle hatch. It was grand going, smashing through the short seas kicked up by the weather-going tide, winding and filling with hardly a check. We hardened in the mainsheet and worked on the vang falls until we were satisfied we could do no better. Then we punched down almost to the Nore Towers before squaring away for the Medway on the port gybe, with the lee backstay and runners slacked right off.

There was still plenty of strength in the ebb and *Henry* tended to sheer about until I stowed the mizzen. She settled down then, and we came surging in past Garrison Point, with the sky gradually clouding over, and made over towards the West Shore where the *Scotsman* lay at anchor.

"Where you for?" they shouted, and must have wondered what a light barge running up the Medway would be after.

"Bringing up," I replied and slacked away the mainsheet for Nick to brail up.

We brought up just above her, and as I lay aloft to stow the topsail, *Pretoria* came running in from sea, a wonderful sight with sprit squared off. She sailed on past us for Chatham.

That night I looked out at eleven o'clock. It was quite dark although the sky had cleared. Away on the other side of the river was the dark shape of a barge under sail, with her green starboard light showing as she made up for Queenborough.

The surf breaking on the flats sounded loud and sinister in the quiet of the evening.

☆　☆　☆　☆

We turned out to a cold and dull morning, with an easterly breeze blowing in from sea. While Nick squared off the fo'c'sle after breakfast I scrubbed out the cabin, polished the brasswork and black-leaded the stove. A woman would have taken half the time and got herself less dirty in the process.

On the flood we lay head to wind and tide, with the mud close abeam. We shortened in, then set topsail and mizzen and a few cloths of the mainsail. With a good sheer out and a backed foresail *Henry* broke out her anchor unaided. Soon we were running up the Medway all squared away.

We gybed over several times that afternoon. In a breeze of wind most barges will ruck topsail or pick up the skirt of the mainsail, but there was no need of that with *Henry*, although for the first gybe in Long Reach we set up the lee vang, hove in the mainsheet and took a turn round the mainhorse chock. We hardly felt it.

The next time, coming through the Forts in Kethole, we grew bolder and scarcely bothered about the mainsheet. And in Gillingham Reach we really hardened our hearts and let her bang over on her own. It may have been the extra beam or the hollow sprit, but gybing was less terrifying than with the little old *June*.

Cockham Woods, just above Hoo, makes a delightful background for an anchorage. That evening I lingered on deck fascinated by the dark wooded slopes that seemed somehow to be invested with an air of mystery. The tree tops were silhouetted against the after glow of the western sky, and from time to time the song of the nightingale came clear and sweet above the twittering of the vast unseen bird population settling for the night.

We pottered about in the Medway for a couple of days. Some old-fashioned ironmongers produced my precious stockholm tar. Farmers bought it, so they told me, as a specific against foot rot. It was also rubbed on dogs' muzzles for distemper.

It was a great joy dressing the shroud lanyards. I warmed up the tar on the fo'c'sle stove and it smelled so good that I felt constrained to abandon my brush and work it in caressingly with my bare hands.

I felt we had got to know each other — *Henry* and I.

The author and Harry Blaxland of Daniels Bros., Whitstable, aboard *Henry*. *Petrel* beyond.

Running out of the Garrison. Elizabeth on the main horse. The boat has been lowered to act as a sail.

Chapter Fifteen

MEDWAY BARGE MATCH

There was quite a good entry for the 1949 yacht barge race organized by the Marina Club, Hoo:

"*Arrow* (Thames Barge Sailing Club)
Gladys (D Biddulph)
Winifred (C H Burge)
Spurgeon (Marina Club)
Russell (Marina Club)
Iota (G Duttson)
Henry (A S Bennett)
Dipper (J R Elliott)
Leslie (T A Lapthorn)
Petrel (D G Rootsey & T R Foister)
Lady of the Lea (W Aslett)
Dinah (J H Briant)"

Dinah was a 45-ft. barge yacht built at Rochester in 1887 and rebuilt by The Whitewall Barge Company since the war. The rest had all been built as trading barges, many of them converted to well-appointed yachts and ranging in size from the 75-ton *Dipper* to the 160-ton *Winifred*.

The race was to be sailed under Y.R.A. rules and only amateur bargemen were allowed to take the wheel. We all mustered at the top of Long Reach, except for *Lady of the Lea*, for she had grounded at Kingsferry Bridge on passage to Hoo. A last-minute entry, albeit unofficial, was the 29-ft. barge yacht *Nancy Grey* (Ralph Rogers), built by Frank Shuttlewood at Paglesham just before the war and probably the best of her type afloat.

The official forecast was a moderate to fresh northerly breeze that should have sent the whole fleet out of the Medway, round the Nore Towers and back on a broad reach for most of the twenty-two miles. As it was, we started with a light to moderate north-easter that gradually fined away and veered so that we had a nose-ender on the long beat seawards.

Canvas was limited to the five working sails; mainsail, foresail, topsail, staysail and mizzen, though *Nancy Grey* sailed with her large new mainsail, foresail and jib. To avoid jostling in the comparatively narrow reach, the racers were to be timed over the line within fifteen minutes of the gun. Even so, *Winifred*, slow in stays with her steeved-up bowsprit, had the misfortune to get aground just below the Darnet Fort. Her owner-skipper was loth to disqualify himself by using his engine and tried to kedge off. By that time she was well and truly on the mud; it was a great pity for she was beautifully fitted out and would have given a good account of herself.

The ex-Goldsmith's *Gladys,* a fine powerful barge that had made a remarkable trip to the Clyde since the war, led the fleet over the line. All made a long board close-hauled on the port tack. *Nancy Grey* was in the best of the tide and soon worked out ahead. *Leslie,* too, was going well, but a new wire headrope in her mainsail had left the sprit peaked up too high for the topsail to set as it should; even bowsing down the topmast forestay failed to take out the bag. *Iota,* with her new well-cut staysail, held a nice breeze but, sailing without a mizzen, she was inclined to fall away each time she winded.

Astern lay *Petrel,* the Ipswich coaster with the dainty lines we might have bought a year back. At one time it looked as if she was going to start a luffing match with *Russell,* manned by a crew of small boat enthusiasts.

We were lucky aboard *Henry* for she had only recently finished trading and had come off the yard freshly tarred and with a clean bottom. I was hoping my old friend Jack Waterhouse would have come with us as pilot for he was probably the most famous of the Medway barge racing skippers. He was first home in *Daisy Little* in 1893 and again in *Harold Margetts* when the Barge Match was revived in 1927. Unfortunately he was not well enough to come, but when I went to see him two days before he had given me many invaluable tips.

"... The tide runs from point to point. Mind you don't stand in too far out of it ... Another thing, if you're carrying stays'l, lead your sheet right aft to the mainhorse so's to set it nice and flat ... "

And that is what we did, leading the sheet to the warping drum on the leeboard winch and heaving in the staysail till it set like a board.

Ahead of us was *Gladys* standing on right out of the tide. We could see the line of scum astern of her marking the edge of the slacks.

"Ready about! Down with the weather board! Lee-oh!"

Staysail sheet was cast adrift. *Henry* came surging up into the wind with a mighty flogging of canvas. The foresail snatched at the bowline and was quiet.

"In with that stays'l sheet!"

The mainsail and topsail slatted and slammed as the sprit lurched over; block and traveller clattered across the mainhorse.

"Leggo fores'l!"

Off came the bowline and away went the foresail, loose-cut on the foot like a great bag, and filled with a crack.

We were away on the starboard tack with the weather board hove up. That was the first of many trips we made on the long beat out to the Nore. A few short dodges through Kethole and we drew clear of *Leslie* and *Gladys* and there only remained *Nancy Grey* ahead. We came up with her just below the coaling hulk, but she managed to weather the reserve fleet on the buoys; soon she was half a mile ahead again.

I could almost hear old Jacko: *"Watch yourself now ... And look out for the tide a-running off Port Victoria away over towards Garrison Point to fetch you out o' the Ness ... "*

And that's what we did, so we came up again with *Nancy Grey* in the popple

116

Henry rounding Nore Fort (Newcombe).

kicked up by the weather-going tide in the mouth of the Medway. Astern, a whole lot of barges were coming down in line abreast. *Iota* had overtaken *Dipper* in Kethole and worked the West Shore until making a long leg across towards Queenborough in the hope of picking up the ebb out of the Swale. Instead, Geoffrey found himself practically becalmed, while *Gladys*, *Leslie* and *Russell* hugged the other shore and kept on coming.

Coming out of the Ness, *Leslie* caught *Petrel* on the wrong tack. With bowsprit steeved up and head in the slacks *Petrel* was slow in stays and *Leslie* was wise to come about. Even so, they caught each other a glancing blow on the bows but no damage was done.

Dinah, of the egg-shell blue topsides, found a slant all to herself and drew up on the others. But the breeze was taking off and fluking, though generally speaking, we found enough outside, even to look up for the Nore at one time, until the big yacht barge *Santille* (ex *Beryl*), fresh from the yard with *Vicunia*'s lofty gear, came motoring up slowly on our starboard quarter on her way to Holland and planted herself immediately ahead of us, her boat towing astern right under our bows. After enduring her wash for a few minutes hoping for an extra puff that would have made her sit up, we came about.

Nancy Grey, meantime, had found the lop in the main channel unprofitable and went away over the Cant into quieter waters, but we drove *Henry* between the Medway approach buoys, making the most of the ebb.

A barge seemed to be coming up on us. It was *Russell*, sailed by our old friend Benny Benton. For a while *Russell* dropped the rest of the fleet astern, then she struck a bad patch and was practically becalmed. We lost the tide soon after mid-day; there never had been much strength to the ebb and *Nancy Grey* went away on a long board towards Warden Point to get some easting before the tide began to flow.

The breeze was veering now and still fluking from time to time. On several occasions we were caught out and had to bear away in a hurry. My shoulders

117

began to ache; it is surprising what a kick the wheel has at times even with so light a breeze. But once we picked up a slant that enabled us to look right up for the Nore Towers while *Nancy Grey* was pointing yet for Warden. Presently she, too, luffed up. Within a little though, the breeze flew back easterly again and we were left with slatting canvas and a spinning wheel, while *Nancy Grey* bore away easily with her tiller steering.

The last half mile to the outer mark was tantalizing. A trip towards Warden: "Lee-oh!" and away we went on what we fondly imagined to be the last board. But we fell off to leeward as the flood began to make. Again ... and again ...

Meantime *Russell* was away on a long board in the direction of Shoeburyness. *Spurgeon*, not to be outdone, seemed to be heading for Southend. And astern, *Petrel*, *Gladys* and *Arrow* plugged away over the Cant. But *Nancy Grey's* long board in the general direction of Whitstable paid handsomely in the end, for she judged her winding to a nicety and fetched the Nore Towers hard on our tail. She followed us round as we bore away and gybed over on our weather for the run home.

"Ease off the mains'l! Up leeboards!"

With the breeze on our port quarter and the tide under us, we seemed to ghost along as steady as the proverbial rock. Suddenly we realized the sun was shining and peeled off our jerseys. And all the way up the Medway approaches *Henry* and *Nancy Grey* kept close company as if loath to be parted.

And what had old Jacko said about reaching? "*...Don't forget to have a bit o' line handy so's to unshackle the chain sheet and ease off the fores'l...*"

We called across to *Nancy Grey*. "What about switching off that engine?"

There were answering sallies and an invitation to step aboard for a tot of rum. It was a pity that the course could not have been shortened when the breeze fell away, for the other barges had been beaten by the tide. Three hours' ebb of a sluggish tide is not enough for eleven miles to windward in a light breeze. *Gladys, Dipper, Leslie, Arrow, Petrel* and *Dinah* had punched away out by the Cant until we came running back, then they, too, turned for home.

Nancy Grey seemed to be gaining slowly, but she lay between us and Garrison Point.

"Watch out for the slacks," we called cheerily.

"I'll be calling for water soon," came the reply.

Nancy Grey was never really out of the tide, but our lofty rig kept us going while she lost the wind under the lee of the Point and fell astern. Up Saltpan Reach we squared off everything and boomed out the foot of the mainsail. We even lowered the stern of the boat in davits.

One by one the other barges sent up their spinnakers. We did likewise. None of us carried a real spinnaker but staysails were unhanked from topmast forestays and hoisted with the luff up and down the mast and the sheet led aft outside the shrouds. It was a sight to gladden the heart as the entire fleet came running up through Kethole, gear squared off, sails full and bulging in the bright afternoon sun.

118

The author and the Barge Match Fleet.

We got our gun at half past four to beat *Nancy Grey* by seven minutes. That night at Hoo all the crews foregathered in the Marina Club for supper in time-honoured fashion. Standing on the balcony of the Clubhouse so ideally situated on the rising ground, with superb views of the river on all three sides; over the creeks and saltings down to Sheerness; Gillingham and the barges in the fore-ground; away up river where the training ship *Arethusa*, once the four-masted barque *Peking*, lay in the bight under the wooded slopes of Upnor — standing there in the peace of the evening, it was good to listen to snatches of conversation from inside. Old Jack Waterhouse would have delighted in it all; he had had so many such celebrations in his time.

"... I got my head in the slacks. Thought she'd never come..."

"... She wouldn't quite fetch. Had to make a trip after all... "

"... And what's all this Y.R.A. business about, I'd like to know. Stand on when the spreet's over your cabin hatch. That's good enough for me..."

"... Thought you were off to Southend, Jock... "

And back would come roar after roar of full-throated laughter.

Yes, we'd had a 'good owd sail', as my old friend Billy Austin would have put it, but the part I enjoyed most was at the very end when we picked up the mainsail and stood in across the flats to fetch up alongside the quay at Hoo with such a quiet air of purpose and inevitability that none of us felt the slightest misgivings. Indeed, there was scarcely need for a fender.

119

Chapter Sixteen

ON THE YARD AT HOO

We left *Henry* at Hoo after the Barge Match and the following Saturday Dorothy and I called on John Briant, Managing Director of the Whitewall Barge Company, from whom I had already received a rough estimate of £1,050 for the conversion. We found him in Whitewall Creek aboard the old sailing barge *Alfred*, which we had known before the war when she lay near *June* on the flats off Bennett's Wharf at Gillingham. *Alfred* now served as an office.

"That's one thing I want," said Dorothy.

"And what's that?"

"Why, a staircase like *Alfred*'s instead of a companion ladder."

"All right," said John. "That could be arranged easily enough. How about the general layout?"

Dorothy spoke again. "To start with, I don't like the idea of a keelson in the saloon."

"Neither do I," said John. "If it's steel we can cut it out level with the ceiling."

I shook my head. There were two schools of thought about the necessity of retaining the keelson in a barge that will never load cargo again, but I disliked the idea of disturbing the main structure of the barge any more than could be helped. Besides, Percy Shrubsall, the surveyor, had advised against it.

"No," I said. "We're not cutting out the keelson."

"Not even to please your wife?"

"Not even to please Dorothy."

"That's fair enough," said John with a laugh. "What do you propose then — flooring over the top?"

I shook my head. "I thought we might pad it out, as it were, so as to make a bit of a hump under the carpet."

John Briant leaned back in his chair and drummed his fingers together.

"I suppose it *could* be done. Well, let's say wedge out the keelson in the saloon about eighteen inches each side. Anything else special?"

"Just that we don't like skylights. They leak and they get foul of the gear, and we're scared stiff of the children putting their feet through them."

"What will you do for light then?"

"Why, have lifting hatches in the cabin top, and ports in the coamings."

John Briant could see no real snags, although he obviously thought skylights more usual. We should need quite a number of ports, but I said ex-naval ports suited better than new metal ones; 10-in. or 12-in. like those fitted to *Five Sisters* could be had quite cheaply, and if need be we could always fit deadlights in the lifting hatches.

We knew pretty well what accommodation we wanted, though *June*'s layout was no great help as she was so much smaller. A more suitable model was the post-war conversion, *Iota*, the barge we had seen in Oare Creek.

The general layout was fo'c'sle with central heating boiler, then two bed cabins in the fore hold; fresh water tanks and airing cupboard under the mast case; the large saloon amidships opening off the galley, bathroom, and so on. All this was similar to *Iota*.

"Right," said John. "I'm with you so far. Usual cabin fittings I suppose — bunks with drawers under, wardrobes and dressing tables."

"A kidney-shaped dressing table for me, please," said Dorothy. "That's something I've always hankered after."

John's pencil was working overtime. "Jubilee boiler in the fo'c'sle for central heating, Rayburn in the galley for cooking and hot water supply. And usual bath fittings —"

"One barge we saw had a green bath," Dorothy broke in. "I rather liked that. She had flush doors, too."

"Simple enough," said John. "What about the engine?"

This was where we differed from *Iota*. She had an engine and a sunken wheel-house aft. We wanted neither.

"No thanks," I said. "Abaft the saloon we'll have a bed cabin to port and a study to starboard. And right aft we'll stick to the skipper's old cabin."
"You mean just as it is?"

I nodded. After all, why not? It was a pleasant cabin with its graining and brasswork and blue cushions. The whole character of the barge was there, the very thing we were so anxious to retain. Besides, it was ideal for the children with its table and horseshoe-shaped locker seats and all the cupboard space in the Yarmouth Roads for toys. And we still had the roomy, curtained, built-in bunks for visitors to sleep in.

"All right," said John with a smile. "The cabin stays. Let's see, we gave you £1,050 as a rough idea. There's a few more things here than we bargained for. We'll have to go into figures carefully, but I should say we'll be able to get pretty close to our rough estimate. We're moving down river to our new yard at Hoo in a few weeks. If you like we'll make *Henry* our first job. Let's say three months from the middle of July, that should take us up to October."

Dorothy looked at me dubiously.

"We want to be in before the winter," she said.

"And so we should," I replied, and John nodded agreement. After all the biggest job is usually the raising of the coamings and ours had already been done when *Henry* was re-built at Sittingbourne. Nor did we require any panelling inside, for the linings were practically new.

"There's one other thing," I said. "You thought you'd be able to find us a barge to live aboard should we sell the house before *Henry* is ready."

"That's right," John replied. "I had the *New Acorn* in mind. She was one of our earlier conversions."

Henry: main hold showing tie beam, keelson and port chine keelson.

We came away from *Alfred* and walked through the ruins of Formby's old cement works to the creek, where a number of yacht barges lay moored alongside.

"Here's the *New Acorn*. I think she'd suit quite well."

"Isn't she in use then?"

John shook his head. "No. The owner got into trouble out sailing. Mains'l block came adrift. You know the sort of thing. He's never been aboard since."

"M'm," said Dorothy cautiously, as John pushed back the scuttle hatch. "You see what I mean about ladders and stairs?"

"After you," said John, and I was about to follow Dorothy down the ladder when she came chasing up on deck.

"If you think I'm going to live in a place like this," she stormed, "then you've made a great mistake. It's nothing but a pigstye."

John was at fault really. He should have seen for himself just what state the barge was in, for anyone less hardy than Dorothy might well have been put off barges for good, coming on such a litter of dirt and rubbish and empty bottles, apart from that dank and foetid oppressiveness that any boat acquires left shut up and unattended for any length of time.

A few days later I went down to Hoo one evening to meet Tony Lapthorn, naval architect and yard manager, as well as owner of the yacht barge *Leslie*. Armed with chalk, we went on board *Henry* to lay out the cabin accommodation.

122

"That's the best way of doing it," he said. "You can see the snags that way. I can measure up afterwards for the drawings."

We started aft in the skipper's cabin. We wanted a door cut in the bulkhead, and the stove was in the way.

Tony looked at me expectantly.

"It'll have to come out," I said, and Tony chalked instructions on the bulkhead. After all we were having central heating right round the barge and there was no real need for a stove.

"And what about this?" Tony asked, as he opened a locker door to port of the companion ladder. "Do you want to keep this water tank?"

It seemed hardly worth while. The skipper's wash basin had its own tank. No, the space could be better employed for coats and oilskins.

Then we started on the hold, fifty-two feet in length, with a beam inside varying between fifteen and sixteen feet. There was full headroom under deck both fore and aft, but owing to the sheet, there was no more than five feet amidships. But the main hatchway was thirty feet by twelve feet and the fore hatchway ten feet by nine feet, giving over seven feet headroom.

We chalked out the bulkheads for the study and aft bed cabin. The saloon, too, was quite easy to visualize, about sixteen feet square in the middle of the main hold. The keelson was to be made into a hump, but there was no camouflaging the middle tie beam. Aboard *June* we managed to work a door frame, but in *Henry* it cut across the proposed saloon.

"You'll want that out, of course," said Tony. But I was not happy about doing away with it altogether. The surveyor had recommended that it should be retained in the form of a solid coach roof beam for although *Henry* would never load a cargo again, should she come to sit on a really bad berth the tie beam might make just that difference in holding her together.

Tony was quite amenable. "We can manage that all right. Those hanging knees could be worked in upside down. That would stiffen her up."

We decided on port holes — thirty-two all told — and coachroof hatches; bulkheads for galley and bathroom, and positioned the companion hatch and Dorothy's staircase.

The galley more or less sorted itself out; sink on aft bulkhead; dressers on either side, Rayburn, coal bunker, Calor Gas stove; saucepan cupboard, refrigerator; full length broom locker and so on.

"Now what about the header tank? You really want it under the deckhead and not on deck?"

"If it's, at all possible," I replied, for I had a horror of decks cluttered up with extraneous gear and fittings.

Tony took a few measurements. "We'd probably manage to work in a fifty-gallon tank. Anyway, that's where you'd like it, up in the corner of the coamings with shelves under."

Owing to the restricted headroom, the space under the mastcase between the two hatchways always proved a problem for working in cabin accommodation in

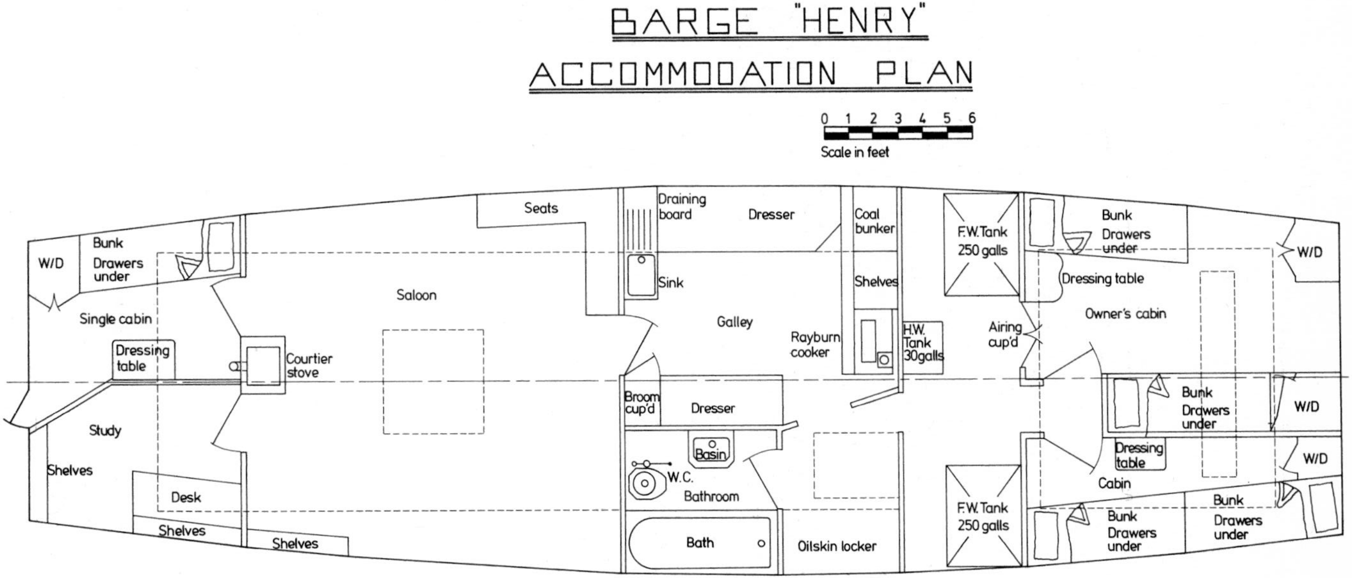

BARGE "HENRY"

ACCOMMODATION PLAN

0 1 2 3 4 5 6
Scale in feet

W/D
Bunk
Drawers under
Dressing table
Owner's cabin
Airing cup'd
W/D
Bunk
Drawers under
Dressing table
W/D
Cabin
Bunk
Drawers under
Bunk
Drawers under

F.W.Tank 250 galls
F.W.Tank 250 galls

Coal bunker
Shelves
H.W. Tank 30 galls
Rayburn cooker
Dresser
Galley
Draining board
Sink
Seats

Dresser
Basin
W.C.
Broom cup'd
Bathroom
Bath
Oilskin locker

Saloon

Courtier stove

Bunk
Drawers under
Single cabin
Dressing table
W/D
Study
Shelves
Desk
Shelves
Shelves

Whitewall Barge Company's first plan for the conversion of the hold. There were only minor changes in the final plan.

Henry: carlines being fitted.

all but the very large coasting barges. In *Henry* It was the obvious place for the two 250-gallons fresh water tanks and the airing cupboard.

Forward, we chalked out the two bed cabins. The children's cabin was fairly easy to plan with bunks end to end under the starboard deck. Our own cabin proved more difficult; the problem was to work in a double bunk without taking up all the floor space.

In the end we were sitting on the keelson with chalk lines all around. We looked at each other and shook our heads.

"I don't know about you, Tony," I said. "I'm tired and thirsty."

We left the bed cabin to a later date and adjourned to the Club house.

☆ ☆ ☆ ☆

It was a magnificent summer in 1949 and the family needed no persuasion to come to Hoo again at the weekend. Even Spanker, the dog, came, all of us arriving in the village about mid-day. Dorothy went shopping. There was thunder about, and by the time we had Peter perched on top of the bag on the push chair we had bought for five shillings especially for this pilgrimage, it started to rain, and we stood under a tree close by the church. For a while it was not too bad and the children sang to keep themselves amused. Then the heavens opened and the gutters became a roaring torrent.

125

Peter gnawed at a loaf, then he began to get wet, which was not so pleasant. Just as Dorothy and I were wondering what to do, a lady called to us from a cottage opposite, and we left the pram and bag under the tree and took shelter indoors. Peter and Elizabeth made themselves at home and cheerfully helped themselves to biscuits. When we finally got down to the Whitewall Yard we found the wharf where *Henry* lay was a quagmire and I had to put down hatch covers to form a catwalk, much to the children's delight.

We all slept in the cabin — Peter in the starboard bunk and Elizabeth in the spare berth to port. Dorothy slept on a camp bed and I dossed down on the lockers.

On the whole it was a quiet night, though Dorothy and I lay awake for quite a while listening to the once familiar sounds of water gurgling under the bottom and the slight creaking as *Henry* lifted on the tide. Peter woke twice; he had got himself curled up at the foot of his bunk and hit his head on the water tank. Elizabeth nearly fell out once. Spanker spent the night with Dorothy. I managed to persuade the children to stay in until nearly 8 a.m., but eventually they got dressed and I took them for a walk on the sea wall while Dorothy cleared up and prepared breakfast.

We collected bits of coloured crockery from the foreshore where the brick-field had been years before, and made a mosaic garden in the grass which Peter ringed with bricks. The *pièce de résistance* was a headless and footless lady carrying a small child which Elizabeth and Peter christened the Vergant Mary and treated with great respect. They also found handles from one-time chamber pots which they used for telephones and conducted long conversations in a peculiar, high-pitched voice after the style of a ventriloquist.

Dorothy gave her approval to the proposed layout, although we decided to make the galley larger and the bathroom smaller. Our cabin forward, however, proved more intractible. It seemed quite impossible to work in a double bunk. In the end we decided on two single bunks.

It was a most successful week-end. The weather was glorious. Neither Peter nor Elizabeth showed the slightest sign of falling overboard; indeed, as Dorothy remarked, we were the ones who had to watch our step across the narrow gangplank, whereas the children skipped to and fro without faltering.

We were a thoroughly grubby, tousled-headed family that wended our way home late Sunday afternoon through the back streets from Whitstable station.

Peter was soon bathed, and tucked up in his cot, thumb in mouth, murmured drowsily; "We's *Henry* boys."

☆ ☆ ☆ ☆

The Whitewall Barge Company made a start on *Henry* Monday, July 11th; their estimate for the job was £1,125 with the wiring for shore lighting extra.

I went to Hoo midweek to find the hatch covers off and the heavily cambered oak carlines cleaned up as new for cabin top beams. And when the family

126

went aboard again the next weekend many of them had been placed in position and some were already dovetailed into the shelf. The new beam to take the place of the middle tie beam had also been fitted and the fresh water tanks installed under the mast case.

Ten days later all the beams were in place and varnished to keep out the weather. Electric power had not yet been installed in the new yard and the port holes in the five-inch coamings all had to be cut by hand, a most tedious and arduous job. The bulkhead framing was all ready for the hardboard panelling. The old coal range had been taken out of the fo'c'sle and a modern enamelled boiler put in its place. Indeed, the whole of the central heating was finished, the pipes making a complete circuit of the barge through bunks, lockers, drawers and cupboards.

Tony said they were waiting for the cabin top planking. It had already been cut and was only waiting to be machine planed, but Drake's timber yard at Strood was on holiday.

"There's something here, though, I'd like you to take a look at," Tony went on, and opened up the newly fitted oilskin locker aft where the water tank had been. "D'you see this?"

He brought out his knife and stabbed at the upper part of the beam. The paint crumbled and the knife sank right in.

"Phew!"

"I thought it might have been sap wood," he added, poking away with his knife. "But the top of the beam has certainly gone and I wouldn't mind betting the dry rot's followed the camber down to the knee." Then stabbing upwards at the deck planking: "It's up here, too."

With the surveyor's enquiring mind, Tony tried to puzzle out the cause. There must have been water getting through to the beam and rot was setting in for want of ventilation.

"I tell you what," he exclaimed after a moment's reflection. "We can't see behind this panelling in the companionway, but I reckon we'll find some of these plank ends gone."

He found a hammer one of the joiners had left in the skipper's cabin, and we went on deck. There was a grating by the wheel, with the compass binnacle attached to it. We lifted it clear, then Tony went down on his knees and started a series of smart taps.

"D'you hear that?"

The plank ends right up by the cabin coaming sounded dull compared with the rest of the deck. "There's trouble here, I bet ... and here!"

Then out came his knife. Six planks, at least, were affected.

"What's to do?"

There was no choice really. The planks would have to come out. It was a pity, apart from the cost, which we could ill afford, but better face up to it right away than later on when we were living aboard.

Before I left I took another look at the saloon. That keelson was worrying

Henry's saloon, with galley beyond and the oak-capped keelson.

me. With the framing and doorways up, it was becoming increasingly obvious that the idea of wedging out the keelson on either side was impracticable, for the doorways at each end of the saloon would have the most awkward sloping steps imaginable. I could picture Dorothy's reaction.

"I suppose a complete new floor is the only alternative, Tony?"

But Tony looked doubtful. "It could be done of course. Probably cost you another forty or fifty pounds and you'd still have steps down at each end. You'd lose headroom, too. Best thing would be to get your wife to accept the keelson. With a nice bit of oak capping it would look quite well, you know."

I knew Dorothy's intense dislike of keelsons. However important and decorative they were a trap for the unwary, in her opinion, and an unmitigated nuisance. Yet I could see no alternative.

128

"All right, Tony. Leave it for the time being and I'll see what can be done."

I caught the last train home to Whitstable. Dorothy was in bed and I tried to sneak in without waking her, but she sat up and wanted to know how things were going.

I tried to talk round the keelson; eleven o'clock at night was hardly the time for such contentious matters. But Dorothy was fully awake by then and not to be put off.

In the end I had to tell her.

"You can do what you like," she said, refusing to be mollified. "But I'm not coming aboard *Henry* with the keelson as it is, and that's final!"

"There'd be a nice oak capping to sit on," I murmured.

"Pah!" Then settling to sleep: "I'll have a cottage in the country and you can keep your old barge."

There was a tense atmosphere at breakfast. And we were still not speaking next night. The battle of the keelson was on!

The following evening I got home to find Tony had been on the telephone.

"What's this about the deck planking?" Dorothy demanded. "Tony says it's worse than you thought and he'd like you to see it again."

I explained the position and she pondered over it for a few minutes. It was one of those unpredictable items which upset our budget. Then her face cleared and she smiled. "About the keelson," she said. "I don't mind leaving the keelson for the time being if it's going to help."

My heart jumped. Relief must have shewn on my face, for Dorothy quickly added: I'll have the floor in the Spring, though."

"My dear, if you still want it by the New Year, so you shall."

"I'll have that in writing — with two witnesses, please!"

But I knew quite well that the keelson would be accepted within a week or so. And I was quite philosophical about the deck planking. That keelson had worried me far more.

There seemed to be at least eight planks affected; worse still, the rot had spread along the beam to the inside of the great oak knee. The beam still had plenty of strength and so had the knee. Bill Andrews, the white-haired foreman shipwright who had served his apprenticeship with Ginger Gill at Bridge Yard, Rochester, was against disturbing it. Indeed, the normal barge practice would have been to leave well alone, for one thing tends to lead to another. But *Henry* had been rebuilt only five years back and I hated the thought of insiduous, creeping dry rot. The curious thing was that new timber only five years old should be affected.

"It often happens like that," Tony assured me. "War time timber and not properly seasoned in all probability. I can clean up the top of the beam, but can't make a proper job unless we have the knee out, I'm afraid."

We dug around with our knives, then looked at each other.

"What would you do, Tony?"

"I'd scarph in a new lodging end of the beam and fit a steel knee."

129

Bill Andrews, foreman shipwright, caulking.

"Pretty expensive, I imagine."

It was Tony's turn to purse his lips. "That's the devil of it these days. And you can't say how much till you get down to the job. The leeboard winch will certainly have to come out — and the bollard, maybe. You might get away with it for about fifty quid."

"Ah well, we'll save on the keelson, anyway."

Tony's face lit up. "Really. That's grand. So you got round Dorothy after all!"

Thereupon we adjourned below where the cabin accommodation was rapidly taking shape. The tie beam had been cut out, ports fitted, and much of the joinery work such as bunks and wardrobes completed.

"Now what about this galley?" and we fell to discussing table heights, dressers, details of shelves and drawers, broom cupboards and so on, just like a couple of housewives.

I think we both felt we owed something to Dorothy.

Soon it was mid-August and Tony was pressing us to decide on electric light points and colour schemes.

Dorothy could not understand the hurry. "They're not ready for that sort of thing yet," she insisted.

But they were. Tony hoped to have *Henry* ready for us by the end of September, which was a fortnight ahead of schedule.

We soon settled the lighting question; coaming lights for the saloon; deckhead lights in the other cabins; bunk lights, too, of course. Nor was there much argument about the painting. We wanted to keep the saloon as light as possible, so cream was the obvious choice to go with the varnished oak beams, keelson and dinette seats. The pitch-pine ceiling, now that we had decided not to floor it over, was to be sanded and polished.

Dorothy had a hankering after eau de nil, so we made that the secondary colour, except for Elizabeth's cabin, where she wanted rose pink — and a very good choice, too!

The fine weather held right through to the autumn and work proceeded smoothly. It was quite an event when Dorothy was invited to pass judgement before the final touches. She said very little, but obviously found the bed cabins to her liking. The bath was not the green she had chosen, but she passed that over. The keelson in the saloon evoked a snort — but no condemnation.

The galley — our joint masterpiece — was the chief concern. Tony and I stood back while Dorothy made her inspection. Would she endorse our handiwork?

Then Dorothy smiled and we knew the galley had her blessing. Tony and I exchanged a surreptitious wink.

Coming ashore, we met John Briant just back from holiday.

"Everything all right?" he asked. "I do hope you're both satisfied with *Henry* now she's just about finished."

"Yes," Dorothy replied. "It's all very nice — except for one thing."

I grabbed her by the arm and led her away.

John called after her: "You know what I'd do with it if I had my way!"

☆ ☆ ☆ ☆

We sold our house at Whitstable in August, with completion by the middle of September, and to bridge the gap we took over Ken Hewett's *Swift* for three weeks, laying her alongside *Henry* and taking our time moving in aboard. We actually commissioned 5 October 1949 *and* we had our party for the men who had worked on *Henry*, and their wives and sweethearts. I really believe they were as proud to show off the barge as we were. Twenty-four sat down to tea, and afterwards Elizabeth and Peter demanded that we should play Hunt the Thimble. To them a party was only a party with all the usual frills and trimmings. It was with difficulty that we dissuaded them from organizing Postman's Knock.

131

George Battershall and Peter.

Chapter Seventeen

WINTER BERTH

It surprised us to find how readily the children accepted living afloat. True, Peter fell into the mud one day but there were extenuating circumstances. He was happily trundling his wheelbarrow across the gangplank with his Bible in it, both of which he had just come across in the store, when he went over the edge.

And a month or so later when there was quite a nip in the air, Elizabeth got tipped off another barge's gangplank that had been displaced during a very high tide. She had never been out of her depth before, but as soon as she broke surface she struck out for the shore in great style.

Indeed, she did so well I just stood and watched. She was in shallow water before she really had time to get frightened. Then she stood up and her lips drooped tremulously.

"You're a fine one," I said, forestalling her tears. "At least you might have taken your clothes off first," whereupon she laughed, and after a hot bath came to feel quite proud of herself.

Peter felt himself cheated though. He was down below at the time and missed the performance.

"Will you fall off the glangplank 'nother day?" he urged. "Will you, Elizabeth?"

Apart from these early mishaps which probably had a salutary effect, we had few misgivings about the children. In many ways they were more sure-footed than grown-ups. It was Pat who was living with us for a few months to look after the children who slipped off the gangplank at low water and sprained her ankle!

The weather was kind during those first autumn months and we got over the usual teething troubles such as airlocks in the hot water system and a scuttle hatch that periodically refused to run in spite of patent metal rollers. We had some exasperating deck leaks here and there in spite of recent caulking.

Before the weather finally broke we managed to scrub the sides and slap on a coat of tar with long-handled brushes that always seemed to cover with such little effort. It took us a day to do each side, which was quite good going though I remembered Dorothy and I had managed to tar the whole of *June* in a tide. But of course, the quality of labour deteriorated with the war. Or perhaps we were younger then!

Then there was the colour scheme on deck to decide. *Henry*'s rail had always been black in the old days, with a gold sheer line. It was grey now. George Battershall told me he had intended the grey for an undercoat but decided to leave it as he thought it livened her up.

Yet I always thought a black rail became a barge, especially with white bow-boards and quarterboards: white collar and cuffs was what one old bargeman

133

called them. Our transom was black but used to be green before she was rebuilt, so Sam Fisher told me. But all this had to wait until the spring. Painting during the winter is usually a waste of time and money, although we did manage to dress the decks on the last really warm and sunny morning of the year. Peter helped. He managed quite well, too, carefully watching the way I held the brush and tapping it against the side of the pot to make sure he did not take too much.

Elizabeth demanded a brush as well, but she found the decks rather uninteresting so I gave into her especial care the blue-white-blue house flags carved on bow and quarter badges.

It was surprising what peculiar pastimes the children found attractive. Whenever there was a silence for any length of time we began to wonder what they were about. One day there came suspicious sounds from the bathroom and Dorothy called to Peter; "What are you doing in there?"

"Something."

"*What* are you doing?"

"Scrubbing the floor."

"What with?"

"Brush."

"What brush?"

"Toothbrush."

"Whose toothbrush?"

"Daddy's toothbrush."

"You rascal. You'd better stop before Daddy comes in."

"I better hadn't. D'you mind, Daddy?"

"Yes, I jolly well do."

"Well I've locked the door."

Another time Peter was busy stuffing putty in a knot hole, when he suddenly demanded: "Which is your back side, Daddy?"

Dorothy and I looked at each other in consternation.

"Whatever do you mean, Peter?"

"Is your cabin back side, Daddy?"

"No. It's in the bows."

"Oh. Well, I've bumped my head in the bows."

All too soon the days began to draw in. *Venta*, that lovely old coaster, had gone to Strand-on-the-Green; *Iota* to Oare Creek; *Atlas* to Sunbury.

We had our first taste of winter gales and driving rain that made the half-mile or so along the bleak open lane to the village somewhat trying. *Winifred*, *Leslie*, *Swift* and *Lyford Anna* all intended wintering at Hoo, but Dorothy began to concern herself over my daily journey to London. It meant cycling to the village, bus to Strood and train to Cannon Street. Not that I minded it. But there was always the shopping and Elizabeth had to be met from school. And there was Pat. Perhaps we *were* rather cut off from town life ...

In the end Dorothy found a berth above bridges among the yachts close under Rochester Castle, and we arranged to move up river on the next spring tide.

134

Peter and Elizabeth.

The breeze was westerly that Friday night three weeks before Christmas, and just touching on as we lay head up stream. We had to move out into deep water over night to take the flood up river in the morning.

I was thinking of running off the dolly wire to the lighters moored head and stern to act as a harbour breakwater, but Ralph Rogers from the *Nancy Grey*, who had joined us that evening to give a hand, thought we could sail *Henry* away from the berth.

"If we shove her bows off and back the fores'l I reckon she'll go," he said.

It would certainly save us a lot of messing about in the boat and was worth trying, so we set topsail and foresail and cast off our lines leaving only the spring to stop us from dropping astern on to *New Acorn* and *Lyford Anna*.

Ralph bore off forward with a boathook. We were head to wind; the foresail on the bowline gave a kick and almost filled aback. Then came a pause and our bows swung in again.

We tried bearing off together. She came at last but only after dropping the topsail headstick and by dint of much grunting and shoving. Once away we had to get sail on her to fetch past *Russell* and *James Piper* and out through the gap between the lighters.

"Shake out the mains'l, Ralph," I called as I brought *Henry* on the wind, and while he slacked away on the brails I ran aft with the mainsheet block. There was no great weight in the breeze. I quickly took in what slack I could. The rest could wait until we came about.

With the Hoo saltings close under our lee, it was high time to wind. There was insufficient water for full leeboard and I hurriedly set the mizzen to help her round.

"About-O!"

Henry came driving up into the wind with foresail on the bowline. Topsail and mainsail flogged lazily as I took a swig on the mainsheet.

"Let draw."

We were paying off on the fresh tack. Ralph cast off the bowline. The mainsail clattered over the horse, flogged once and was quiet. *Henry* heeled a little.

There is a wonderful detached sense of power sailing a barge at night, especially to windward. *Henry* was still the same in spite of her conversion. She had ports in her coamings but her decks were no more cluttered up with gear than before; outwardly she was unchanged, with her own distinctive rig.

Peter was asleep, but Elizabeth, wrapped in a blanket, stood with Pat in the cabin hatch. She was somewhat awed at the sight of all the other barges she knew so well lying there in the moonlight beyond the pale line of the concrete lighters. I sensed how she felt. Over there lay the world she had come to know. And yet we in *Henry* were also in a world of *our* own.

Another sailing barge, the *Arrow*, lay at anchor on the flats; she was already swung down. The flood was about done as we made a trip close under her stern and stood over towards the moored frigates of the Reserve Fleet. There was plenty of water hereabouts to lower our leeboards, and when we winded again we were able to look up for our anchorage off Cockham beach.

"We'll have the mains'l off," I called and eased off the sheet while Ralph hove away on the brail winch. Then he straightened and looked around.

"We should be all right anwhere here," he said.

"Rounding up now."

The foreseail came down with a run. I took a sounding: five fathoms.

"When you like, Ralph. Give her plenty."

By the time we had everything stowed on deck Dorothy was waiting at the companion hatch.

"Come on you two," she exclaimed. "You wouldn't have been so long in the old days. Supper's been on the table this last half hour."

☆ ☆ ☆ ☆

That night it came on to blow. There was plenty of wind still when we turned out at daybreak, and the weather forecast talked of south-west gales. We had only three or four miles to sail but it was a dead beat up Chatham Reach.

After a cup of tea we got *Henry* under weigh. Topsail, foresail and mizzen, with a few cloths of the main was all we gave her, though doubtless she would have stood up to full sail if we cared to drive her. But it was six months since we sailed *Henry* last; her gear had been good then but it was hardly wise to take chances.

136

We turned up past the Dockyard in company with a small tug towing a couple of lighters. It was not too uncomfortable, though once or twice there came the ominous sound of crockery on the move below. The children were both standing in the cabin hatch with their lifebelts on and highly intrigued with *Henry* sailing hard.

Off Chatham Point we had to make a last minute board to clear the tier of lighters, and stood over towards Ship Pier. As we winded, out of the corner of my eye I caught sight of somebody waving from sailing barges on the buoy.

There came a hail down wind: "Where you bound?"

It was George Blake of the *P.A.M.* with his father Tubby. Both *P.A.M.* and *Lancashire* were loaded — with stone, no doubt — and waiting for the weather to ease up. Tubby seemed to have a hitcher in his hand and dashed it to the deck when he recognized us, as if to say — which he probably did — "Well, I'll be — — —!"

Yelling that we were bringing up at Strood, we bore away up Limehouse Reach like a scalded cat. When we came to pick up the mainsail I was glad we had no more than half of it set. For a few moments we were almost blanketed under the lee of the gas works, only to meet a furious gust as we opened up Bridge Reach. I was deciding to bring up alongside a motor barge on a buoy off Strood Dock when there came a great cracking of canvas. The topsail sheet had somehow come adrift and the sail was suddenly possessed of the devil, flailing away and threatening to bring the topmast down.

"Drop the headstick, Ralph," I shouted.

We blew in alongside a tier of lighters just short of the motor barge and I ran forward to make fast and to give a hand with the sails. The topsail sheet cleat had pulled out from the heel of the sprit. Both standing part and fall, together with the block had threshed their way aloft up the stanliff. As I stood there groping for the tail of the sheet, the cleat came tumbling down at my feet with the two great spikes protruding from it. It was close enough to be unpleasant.

After we had stowed the topsail — luckily it had come to no harm — we found the port crosstree had bent aft with the strain. All things considered we were lucky not to have lost the topmast.

We lay alongside the lighter broadside to the wind which was howling down the reach, and after securing the gear I went across in the boat to speak to the skipper of the motor barge *The Flame*. He and the mate had only just come off and were away up to Halling after cement.

"I'd come on this buoy if I were you," the skipper said. "I don't reckon the lighters will trouble you much here, but by and by like as not there'll be some more fetching up where you're laying and they ain't exactly pleasant neighbours."

As soon as *The Flame* had gone Ralph and I ran our dolly wire to the vacant buoy and hove *Henry* against the strong S.W. wind. We had just cast off our last line to the lighter when the shriek of the wind rose in furious crescendo, and the wire parted. In a flash we had swung down athwart the tier of lighters and lay pinned there with the swim of the outside lighter grinding on our rail.

137

Dressing the mainsail on the grass as Buttercrock Wharf, Hoo.

For a few minutes we could do nothing but wait. When the worst of the blow had eased I ran out a new track line to the buoy and we started to heave ahead on the mast winch. It was a huge mooring buoy. I acted as jumper and passed a stout three-inch slip rope. Ralph had just slacked off the track line and we were working on a mooring wire then another gust hit us and the rope parted.

I was sitting astride the buoy and was nearly jerked into the water. Luckily I was able to take a couple of turns round the ring, and yelled to Ralph to hold on. In the end we passed a bight of our anchor chain and lay to that. It was just as well we shifted, for later on a tug came down river with a string of empty lighters. They secured in turn to the tier we had recently vacated, clanging and groaning as they rode up on each other. We were thankful none came alongside us.

After a belated breakfast we struck the topmast and made ready to lower away, but there was no sign of our tug which was to take us through the bridge.

"We ought to shoot her through like they did in the old days," said Ralph with a grin.

"And so we shall — but not to-day!"

Indeed it had always been one of my ambitions to shoot a barge through the bridges. Time was when all the Medway cement works had their own fleets of sailing barges and there were hufflers at Strood — Lucky Brown was one of them — who did no other work than to lend a hand lowering the gear as the barge shaped up for the middle arch. As soon as they were through it was a case of scrambling the gear up to get the barge sailing again. The only snag was our cabin top and even *Henry's* hollow sprit was a hefty spar to come thumping down.

That night Goldsmith's old *Lorna* came away from the Oil Cake Mills just above Strood Pier, hoisting her topsail as she came. She headed right for us, both lights showing, then at the last moment bore up and gybed over with a shudder and rattling of gear and was soon out of sight down Chatham way. It blew hard that night. At times we came riding up on our buoy. What with the noise reverberating through the barge, the howling of the wind and the trains as they crossed the bridge our night was anything but peaceful.

Sunday morning we lowered the gear on deck. It came down easily enough though the sprit tended to blow off to starboard until the full weight came on the headrope; then it settled quietly between the mizzen mast and the boat davits.

The tug came for us just before high water and towed us up through. It was blowing too hard though to attempt to reach our berth among the yachts. We had to lie yet another night to our anchor out in the river and the next day found another berth on the Strood side by Temple Farm, where we lay outside some derelict lighters bridged by a gangway to the shore.

The wind dropped late Monday afternoon and Dorothy gave me a hand to heave up the gear. We sent the topmast aloft by the light of the moon and went on working about the decks. Presently the tide came creeping in over the mud flats. The Cathedral clock on the far side of the river struck midnight as I finished scrubbing the decks. Next morning I caught my usual train from Strood. I felt incredibly fit in spite of the hard work and the carriage seemed stifling. At Woolwich the train filled up; a man opposite was wearing spats. I fingered my calloused hands, as the thought flashed through my mind: "There but for the grace of God go I."

☆ ☆ ☆ ☆

At first the family enjoyed themselves. Dorothy and I went to a symphony concert, and Pat to the pictures; Elizabeth visited school friends and Peter fed the pigeons in the Castle Grounds.

By the end of the week the novelty had worn off. Pat found the pavements narrow and she disliked the crowded streets. It was much nicer at Hoo.

Dorothy looked at me meaningly.

"Don't look at me," I said. "I was quite happy where we were."

"Well, it seems so silly going back after all this trouble."

I shrugged my shoulders. It was all one to me. Besides, we would have another sail. "Get your shopping done," I suggested. "We'll slip down to Hoo for Christmas."

And that is exactly what we did.

139

Henry at the Hythe.

On Basin Reach Buoy: *Sea Spray, Mayland, Saltcote Belle, Ready* and *Gladys.*

140

Chapter Eighteen

MALDON

We had come away from Hoo for our summer cruise as soon as Elizabeth broke up at school, and spent three sunlit days gently cruising round to the Blackwater. There were two of us spritties early in August 1950 at Town Quay, Maldon: our own *Henry* and the fine, powerful Colchester-owned *Centaur* flying Francis & Gilder's attractive gold and purple bob. She had brought Canadian wheat for the Mill from the London Docks and dropped down alongside us on the day tide.

The children were quick to make friends with Stan Yeates, the skipper, and his wife Chick, and Jack, the mate. As I stepped aboard *Henry* that evening Peter came clambering up *Centaur*'s companion ladder. It was his first visit to a trading barge and he was much impressed. *Henry*'s cabin had been given over to the children and their toys, and was only used for meals on birthdays and other special occasions.

"Liz! Liz!" Peter shouted to his sister who was scampering about the hatch top. "Do you know, Liz? They sleep and eat in their playroom even!" But Elizabeth, with all the superiority of a nine-year old only laughed at him.

"Isn't Peter silly, Daddy? He calls the skipper's cabin a playroom."

"So it is, Liz," Peter maintained stoutly, " 'Cos I know it is."

I refused to take sides but looked across at Chick who had followed Peter on deck, and smiled.

Centaur was built in 1895 at Cann's Harwich yard where many a fine coaster was launched. The Colchester barges depended largely on imports, loading trans-shipment cargoes in the docks for the East Anglian outports of Maldon, Colchester, Felixstowe and the like, with an occasional freight for Great Yarmouth. There was not much grain moving and the timber season was late to open up; barges were once more having to lie at Erith or North Woolwich sometimes for a week or more waiting for a job.

Return freights to London were few and far between at the best of times. It was early yet for much English wheat but sometimes there was maize or barley coming out of store for account of the Ministry of Food. Sand and ballast could usually be had out of Colne, but the Colchester barges preferred to be without such cargoes since the heavy grabs used in discharging were apt to damage the hold ceilings and take bites out of the keelson.

"No," said Stan. "It's pretty certain we'll be going round to London light. It's Maldon Town Regatta tomorrow and Chick's keen on stopping over for that."

I turned out in the early hours next morning and got busy with the dip bucket before the tide went. In hot weather it was the only way to keep decks tight by sluicing them with water night and morning.

Everything was still; there were wisps of mist over the saltings opposite, where the hulk of the old sailing barge *Herbert Gordon* rose wraith-like from a sea of white. And down below Cook's barge yard, the smacks lining the beach and the trees beyond lay mirrored in the placid water.

They had been busy, these little Maldon smacks with their lovely flowing run, and the Income Tax man was said to be paying his unwelcome attentions. It was on account of oysters, though, not fish, for the biggest fall of spat within living memory had meant much dredging for the young oyster brood. The oyster companies took most of them for re-laying on the beds; after four or five years of careful tending, and should they survive the hazards of frosts, limpets and five-fingers, they would be ready to tickle the palate of the gourmet. The initial price for the young oyster of 3/6d per hundred was too good to last; prices began to drop so that some of the men were tempted to lease patches of the river bed and lay down young oysters to fatten for their own account. But human nature being what it is, and with all the ingrained rivalry between the local families, perhaps it was not altogether surprising that some folk hinted at poaching and other nefarious 'goings-on'.

As I stood on deck that early morning, bucket in hand and watching some gulls lazily contending over some tidbit on the river, there came the sound of a mainsail halyard block. The smacks were getting under weigh. One after the other, a dozen or more made sail and dropped down on the ebb. All but one had a motor that morning. There was a light westerly air and the tide served.

Presently the skipper of *Centaur* came on deck and went forward to call the mate. "Nice day for the Regatta," he said to me. "We'll have to get the flags out. I reckon you'll be dressing ship, too, won't you?"

Henry boasted a set of signal flags, but unfortunately the staysail luff wire had parted by the head on our way up to Maldon the previous week and the fall of the halyard was away up aloft in the block. It meant striking the topmast to retrieve it before we could bend on the flags.

"That's all right," said Stan. "We'll set the tops'l this morning and my mate can climb up the mast hoops. That's the easiest way."

But the young mate had other ideas. He came across and squinted aloft.

"Got much grease on your topm'st?" he demanded, and when I shook my head, he hitched up his trousers and climbed quickly up the ratlines to haul himself on to the crosstrees and mainmast cap. Then he wrapped his arms and feet around the topmast and went straight up the bare pole like a monkey. In less than a minute he was back on deck with the halyard in his hand.

That evening as I came down the High Street past the church and over the brow of the hill, the two barges lay festooned with bunting, and *Henry*'s twenty-five foot pennant flying from her sprit end. They made a gay, enheartening sight at the quay opposite The Jolly Sailor, set against a background of saltings and a

142

cluster of trees, roofs and masts that was Heybridge Basin, with Osea, Mersea and the broad waters of the River Blackwater stretching away into the blue, hazy distance.

The Regatta had been a great success in spite of the thunderstorm that cut short the antics on the greasy pole — to Elizabeth's disappointment.

We saw a lot of *Centaur* during our month at Maldon. Sailing light to London, she got orders to return to Maldon for English wheat and we found her coming back alongside us early one morning to await a berth at Haslar's Mill further up river by the Fullbridge. Eventually *Centaur* loaded and sailed for Felixstowe. Then bound light for London River, she sprang a leak in the Wallet and finished up once more at Maldon to go on Cook's Yard for the bottom to be re-fastened. Whilst there, she went down to West Mersea as Committee boat for their Regatta.

Elizabeth went with them for the weekend and had a grandstand view of the greasy pole, miller and sweep, the traditional duck hunt with one man chasing another in and out of the water and up and down the rigging, and ending up with the fireworks. Elizabeth returned on board with suspicious-looking tide marks round her neck, but thoroughly happy.

August was the month for all the local regattas — Tollesbury, Steeple, Heybridge, Bradwell, Wivenhoe and others besides. They were traditional and always well supported by yachts and working craft including the narrow, coffin-like duck punts that competed in sailing, pulling and shovelling races, as well as pull devil pull baker tugs-of-war.

☆ ☆ ☆ ☆

We always found the atmosphere of Maldon peculiarly attractive. Unlike so many old-time ports whose trade has fallen away, there has always been plenty of life. I doubt if there ever was another place so boat-minded, and it was said with some truth that half the population went afloat at weekends, and the other half thronged the promenade to watch and criticize.

The sail loft between Town Quay and Howard's old barge yard was a fascinating place with its polished floor and heaped-up sails. Before Fred Taylor's father came from Brightlingsea in 1891, there was Joseph Sadler who hailed from Heybridge Basin in the days when it was packed with billyboys and brigs. He died in 1923 at the ripe old age of ninety-three. Nor was he the founder of the firm for there was Gowan before him. And originally, well over 100 years ago, the wooden building on the river side had been a granary.

Fred Taylor used to have records of original sail plans drawn out to scale for all manner of craft from 1897 onwards, and it was interesting to note the way barge sails gradually changed over the years; the shortening of the sprit, the squarer head to the mainsail and the larger topsail. Bill Raven made sails there for over sixty years and remembered the time when no stackie was considered fit to go up Swin with anything less than a 60-ft. sprit plumbing the scuttle hatch so that the leach of the mainsail actually led *aft* from the horse, and the vangs too. In those days the mizzen was stepped on the rudder post and some-times had a lug sail. But wheel-steering allowed the mizzen mast to be stepped inboard and the sail made larger, so that there was no longer any need for such enormous sprits and mainsails. Foresails changed from the flat smack type to a baggy sail stretching some foot or so abaft the horse, and barges were all the better for it. Not that a baggy sail suited every barge; when David Hedgecock in *Leofleda* came to Taylor's for a Maldon foresail the barge just would not have it and eventually Bill Raven had to cut a foot off the luff.

Those were the days when the jackstay was only just taking the place of mast hoops. And there were some barges still using hemp stayfalls; the *Oak* had one, together with huge stem head blocks, until she passed from Sadd's to Francis & Gilders in the 'twenties. In 1898 a new mainsail for Eve's *Jess* cost £22.10.11; headrope and dressing cost another £3.10.0. A complete suit for *British King* in 1901 cost £8 including stack cloths. *Leofleda*'s new mainsail came to £187.5.0 in 1951. And now ...

Barge work fell away in the 'fifties. Although barges still came to Cook's yard and usually sent their sails along to Fred Taylor to be overhauled, yacht sails became their speciality.

The ketch-rigged, boomsail barges bringing North Country coal had fallen to the railways years ago. And spritsail barges were declining too. It is a long call to the days of the old horse-drawn bus, when Essex stackies kept London supp-lied with vast quantities of hay and straw. By the early 'fifties *Ethel Maud* was the only remaining Maldon-owned barge; even she came to Green Bros' Mill while we were there to lay up. But Colchester barges, and quite a few outsiders, still traded to Maldon with grain and timber and an occasional freight of sand. But in the old days there were lots of local barges and it was surprising how well some of the smaller ones like *Diligent* and *Keeble* used to get along. Both were built in the 'seventies by Shrubsall of Milton. *Keeble* was never empty through-out the whole of her first twelve months when she worked to Mill Beach just below Heybridge Basin. As soon as the forehold was clear of manure, they started loading hay or straw for London, and the same thing happened at the other end.

Barging and farming were always closely associated on the Essex sea borders. Barges were the logical means of transport for farm produce before the coming of road transport. Early on, the local owners used to go to Kent for their barges. They were well built, too, handy-sized, full-ended craft, with rounded bows and tucked-up quarters. They must have been strong to be working, as they were still in 1950, lightering timber to Heybridge Basin and Sadd's.

By 1879 John Howard had started to build barges at the Hythe Slipways, taken over later by Dan Webb and Feesey. *Surprise* was Howard's first, built for "Farmer" Strutt, who lived in the High Street where the Post Office now stands. Then came the 105-ton *Rose* for Charles Hawes, Hay and Straw Merchant; the little *Oak* with the unusual, rounded, counter stern; *Saltcote Belle* for Alfred May of the Saltcote Maltings just below the Basin; *Mayland, Mermaid* and

D'Arcy for Richard Seabrook who farmed at Tolleshunt D'Arcy; *Emma* reputed to be one of the fastest barges that ever sailed up Swin, and many more besides.

Howard was always experimenting. It is said that, except for *Hyacinth* and *Violet*, he never built the same ends on any two barges, and he sometimes had as many as four barges on the ways at the same time. Like many another artist, he was often in debt. Eve picked him up with the *Jess* in 1899, and the following year Seabrook helped him out when he ordered the *Defender* that cost £2,150 as compared with £1,400 for the *D'Arcy*. But Seabrook had only the best put into *Defender*. Her sails were made by Ratsey & Lapthorn, but they were more suitable for a yacht than a barge, and Bill Raven had to have them in his loft twice before they served.

John Howard built only first-class barges; each had a limited yet pleasing sheer and well faired runs both fore and aft. They were a departure from the more usual full-ended, long-chine, Kentish craft, and were invariably rigged out with bowsprit and jib. Additional headsails were essential in the stack work, with hay or straw piled six or seven trusses high halfway up the mainmast.

Lying there at Town Quay and working on deck most evenings sewing a new luff rope to our staysail, I was often joined by one or other of the retired barge skippers so that I came to hear something of the old Maldon barges that were so long-lived and well remembered.

Surprise eventually crossed over to the Kentish shore and was worked out by Burley in the Sittingbourne brick work. Her hulk lies in the mud off Queenborough, so Arthur Keeble told me.

Rose went lightering at Heybridge; some of her gear was hoarded at Francis & Gilders' store at Colchester, as Stan Yeates discovered when he went rummaging through the sail loft after a staysail for *Centaur*.

D'Arcy passed to Horlock's of Mistley. She was taken up for mine spotting like *Henry* during the war, but she was never fitted out for service again. A few years without proper attention did more damage than years of regular trading.

Cromwell Horlock sailed *Defender* until she wanted more done to her than trading prospects warranted, so she was laid up on the flats at Pin Mill, where we came across her when we sailed that way. She was a beautiful model of a barge even then, fully rigged and with bowsprit down.

Emma was lost during the war. She was loading alongside a steamer at Bellamy's Wharf, Rotherhithe, when a mine went up and blew off her stern. Both Dick Springett and the mate got clear.

It was not surprising that these shapely Howard barges were much sought after for conversion to yachts. *Mermaid* was a regular trader between Maldon and the Medway. Billy Austin was Master of her for twenty-eight years and won the Maldon Barge Match on several occasions. Before the race he used to sit his barge on blocks placed beneath bow and stern so as to give her bottom an inch or so of rocker after the fashion of the famous racers *Giralda* and *Veronica*, both expressly built that way. But with *Mermaid* the next time she took the ground she straightened out again.

145

Mirosa bound for Sadd's.

There was *Venta*, too, built as the *Jachin* in 1893. She was a real Channel banger if ever there was one, with good old-fashioned bulwarks and over seven feet depth of hold. Her hollow fore run and fine lines aft were more reminiscent of a schooner than a Thames barge. She got athwart a groin in the 1914/18 war and was bought by Percy Shrubsall's father, who repaired her and renamed her *Venta* in conformity with the rest of his fine fleet of that day: *Veravia*, *Veronica*, *Verona*, *Valonia* and so on.

Venta's cargo book covered most ports on either side of the English Channel. In twelve months from March, 1927, she made twenty-six consecutive trips with stone from Cherbourg to Hayling Island and Bosham, but Channel work began to fall off in the 'thirties, for the full-powered motor vessels were ousting the sailorman. Right through the last war *Venta* was in the East Anglian and Kentish work, but repairs were proving more difficult and barges were out of favour. So *Venta* was put up for sale. Francis & Gilders, who had been working her on the market for some years, would have bought her but that two of their barges were laid up for the want of crews. She was sailed to the Medway and sold for conversion to a yacht. When we saw her at Hoo the Howard hallmark still stood in the form of a little carved rail or balustrade round the semi-circular ledge in the Yarmouth Roads.

Saltcote Belle won many a Maldon Barge Match and was probably the prettiest of all Howard's long line of barges. Bill Quilter had her new when she worked to the Saltcote Maltings; like most of the privately-owned Blackwater barges she eventually passed to the ownership of Francis & Gilders. With an inexperienced young skipper and mate she collided with a steamer in the Thames Estuary which nearly brought her gear down. She ran back to Holehaven and effected temporary repairs, then putting to sea again, ran into trouble on the Spitway, dragging over the sands with two anchors down and making water to the extent of eighteen inches in the cabin. The crew flared and were taken off by the lifeboat. But *Saltcote Belle* stayed afloat and was eventually brought in by a couple of fishing smacks. Her cargo of maize was discharged and the bilges stoked out.

Stan Yeates took her over with his wife as mate, for they had lost *General Jackson* timber laden in collision with M.V. *Grampian Coast* off Erith November 1948. But they found *Saltcote Belle's* cabin unbearable, for some of the maize had washed up under the cabin sole and lodged there to rot and stink. The cabin sole or floor boards were spiked down and to raise them would have meant a new floor. It was the owners' intention to have the barge on the yard for a thorough refit as her top and chines were in need of attention, but at that time Francis & Gilders had two more of their barges laying at The Hythe, Colchester, without crews. Stan Yeates was given *Centaur* instead, one of the biggest of the Colchester fleet, and the little *Saltcote Belle* was sold away for a yacht on the Ipswich river.

It was Howard, too, who built the graceful clipper-bowed ketch barge *Record Reign* in 1897. Originally she was rigged with two square topsails but was much cut down in later years. But the real pride of Maldon was *Thoma II*, a barge

Henry in Basin Reach.

yacht built in 1909 on similar lines to but slightly smaller than *Record Reign*. She came out with a centre board, but this was soon discarded in favour of the traditional leeboards.

Jack Keeble remembered her building. The timber cost £345 and he fetched it in his barge *Emily*, the freight amounting to £9. The oak had been seasoning for five years and was so hard that holes had to bored for every fastening. Yet when she lay for some months in the fresh water of Heybridge Basin rot set in at the water line and a number of planks had to be renewed.

There were several of Howard's barges still trading in 1950. *Mayland* was one, owned by R. J. Prior of Burnham. She was in Heybridge Basin with timber during our spell at Maldon. George Bowles and his mate had gone off home for the week-end. The cabin was padlocked and an old saucepan was turned upside down on the cabin chimney stack. *Mayland* was deserted and was so hemmed in by duckweed that she might have been there for months. By Monday night, though, her timber was unloaded and she was away next day.

Violet, too, with her carved badge of oak leaves on her bows, was also trading. She belonged to Marriage of East Mills, Colchester, but eventually went across the estuary to work out of Whitstable. She was a pretty 110-tonner with Howard written all over her.

Yet another was *Mirosa*, built as *Ready* in 1892 for Charles Gutteridge and renamed at the request of Trinity House who wanted the name for their Lights tender.

She was a typical Maldon stackie, very beamy, and carrying about 120 tons on a bare 5-ft. 8-in. side. Her original spars were quite fantastic by later standards, Mainmast measured 33-ft. to the hounds; topmast 44-ft.; sprit 63-ft.; bowsprit 32-ft. John Howard shipped aboard for her first trip round to the Thames and took the wheel as she turned to windward up Swin. The barge was not going too well; John Howard was pinching her and at last old Jim Keeble could stand it no longer.

"I grant you can build a good barge, John, but you can't sail 'em. That you can't. Just you let my young nephew take her. He'll sail her, he will."

But *Ready*'s gear was too much for her. She went back to Maldon and had three feet cut off her sprit. Even so she was a smart barge and at the turn of the century she raced against Seabrooks *D'Arcy* and *Defender* and Marriage's *Fleur de Lis* at the Brightlingsea Regatta.

"That's right," Jack Keeble told me. "*D'Arcy*, she went on the slip and had her bottom black-leaded, but the *Ready* was up at Osea unloading dung. We gives her a quick tar round an' beats the lot on 'em."

Billy Austin took her when he left the *Mermaid* and there were few barges that could show her the way up Swin.

☆ ☆ ☆ ☆

149

Maldon River was full of surprises. There was a crystal salt works; bungalows overhung the water; handsome yachts lay cheek by jowl with derelict barges. The little *Canvey* lay in Hedgecock's Yard; *Golden Hope* which appeared as *Ark Royal* in that odyssey of barge life "A Floating Home" was there, too. And across the river were flour mills and Sadd's timber yard and a wonderful collection of old barges engaged in lightering timber; there were well known names among them — *Agnes & Constance, Falcon, Cypress, Oak, Briton,* and many more besides.

Barges still came to Cook's Yard — mostly motor barges — but many of the old craft had been rigged again and turned into yachts. Walter Cook and Arthur Woodward both worked for John Howard until they took over Finch's small yard and built the *Dawn* for Ebenezer Keeble in 1897. It was a big day when they dug away the sea wall to launch her. *Dawn* was quite different from Howard's dainty craft. She was square and had a long chine that made her a difficult barge to catch to windward, especially when light. Horace Keeble — universally known as Hob or Hobby — was master of her for many years and could get any barge along, for he was a rare thruster.

Arthur Woodward was a wonderful craftsman. "If he cut a piece of wood, that fitted, that did," so his cousin, Arthur Keeble, once told me. "And years ago he trimmed a chap's finger nails with his adze."

He and Walter Cook built the *Lord Roberts* for James Meeson, farmer and miller at Battlesbridge, as well as the 160-ton *British King*, later owned by the Keeble family, at a cost of £1,400. During the 1914/18 war, when she was trading regularly from Thames to Calais at 32/6d per ton, she could have been sold for over £2,000. Even in 1924 she fetched £1,000. They were well built, those barges, but they were the last. Arthur Woodward left. Walter Cook's son Clifford carried on the yard under the style of Walter Cook & Son. Hundreds of barges have been on the yard over the years. We put *Henry* on the blocks where Peter and I crawled under her to scrape the bottom; *May Flower* was fitted with a new wooden keelson; *Oak* and *Grange* were rebuilt for Sadd's; and Rankin's *Joy* was turned into a very fine yacht. It always amazed me how much could be accomplished by experienced shipwrights in such a small yard and with such primitive tools.

There was only one other firm of Maldon barge builders in recent years. During one of Howard's spells of financial difficulty Barr, Payne & Hocking had his yard. They were building small craft and naval cutters mostly, but in 1900 they launched the *Columbia* for Cory's, a big boxy barge, quite unlike Howard's beauties. She was in trouble from the start, for she sank at her launch and eventually had to be doubled in the London River. She finished up lightering for Cory's.

150

Chapter Nineteen

MALDON BARGE MASTER

Oftimes in the evening, while we lay at Maldon, Arthur Keeble would come aboard for a chat. Essex barges were in their heyday when he started in 1897. Life afloat was hard and wages poor yet he cherished a soft spot for those early days. "I was thirteen when I went third hand or cabin boy along o' my father in the *Emily*. I got two shillings a week and when my brother come mate they give me a shilling rise."

The 115-ton *Emily* belonged to his uncle Jim who also had the *Eva Annie*, *Burnham* and *Keeble*, all tiller steering and built by Shrubsall of Milton for the Maldon hay and straw work to London. Later on came the *Ready* from John Howard's yard and the *Dawn* from Cook's. There were four Keeble brothers — James, John, Ebenezer and Samuel — James was the eldest, but they were all in the barges and their sons, too. When Jim died, his nephews James and Ebenezer took over the business, which continued until the barges were merged in the Colchester firm of Francis & Gilders. Horace Keeble, grandson of old Ebenezer and the last of the Keebles in the Maldon barges, had the *Dawn* and drove her as hard as any of the old timers. She eventually went on the yard at Rowhedge for an auxiliary engine to be fitted, and Hobby — as he was invariably called — so mistrusted power that he set sail to round up for the dock head. But a year or so later he was complaining that the 44 h.p. Kelvin should have been twice as powerful!

Arthur stayed with his father, Samuel Keeble, in the *Emily* for three years before he went mate with brother Alf in Seabrook's *Pride of Essex*. "She was a lovely little thing, shaped just like an egg on top and flare-sided. You could row her about like a boat. That thing could sail, too, and they do say she come up from Newcastle once in thirty-six hours."

The *Pride of Essex* was built at Limehouse in 1857. Richard Seabrook, farmer at Tolleshunt D'Arcy, bought her from William Green of Hullbridge, and later had the *D'Arcy* and *Defender* built by John Howard at Maldon, both shapely, well-lined stackies. Yet the old man was once heard to declare that if he had his time over again he would build a couple of barges like the *Pride of Essex*, as well he might, for she must have paid for herself over and over again.

Seabook's barges flew a red-and-blue bob with a blue 'S' in a white ball. They used to go to Maldon for shipwright work and repairs, but Seabrook had his own place at Skinner's Wick at the head of Thirslet Creek, where they lay for painting and doing up generally. The barges loaded from there or one or other of the numerous farm wharfs on the many creeks on the Tollesbury side of the Black-water, and a hold full of mangels with a stack on top was a favourite cargo. The *Pride of Essex* loaded about forty tons of hay with a stack on deck some six

Arthur Keeble ('Sorbo').

or seven trusses high, a good twelve feet up the mainmast. Only a beamy, shallow-sided stackie with a tall, high-peaked mainsail and brails led to the dolly winch forward could load such a cargo in safety and turn up Swin for London River.

The stackies bound above bridges used to bring up just below the Tower. "That's where our work started. Had to pull the guts out of the stack, cover up again and lower the gear." A huffler was shipped for the trip up to Nine Elms where the *Pride of Essex* and most of the Maldon Barges used to discharge. He steered from the top of the stack with tiller lines rove through blocks on outrigger irons shipped in the quarter rails, while skipper and mate rowed from the bows. If the breeze served they set a bridge sail on the bowsprit which was lowered for each bridge by the roller winch, as the dolly winch on the windlass bitts was usually known in those days.

Once Arthur Keeble helped to bring both the *Pride of Essex* and *Ann Elizabeth* up through bridges on the same tide. Billy Austin was mate of the *Ann Elizabeth* and he gave a hand first with the *Pride of Essex*, two towing in the boat, two rowing on board and 'flying jib' set as well. As soon as they made Nine Elms, back went Arthur Keeble with Billy and the huffler to give a hand with the *Ann Elizabeth*. "That was all on account of a misunderstanding. Somebody said the *Ann Elizabeth*'s huffler had gone away down to Greenwich. That was a lie, so it turned out, but we worn't to know. I never did hear of two barges fetched up one after the other on the same tide before. One thing we never did take a tug. That cost too much." The freight on a stack to London averaged £12 to £14, half of which went to the crew who had to pay their share of the huffler's charge of 7/- each trip.

They once took two stacks away from Maylandsea to Greenwich in the *Pride of Essex* and unloaded both within the space of five-and-a-half days. More often than not, though, the stackies used to load back with stable manure for the farms. With the Essex barges so tied up with farming it was nothing derogatory in those days for a smart barge to carry a freight of dung. Indeed, old Richard Seabrook often went yachting in the *Defender* and had her cabin and stateroom tastefully fitted out for that purpose.

The *Pride of Essex* went yachting too. "Seabrook let his farm hands come away sailing with us once. Said he didn't mind what they did provided we got back by the end of three days. Rare owd crowd come aboard. The schoolmaster, he was there, and villagers and the owd farm boys. They lay straw over half the hole to sleep on and brought plenty to eat and drink. We left Tollesbury Pier at five in the morning. Up on Southend a-dinner time. Next day we sailed all round the fleet. Third day we come away dinner time and put them ashore at Tollesbury ten that night. Do you know, they collected enough among themselves to pay us a freight so we didn't lose nothing.

"They enjoyed themselves, those owd farm boys. We had some fun, too. There was one chap asleep down the hole and Alf thought he'd have a game with him so he carefully lifted a corner of the hatch cloth and tipped a bucket o' water down, then covered up quickly. You should have heard him! Woke up a-swearing and hollering: 'Skipper. Skipper. Come quick. We're a-drownding!' I tell you we had a good owd time that trip."

The *Pride of Essex* came to grief at Nine Elms in 1911 when she was burnt out with a stack on board. "We lay fifth bottom. The tide was out and there was nothing we could do for it was the other barges' gear a-falling that set us afire. My wife was aboard; we'd only got married that Whit Monday. Had to get

153

her over the stack and drop down over the bows, across a lighter and through two foot o' mud to get clear. You could hardly bear the heat! That knocked her up for a time, that did."

Parker's *James* and *Triton* were both on fire that day. Arthur Keeble shipped with his brother Alf in the *Charles and Isabella* belonging to Hollington's, clothiers at Colchester. They loaded red flints in Oare Creek, a common freight in those days when a whole fleet of barges — Kentish as well as Essexmen — took flints to the beaches down Clacton way for the Essex roads. This time they were caught out by a south-west blow that flew into the north-west. First the bowsprit went and then the steering gear. *Charles and Isabella* hit the Gunfleet, going ashore at half ebb and settling on one chine; by the time they were taken off she had sanded down to the deck all along that side. "We worn't the only one either. The *Gertrude May*, she was in trouble too. That was the worst year I ever had. I tell you, I was burnt out, washed out and wifed out all in six months!"

Goldsmith's *Trojan* was caught out that day. George Battershall told me how he came out of Harwich and got nearly up the Sheers when it came on a gale of wind and he rode it out in Abraham's Bosom, that great bight in the Maplin Sands just above the Whitaker Beacon.

Two of Arthur Keeble's brothers were lost from barges. Bruce was in Murrell's *Robert* when she was run down off Barking; and Bill had Parker's *Ethel* that was lost early in the First World War at a time when all barges had to bring up at night. "Daresn't move or you soon had the patrol boat after you. Night of the great gale 28th December 1914 Bill was brought up in the Whitaker. That's where they found the barge, but Bill and the mate had clean gone."

From the *Charles and Isabella* — "Still on the Gunfleet for all I know" — the two brothers shipped in the *Blackwater*, owned in the little port of Bradwell by Clem Parker whose fleet of stackies loaded hay and straw from a multitude of small creeks and outfalls bordering the lonely Dengie Flats. Clem Parker combined farming with barging and kept up his craft as well as any of his day. Although kindhearted he was something of a martinet in many ways.

"I got on all right with him and we never had a cross word. Some on 'em were afraid to speak up, but I wasn't. Why should I be? I'd nothing to lose. Him and Alf soon fell out though. Parker said to Alf: 'What I can see of it others have been picking up stones and you've been a-throwing on 'em.' "

In those heydays of barging at the beginning of the century it was quite usual for a lad to sail as third hand or cabin boy for three years and then ship as mate for another eight or nine years before going skipper. Arthur stopped mate with his brother rather longer than he would otherwise have done. Eventually he went master of Parker's *Sophia* and once loaded a stack on the beach outside Foulness in the morning, went away over the Ridge as soon as the tide served and was up on Southend that same evening. Charlie Simmons, Arthur's brother-in-law, had the *Champion* at the time and together they carried sludge from Beckton for the Essex farms. "That was the only time I ever had a weekly job. We got something over four pound ten and that was considered good money in those days."

154

Arthur Keeble also had Parker's little 80-ton *Gillman* for a time, but the shipping boom after the First World War was short-lived. The pattern of Essex barge work was changing. The hay and straw trade to London had virtually died with the passing of the old horse bus; and now motor lorries were serving the farms on the East Anglian sea-borders, where barges were once almost the sole means of getting the crops away.

But across the Blackwater, opposite Bradwell, a new fleet of sailing barges was coming into being. Josh Francis, with over twenty years of practical experience in Medway craft, had returned to Colchester in 1915 to manage the barges belonging to his uncle, Henry Howe, and was managing owner with a half-share in the old stackie *Unity* built by Shrubsall of Milton in 1871. Arthur Keeble left Parker to go Master in the *Unity* in 1921, thus commencing an association with Josh Francis that lasted thirty years.

After Henry Howe's death the barges were auctioned in October 1921 and Josh Francis bought in the *Falconet, Keeble, British Empire* and *Peace,* as well as his uncle's shares in the *Unity* and *Golden Fleece*; with *Roache* and *Excelsior* already jointly owned by Cecil Gilders, the broker, and farmer Littlebury, he formed the nucleus of a comfortable fleet.

Littlebury had taken a half share in the *Unity* while Arthur Keeble was in her. "He come down aboard to see us. 'Which end d'you reckon I ought to have,' he said jokingly. 'Shall it be the bows or the other part?' 'Well,' I said. 'That don't matter so far as I'm concerned. I dunno though. Come to think on it, perhaps you'd better have the starn end seeing the other's chained up!' "

The small owners were beginning to drop out but Josh Francis had the prescience to bring nearly all the local craft under his management. By 1934, when the firm of Francis & Gilders Ltd. was formed he had over thirty barges flying his well known and most attractive gold-and-purple bob.

After twelve months in the *Unity* Arthur Keeble shifted into the *Rose,* one of the earliest Howard-built barges and previously owned by John Thompson, the Maldon hay and straw merchant.

Next came the 120-ton *Saltcote Belle,* another Howard barge. When she was built in 1895 for Alfred May's Saltcote Maltings work the crew were paid a weekly wage; Bill Quilter got 30/- as Master; the mate got 20/- and third hand 10/-. Under Josh Francis, of course, all the barges worked on shares, the traditional system whereby the crew got one-half of the net freight, of which the master took two-thirds.

"That *Saltcote Belle* loaded a good five hundred quarters. Had very little chine and find ends. A lovely barge — she'd go too." She often sailed in the local regattas, and under Young Eb won the Maldon Challenge Cup outright in the mid 'twenties.

But Arthur Keeble only stayed in the *Saltcote Belle* for two years. In 1929 he took the *Agnes & Constance,* built by Curel at Frindsbury, a big barge loading 700 quarters. "She was a comfortable old thing. I liked her rather."

Lying in Colne weatherbound one time, he and his mate went visiting aboard

Centaur running down Colne in a fresh breeze with partly brailed mainsail.

the *Pall Mall* and it came on to blow so hard that they were unable to get back in their boat. Worse still, the *Agnes & Constance* started to drag on to the old wreck just above Mersea Point. "Couldn't do a thing. That was a bare barges's length off the wreck when the anchor picked up on a wire and there she stayed till we got back aboard."

But stranger still was the trip into Harwich one dark night. "That was quite calm with hardly any wind time we come jogging along in. All of a sudden there was a great blowing and threshing all around us. What a calamity!

" 'Good Gawd!' I says to the mate. 'Whatever is it?' But we couldn't see nothing. That was dark that night. Black as a grave. Just the time of that Loch Ness monster. I don't mind telling you that scared me coming so sudden on us. 'Get a torch,' I shouted, and the mate sung out he'd seen a face a-peering at him over the rail with whiskers on him. That was a rum 'un that was.

"We brought up under Shotley and next morning we got against the *Beaumont Belle* and called over: 'Did you see anything last night, Toby, a-coming into Harwich.'

" 'That was mighty queer,' he said. 'I'd never have believed it meself but what we had a seal on the forehatch.' And that's what it was — seals."

The *Agnes & Constance* went mine spotting during the war, and afterwards lightering at Maldon for John Sadd's, the big timber firm and one-time sailing barge owners.

In 1935 Arthur Keeble shipped in the *Centaur*, a 155-ton barge with 6-ft. 9-in. sides. "Six hundred quarters is enough for her; six fifty is too much." Built by Cann's of Harwich in 1905, she has always been a fast barge. "Knocked 'em all acock at Harwich one time. That was over seventy years ago when she belonged to Stone's of Brightlingsea and beat the *Orinoco, Ida, Iverna* and *Primrose* in the Regatta. She's strong. Why, all the floor timbers in the middle of her are a foot square. There's strength in her deadwood too. That comes right aft from the stem into the fore hole, and at the other end that's scarphed in under the cabin stove.

Centaur towed down to Dover with *Lady Rosebery* and *Duchess* to take part in the Dunkirk evacuation. She was lying in the Prince of Wales Dock with *James Piper* alongside on her way round to the Thames, when a tug came in at an excessive speed.

"Some of our chaps started a-singing out. 'Don't you worry,' I said. 'He won't hit us. He can stop her.' But he didn't! He came into us head first. *James Piper* being outside, she got her coamings sliced through. But for a good owd bumping it didn't seem we'd taken any harm, though we had a good look round."

"Presently soldiers come aboard. 'We're going to start a-loading now, Skipper.'

" 'That's all right,' I says, for we'd already uncovered. Presently though, one of the soldiers come down aft. 'There's water a-coming into your barge.'

"I knew that, for they'd started making a bulkhead of cans of drinking water under the mastcase.

" 'No, no!' he says. 'She's leaking, Skipper.'

"Dear oh dear! So she was, too. Water over the ceiling and me and my poor owd mate had a rare owd job a-pumping of her out. We were at it all night long. Then a naval officer come along and took a look at us. The soldiers worn't to put no more aboard, he said. That stuff was too valuable to charnst losing, so they loaded it into the *Lark* instead, and she never did come back from Dunkirk.

"What happened, though I worn't to know at the time, *Centaur's* chine had been damaged against the sloping dock wall. There was nothing they could do with us in Dover. Said we'd better go and get repairs done. Wanted to route us to Gravesend.

" 'That's no use to us,' I said.

" 'Where d'you want to go then?'

" 'Why, back to Maldon. We've got a yard that'll see to us there.'

" 'All right,' they said. 'Clear off!'

Centaur eventually sailed for Maldon at about ten o'clock in the morning, with an extra hand on board to help pump. They shaped up for the West Last then stood on for what they took to be the Mouse and the Blacktail. "That come on as thick as guts. Worn't Mouse! Worn't Blacktail! We fetched up alongside the Sheers. Tide was a-flowing by this time and we came right over the top into the Blackwater and brought up under Wymarks between eleven and twelve that night. Never saw a thing!"

Arthur Keeble had *Centaur* in the East Anglian work during the war. Brick rubble from the blitzed areas of London to Maldon for the construction of East Anglian aerodromes gave employment to a number of barges; there was a great deal of laying about and some of them made more from demurrage than they did from freight.

"Same as at Ipswich. We loaded up at Millwall for Ipswich along with *Defender*, *Oxygen* and a whole lot of others. They all went straight in and tied up at the abutment. When they called out to them to come alongside and load they took no notice, so they loaded *Centaur* first.

"A wonderful lot come away down and brought up under Shotley, so we did the same. George Bowles was in *Veravia* and wouldn't muster till we were a mile past. Up at Ipswich I said they'd come first on turn, but they wouldn't have it. That was a proper racket to leave barges on demurrage. I told the foreman I'd report it to the Ministry of Transport, but he said there was no need to carry on so.

" 'Why should I pay you five bob to take other barges out of turn?' I said. 'That's not right.' And nor it worn't not that it did George Bowles much good that time for they got him out before the weekend anyway, *and* he lorst a freight, what's more!"

Centaur was largely in the grain work, mostly between London and the East Anglian ports of Colchester, Maldon, Felixstowe and Ipswich, with an occasional freight to Great Yarmouth. Like all the Maldon skippers, Arthur Keeble was a great one for getting home whenever opportunity offered and had joined with the others many years ago in laying a mooring off Heybridge Basin so that a

Maldon man could leave his barge there and go off home with an easy mind.

He came up to the mooring at eleven o'clock in *Centaur* and tramped off home along the sea wall. Next morning he turned out early and came down the High Street past the church and over the brow of the hill expecting to see *Centaur*'s sprit and topmast above the cluster of trees and roofs of Heybridge Basin.

"Worn't no sign of her. That's queer, I thought, and went and knocked up Fred Taylor, the sailmaker, who's got an interest in our firm.

" 'What's the matter Arthur?' he said.

" 'I'm a-looking for my barge.'

" 'Where was she then?''

" 'Why, on the mooring eleven o'clock last night. There's no sign of her now.'

"Fred didn't know nothing about her so I set off down river. Oh I found her all right — down on Mill Beach. Seems she parted her mooring during the night. The mate got a scare when he looked out, for he didn't know anything about it till she'd washed up the beach. He couldn't do much for there worn't no bus to Maldon that time o' morning.

"One thing, she lay lovely along the shore between a couple o' breakwaters. I was more worried lest she damage herself a-coming off that night tide. Gawd that blowed a gale o' wind! That worn't no good a-getting off. That rained and blowed but we never floated and a good job we didn't.

"Next day Arthur Wright, the water bailiff, come down with another motor boat as well and just managed to drag us off. Didn't do a ha'p'orth o' damage and we'd still got the mooring hanging from our bows."

Arthur Keeble's last barge was the 120-ton *Falconet* built by Curel in 1899. He shifted into her from *Centaur* for easier working. "That's got a side on her though. Six-foot-three side's a rare lot for a barge that's only seventeen-six beam. Plenty of headroom though and good wide hatches. Just right for a yacht. She's good you see. She'd been doubled during the war and had a new keelson too.

"That *Falconet*'s a handy little thing." Then his eyes twinkled. "Why, I wouldn't say she's all that fast. Old George Watson was owner of her one time. Thought he'd got a flyer till he put her in the Medway race and she came in next morning."

Arthur Keeble retired June 1950 at the age of sixty-five, living in the same house Strutt built about the time he ordered the sailing barge *Surprise* from John Howard. Taking life easily now and putting on weight as if to justify the nickname 'Sorbo' by which he had long been known among his fellow bargemen, Arthur Keeble turned down several offers of barges. One man was after him to take a yacht away, but he shook his head and gently patted his stomach.

"Can't get about like I used to. No. No. I shan't go a-barging no more. Reckon I've had enough on 'em to last me my time."

Chapter Twenty

THROUGH THE WALLET

Henry and *Centaur* both towed down on the morning tide and brought up on the buoy opposite Heybridge Basin. We were starting our holiday and intended laying over the weekend for a scrub and a coat of tar. *Centaur* was bound to Fingringhoe in the Colne to load English wheat, but Stan said the *George Smeed* was already there and waiting to load so he decided to stop over for a tide and give us a hand.

"Besides, Chick loves tarring. That's right, isn't it?" he demanded, and Chick being a dutiful wife, flashed him a meaningful look, but nodded assent.

As soon as the tide had gone we hove the leeboards up clear on the runners. Jack, the young mate of *Centaur*, fetched out his scrubbers, and we all joined forces overside on the firm gravel river bed. There is something very satisfying about paying on tar on a warm summer day. It goes on so easily and shows a barge off to advantage. Chick apparently really did like tarring and we finished everything within reach before the tide made.

That night, after the children had gone to bed, we all lingered over supper in *Henry*'s saloon. Stan and Chick knew George Battershall, for they had sailed with him aboard *Veravia*. They both had a real affection for George, and Chick had a profound respect for his appetite. Apparently he thought nothing of having a fish and chip supper in one restaurant and following it up with meat pudding in the next. But in recent years George had been troubled with indigestion, and his eyesight was not as good as it had been, especially at night.

Stan told the story of *Veravia* drifting down Gravesend Reach in company with several other barges and soaking down on the Ovens Buoy which suddenly appeared from behind the mainsail close alongside. George was visibly shaken. He blinked at the buoy just where the Lower Hope opens up, then touched his cap and said: "Good morning, Mister Hope."

"The Ovens Buoy seems to come in for quite a lot of attention one way and another, " I remarked. "Wasn't it Knocker Hart's yarn about that buoy flashing in an' aht, in an' aht — then we hits it and it goes right aht?"

Stan shook his head. "Knocker swears it wasn't him that put the light out. He was complaining about that one night in The Ship and Lobster. Said someone must have made it up. Quite upset, he was too."

" 'Never ought a-bin allowed,' " broke in Chick. "That's what he's always saying. Same as coming out of Harwich that time. Do you remember, Stan?"

Chick told how they came drifting out of Harwich with hardly a breath of wind, and Knocker in the *Lorna* was half-a-mile or so inshore of them, with a very fair chance of being carried up Hamford Water when the flood set in. They conversed together as the gap gradually widened.

'It never ought a-bin allowed,' intoned Knocker. 'It never ought a-bin allowed.'

"What are you going to do, Knocker?" they called out. "Are you going back in again?"

"It's not what I say," he had roared back across the water. "It's not what I want but what the old girl wants to do. It never ought a-bin allowed. Put the kettle on, boy!"

Chick had a remarkable sense of humour and considerable powers of mimicry. She obviously enjoyed the free and easy life afloat and insisted on going sailing with Stan when he was mate in *Veravia.* "I said I wouldn't marry him otherwise." George wanted them to ship in *Henry* but the fo'c'sle was too small; instead Stan went master of *General Jackson.* But it was in *Saltcote Belle* that Chick officially shipped as mate.

Knocker Hart was in the pub at Woolwich when Stan said he would like him to meet his new mate.

"That's good," he beamed, "That's good," but next day he told them he couldn't stop laughing afterwards.

"I laughed as I went off. I laughed on board. I kep' all on laughing as I turned in."

"What were you laughing at, Knocker?" Chick demanded.

"Him," Knocker declared, pointing at Stan. "Couldn't help laughin'. Suddenly crossed my mind as he's a dirty old bugger a-sleepin' with his mate!"

Presently we felt the barges lift and swing to the flood with much rumbling and grating over the shingly bottom.

Stan stretched his long legs and got up.

"It's been nice knowing you folk," he said. "But it's time we made a move. With any luck we'll get a few hours sleep in Colne before taking the day tide up to Fingringhoe tomorrow."

It was quite dark when we came on deck; the moon was rising and trying to break through the clouds. We stood chatting for a few minutes longer while Jack got the lamps up. Then they made sail together, hauling out the topsail sheet and hoisting away.

"That'll do her, Jack. You can let go when you like," and Stan made his way aft to cast off the stern lines. The barges began to sheer apart.

"Let's have the mains'l."

The mate eased away on the main brails, while Stan, a dim shape on the hatch top, hauled the mainsheet block aft and hooked it on the traveller.

"Let her run."

The heavy folds of the mainsail fell out with a clatter ... slatted and filled. *Centaur* was well away now, forging ahead over the tide. Within a little she was just a black mass down the Reach all but merged in the dim background of the countryside, with only the steady, white, stern light to mark her progress.

"She'll be gybing over in a moment," I murmured, and sure enough there came the faint rattle of gear as the sprit slammed over. Her green starboard light opened up as she luffed up close-hauled round the point, and for a few moments *Centaur* hung there silhouetted against a break in the clouds. Then the moon went in again. It was August, yet the night was chilly. We dropped below and turned in.

Next morning I was out at six o'clock to finish off the port side where we had lain alongside *Centaur*; but the tide beat me. We were in two minds whether to get under way. The light southerly breeze would have served us well for a pleasant sail down the coast to Harwich and Pin Mill. And yet it was a pity not to make a job of the tarring while we were about it, so we let the fair wind go.

Dorothy gave me a hand when we took the ground Sunday afternoon, while the children played about on the river bed chasing flounders in the pools.

Monday morning we cleared up on deck. It is surprising what a mess the decks can become after a couple of days working overside. Peter helped me; we threw water over each other as well as the decks, while Elizabeth scampered about trying to get out of range.

Presently we went ashore in the boat, landing on the beach just below the entrance to the Basin. It was an attractive spot; the Basin itself had been given over to yachts, though there were still a number of old barges — *Keeble, Diligent, Snowdrop, Ida, D'Arcy* — which only voyaged forth on rare occasions lightering timber ex steamers anchored at Osea and transhipping in the Basin to special light draft craft for the canal trip to Chelmsford.

The atmosphere in the Basin was pleasant and informal; hardly a word was spoken except in cheery greeting as the yachts locked in or out. Once Peter was sitting on the footbridge sucking his thumb in thoughtful mood when the gates began to shut, and I had to make a quick grab at him. Nobody worried — least of all, Peter.

That Monday morning Dorothy carted Peter off to buy milk while Elizabeth and I walked along the sea wall to Saltcote Maltings, tucked away in the saltings at the top of Mill Reach. Wakeley's auxiliary *Water Lily* was loading English wheat. Time was when Bill Quilter used to work here in May's *Saltcote Belle*, fetching up the creek as best he could and poking up the last narrow gut stern first.

George Battershall came up here with *Henry* once. And so did Tubby Blake in the *Lancashire*.

"That's right," Tubby told me. "And what a place to git to! I kept sail on her coming up the crik and was just about to shoot up the gut when I sees a little yacht moored right in the middle, so I stands on and hits that there concrete sluice at the head o' the crik a fourpenny one. In the end we gits up to the Mill an' loads an' away we come. I could tell she was making a drop or two, but time we're discharged blowed if she hadn't wet a good twelve inches, an' the gov'nor gits charged up with sixty-five quid for damaged wheat.

" 'Tubby,' he says. 'I'm dockin' you half of it.'

" 'That's a nice thing,' I says. 'An' what for may I ask?'

" 'Because it's your bleedin' fault, that's why,' says the Gov'nor, and I never did git that out of him.

162

"Bugger that for a caper, so I stops a third of it from the mate's money.

"The mate didn't go much on that, but I told him if he'd a-pumped that wouldn't have happened.

"No, he didn't like that at all an' made as if to sock me one, but I perty soon screwed him on the floor.

"After discharging we went up to Tovil after stone. Time we're loaded an' towed down to Rochester I'm away ashore an' never come off till the pubs close at eleven o'clock. Next thing I know there's me a-floatin' out o' me bunk. Some o' the others give me a hand to beach the ol' gal over on the Crown an' Quarry. D'you know what? Why, she must've picked up a damn great lump o' stone in her bows time we hit the sluice — an' the bugger had dropped out!

"I soon had the fo'c'sle floor up an' rummaged round till I found the hole. Then I nailed on a bit o' felt an' tin and away we goes. Gets to Heybridge Basin an' part unloaded on the sea wall jest above the entrance, when the foreman comes aboard that night an' says we're wanted jest below the entrance fer the mornin'.

"It was blowin' hard an' there was a rare run o' tide, but I drops down on a line and puts her on the berth jest where the foreman said. Next mornin', blowed if there don't come a pile right up through her bottom!

"That done it. 'I've jest about had enough o' this,' I says, so we got her up on Cook's Yard at Maldon. 'I've had enough a-patchin' of her up,' I says. 'Now you have a go.' "

☆ ☆ ☆ ☆

We got *Henry* under way soon after mid-day. The breeze had come easterly, and was beginning to pipe through the rigging as we turned away down the Blackwater through the popple of a strong weather-going tide.

Saltcote, Northey, Lawling, Osea, Thirstlet, Tollesbury ... fine sounding names, with a virile and salty flavour on the lips of an Essex man. These creeks and rivers and little communities were very much alive, yet rich in memories and abounding in local lore.

Down below Osea we made a long board of it as far as the old Nass Beacon that smacks of Viking days, then winded and lay over towards Bradwell Creek, once the home of Clem Parker's fleet of stackies.

In the distance a couple of barges were coming out of Colne and luffing up for the Spitway. Soon they would be squaring away for the run up Swin to London River, as barges without number have done these hundred years. But we were bound into Colne for the night, and fetched slowly over the last of the ebb, with the breeze taking off all the time until at last we had to give her the light topmast staysail, on which I had spent so many hours at Maldon re-roping the luff. We anchored off Brightlingsea Creek, and presently there came the rattle of another anchor chain and we looked out to find West's auxiliary *Leonard Piper* just outside us. Peter, whom we thought to be asleep, clambered up the

163

Henry close hauled.

companion ladder to see for himself. There were lights of another small craft coming in from sea, and the red-flashing light beyond which we told him was the Bench Head Buoy, whereupon he dashed below for a torch.

"Yes," he said flashing his torch seaward. "That's what it is," and quite happily trotted off to bed.

Before daybreak I was sorry not to have anchored in the Pyefleet on the other side of the Colne under the lee of the East Mersea shore, for the breeze had piped up from the south-west and we began to roll when the tide turned so that I had to turn out and harden in the vang falls on the leeboard winches.

For two days we lay in Colne. *Gwynronald* came in from sea; both she and *Leonard Piper* were waiting for weather to go on the beach inside Colne Point for shingle. By Wednesday it was blowing no more than a moderate breeze from the south-west, and we got under weigh in the afternoon, turning out of Colne and squaring away to surge through the Wallet past Clacton and Frinton, with rolling vang set up to check the sprit; even then the sails slatted and slammed as she rolled.

Cranfield's *Gladys* came motoring out of Harwich and set her topsail off the Naze as she lay up for the Spitway. She was the only ship we saw that afternoon. There was weight enough in the wind for us to drop our headstick and pick up a cloth or two of the mainsail before we gybed over for the run into Harwich over the last of the ebb, though a trading barge would probably not have bothered.

Horlock's *Portlight* was hauled out on the slip at Harwich, and her steel hull made a great splodge of red lead paint above the roof tops. The old Ipswich barge *Serb* lay on Shotley Spit; she was a yacht now, a great lump of a barge, yet surprisingly handy in spite of her boxy lines. She was reputed to have the biggest spar for a mainmast of any barge afloat.

The light was beginning to fail. A dredger lay moored in mid-stream up the Orwell, and instead of pushing on for Pin Mill, Dorothy elected to bring up under Stone Heaps at Shotley, so that we luffed up and got sail off in a great hurry. It was only after we had anchored and gone below for supper that I remembered there were telephone cables hereabouts and they were certainly marked on my pre-war chart. Dorothy had seen beacons on the shore just below us, but it was too dark to pick anything up even with glasses. I was up at daybreak and found we were clear. Such was my relief I turned in again and slept soundly.

We blew up to Pin Mill on the morning tide and brought up well below the fleet of yachts. We lay opposite the *Golden Fleece*, a yacht barge that had come from Conyer to a delightful berth on the foreshore close under the woods, where they piped water aboard from a stream on the hillside.

We spent three happy days at Pin Mill among the old barges. There was Cromwell Horlock's *Defender* under the trees up towards the Butt & Oyster, with bowsprit down and fully rigged; alongside her was the old-time *Anne Maria* with her little tucked-up stern so typical of the early Kentish barges. The Wood-bridge *Nautilus* lay there too, and the boomy barge *Ethel Edith*, and Eve's old *Jess* that was run down and sunk in Harwich. Webb still repaired barges on the hard and *Jess* served as a workshop.

Wakeley's *Water Lily* was re-built here; and Cranfields's *Spinaway C* had just completed a re-fit. We watched her sail down from Ipswich looking magnificent. We had no regrets; *Henry* suited us well.

The children found Pin Mill just as fascinating as I always have. It was not so much the barges with them as the foreshore itself. They bathed from the beach inshore of us and had picnics. They walked up the hillside and through the woods to collect milk from the farm; they watched the baker ice his cakes in the bakery at the top of the hill; they paddled in the fresh water stream by the side of Harry King's boat yard and sent paper boats on the hazardous trip under the bridge. In short, Elizabeth and Peter fell under the spell of Pin Mill just as I had when I first sailed that way twenty years before.

Our passage up the coast was just as it had been so often in *June* before the war, coming out of Harwich with the promise of a north-westerly slant, only to find the breeze draw ahead off the Naze for a nose-ender up along the land. It freshened all the while so that we were glad to run into Colne on the last of the flood just in time for tea.

Arthur Keeble's old barge — the little *Falconet* — lay at anchor there. On the way ashore in the boat we spoke to the skipper. He didn't go much on the weather, though he reckoned he might have a look at it later, for he was bound up London River. Indeed, old Rookey was inclined to be thoroughly miserable. Even when I suggested he had a nice little barge he sniffed and said he didn't know about that, but he'd had plenty of the other sort.

He was away next morning at eight o'clock and laying out for the Spitway as we got under weigh an hour later at about half ebb. We should have done better to follow the *Falconet*; instead we held on for the Raysand Channel inside the Buxey Sands, and found so little water that our rudder ploughed a sandy furrow for nearly half-a-mile and caused us to lose our tide down the Whitaker while Rookey in the *Falconet* was away outside the sands legging it up Swin.

It was Burnham Week and the racers came running out of the Crouch, class after class of them with spinnakers set, to converge on the S.W. Buxey Buoy. We did our best to keep clear. One after another they handed their spinnakers and went away on the long beat home, while we fetched slowly over the young flood; the breeze died away until the bob hung lifeless ... then came again ... and dropped to the faintest of zephyrs. The flood was setting us over the sands so we dropped anchor in less than a fathom of water, where it lay on its side with stock showing, much to Peter's amusement. I dowsed the staysail and went below for a snooze.

When an hour or so later a light air came up from the south-east and the rigging was quite suddenly festooned with cobwebs; we decided to call it a day for it was too late on the tide to make Whitstable. Instead we hove up the anchor to

166

take the flood up the Whitaker again; drifting past the Ridge Buoy which suddenly appeared from behind the mainsail, Peter called out in a flash; "Good morning, Mr Buoy."

I looked at Dorothy and smiled. It might have been George Battershall greeting the Ovens Buoy.

We brought up for the night under Foulness and landed the family to walk across the fields to the village for stores. Our anchorage was the place old Dick Philpotts called Shell Bay. At one time Dick had Parker's *Victa* that was originally named *& Co* until 1913, when she was re-built on the old bottom with such flared sides that she had an extra 2-ft. 6-in. beam on deck. Although she carried 96 tons fully loaded she drew five feet with but half a cargo on board.

Dick had her in the Foulness stone work and used to beach her with Kentish ragstone all along the sea wall from Shell Ness to the River Roach. One night they came into Shell Bay to find a boat brought up with a light shining from the cabin.

" 'Tain't a barge," said Dick.

"More like a little yacht," said the mate.

After they had brought up and stowed Dick suggested sculling up in the boat to see what manner of craft she was. They came alongside and gave a hail, without reply. With curiosity getting the better of him, Dick stepped on deck and nearly slipped over. There was nobody on board, but the decks were strewn with fish.

They were thornbacks, thick and good eating, so they helped themselves to three of them and went back aboard their barge. Presently two men came off and got their boat under way.

"There's a barge brought up," said one.

"That was there when we come in," said the other.

"No, that wasn't."

"Yes that was," and they went on arguing all the way down river, while Dick stood in the cabin hatch and kept quiet. Next day they went ashore and walked across the fields to the pub.

"I reckon you had visitors last night," Dick said to the landlord.

"That's right. Fishermen, they were, come up here selling roker."

"Funny sort o' fishermen," Dick remarked, and he was right, for later on the police came along, and it transpired that the boat had been stolen from Leigh. "Good eating though, them thornbacks!"

It was fine and sunny and the glass stood steady when we turned out next morning. There was a light westerly breeze, although the weather forecast spoke of it backing and freshening later. Had we known how fresh we would never have sailed at all. As it was we were away before eight o'clock and ran gently out of Burnham River, while the cocks crew ashore and tractors started up in the fields. The S.W. Buxey loomed up out of the mist, then the Ridge. We set the staysail as a spinnaker and the children began to make plans for Whitstable.

It was still pleasant sailing when we cut inside the Whitaker Beacon and hauled

Peter: at the wheel; reeving the staysail sheet; and weighing anchor.

our wind to work up along the Maplin Sands out of the worst of the tide. But clouds hid the sun and the breeze was beginning to freshen by the time we had the flood under us off the Sheers, as the Maplin Light used to be known to bargemen. Before long I had to drop the topsail head to ease *Henry* through a vicious squall. But there was worse on the way; I had to let go the topsail sheet and lay aloft on the next starboard tack to pass the gasket.

Henry was quieter now, but much of her power and liveliness had gone from her. A bargeman would have held on to the topsail and maybe hove up a cloth or two of the mainsail. But I was short-handed and played for safety.

The children were not worried. Peter was sick but his appetite was unaffected. He and Elizabeth played in the saloon and every now and then she would appear in the hatch to ask if we were still making for Whitstable.

"Can't say yet," I replied, for it was touch and go whether we would have to run for shelter, but when we eventually made the S.E. Maplin I reckoned we had sufficient offing to lay across the estuary for the Kent Coast, and the next time Elizabeth popped her head up I nodded, whereupon she exclaimed: "Goody. Goody," and clapped her hands and disappeared below.

Dorothy went down a little later to find Peter playing happily with his cars and Elizabeth sitting on the keelson eating chocolate and singing at the top of her voice: "Put another nickel in."

It was too much for Dorothy and she had to retire hurriedly.

There was a nasty sea running in the big ship channel and steamers were flinging spray over their fo'c'sle heads. It was raining, too, and the visibility was poor. Three destroyers coming out from Sheerness in line ahead had to alter course for us and their wake added to the confusion of the short cross seas.

Elizabeth still looked out from time to time, and when she saw we were still shaping across towards the cliffs of Sheppey she gave me a great wink before slipping below. I was reminded of naval ratings during the war who could go off watch and turn in without the slightest qualm when sleep seemed out of all question to me on the bridge. What it is to have faith!

Savoy lay at anchor under Shell Ness, bound for Dover. The seas seemed easier over by the Columbine and *Henry* drove through them with only an occasional burst of spray over the foredeck. We held on past the Ham Gat Buoy close-hauled on the starboard tack. The tide was done and I was just about to lay aloft to loosen the topsail when another squall came shrieking down the West Swale and I changed my mind, relying on the mainsail set smart to fetch us across the bay.

We made Whitstable just as it was coming dark. Albert Fryer, the huffler, and his mate, Stuart Etheridge, were waiting for us out by the oyster yawls. I was never more glad to see two people step aboard. Within a few minutes we were luffing up for the harbour entrance where willing hands took our lines.

That night it blew a gale. Only when it had blown itself out did we lay up along the coast for the Medway and our winter berth at Hoo. But those three days renewed my conviction that the following year I must bring *Henry* back to Whitstable and learn something of the fascinating story of the local craft.

Chapter Twenty-One

HOO ST WERBURGH

The Marina Club, where we used to berth before Frog's Dock, had grown up on the site of the old Hoo Brickworks, owned by George Armytage of Loo Lodge, and later by Walter Brice. Armytage had the little barges *Conyer*, *Mosquito* and *Bluebell*.

Walter Brice owned the ballast pits, too, but it was another member of the Brice family, Solomon Brice — commonly known as Solly — whose barges did most of the local work. Based on Point Yard, Rochester, he had a fleet of thirty-four barges in the old days, and used to hire many more besides for his farm and mud work. They were Sittingbourne barges mostly, such as the *Henry Wood*, *William Wood*, *Sophy*, the little stumpy *Maria* and the old *Pioneer*, whose bottom lay on the beach under Cockham Woods. Eventually he bought them outright from Charles Wood. He also bought the *Bessie Hart* that won the Thames Barge Match in 1867 and is now hulked in West Hoo Creek, filled in with earth under the sea wall and overgrown with wild thyme.

The ballast pits have long since been worked out and by 1950 there were only six of Solly Brice's barges still working, with their familiar light-blue rail and stern, and blue-white-blue bands in the sling of the sprit. *Violet* was probably the best of them; she and *Nelson* and *G.C.B.* were in the dry work — coal to Queenborough and an occasional freight of cement to the London Docks. There was the *R.S. Jackson* and *Rowland* and the beamy old *Plover* that could only be got to bear away loaded with the topsail sheet hanging over her stern; these three were mostly in the slob work.

All the rest had gone. Most of them had been worked out like the *Partridge* and *Metropolis* propping up the sea wall in West Hoo Creek. Others, like *Pomona* and *Miranda* finished up in the Stoke Mudhole, where the *Glenburn* came to grief taking a short cut and breaking her back athwart the remains of an old German submarine that was towed to the mudhole after the breakers had taken their pick.

Another barge that met an untimely end was Brice's *Busy-Body*. Dick Philpott had her in the stone work during the war and one day he cast off from the quarry just below Allington Lock as the tug came down, but owing to the ineptitude of the mate of the last barge in the tow, their line was never made fast. *Busy-Body* swung athwart the narrow river and grounded head and stern on the banks. Although the tug slipped her tow and came back, they were unable to get her off and Dick had the mortification of watching his barge with 140 tons of Kentish ragstone on board slowly but surely break her back as the tide fell.

The *R.S. Jackson* came to Brice's Wharf when they started to clean out the berth against the time when craft would be bringing in Thames ballast for the new Grain refineries, and they were taking the mud down to the Stoke mudhole where Brice's muddies loaded away thousands of tons of clay for cement and brick making.

I spoke with the tall, young mate of the *R.S. Jackson*, and saw how a barge's hold could be knocked about in the grab work, for her ceiling was in splinters and there was barely anything left of her wooden keelson, except beneath the deck where the grabs were unable to get at it. The wonder of it was that she kept as tight as she did. It must have been the cumulative effect of years of Blackwall caulking, so the mate declared.

Barges are no strangers to Hoo. Henry Everist of Parsonage Farm had the old *Ceres*, built Battersea 1795; *Elizabeth*, built Bankside 1809; *Brothers*, built Stratford 1829; and *Richard*, built Strood 1846. He lies buried in the massive family vault in the churchyard of Hoo St. Werburgh, the church that was founded as a cell of the Abbey of Minster on the Isle of Sheppey, by St. Werburgh herself in the seventh century. The square tower with its slender, shingled spire, stands as a landmark for all who voyage up the Medway, and until recently the Admiralty recognized its value to mariners by presenting two white ensigns every year to be flown from the flag staff. Should ever the custom be revived, it would be necessary first to replace the staff, which had gone the way of all spars and succumbed to the ravages of dry rot.

There used to be plenty of barge work to and from the local farms. Our own berth at Frog's Dock was just one. West's barges brought dung to Crawford's Wharf from the cattle boats moored off Deptford; the farm hands did the unloading for 5/- a day and glad of it, for they earned but 3/- a day on the land.

Welsh steam coal came in by barge to Buttercrock Wharf for both the Hoo Steam Ploughing Company, as well as for the North Kent Haulage Company, whose traction engines did much of the general road haulage before the days of lorries. The coal shed still stands on the wharf in the middle of the saltings.

Another relic of the past is the Hoo Fort. There is only part of the brick wall left on the foreshore, but Elizabeth picked a cannon ball out of the foundations, in all probability fired by the Dutch when they sailed up the Medway in 1667, so the curator of Rochester Museum declared.

W. L. Wyllie, the marine artist, lived at Hoo Lodge from 1885 to 1906. Both he and Mrs Wyllie were keen sailors and they had what must have been the first of the yacht barges, for they bought Keep's *New Zealand* in 1896 and re-named her *Four Brothers* after their sons. William Webb, who lived in the cottage under Cockham Woods, went skipper of her, and years afterwards he took me away sailing in my school holidays aboard the *Three Brothers*, owned at Maidstone by the Medway Brewery. And when I bought *June* in 1933 it was the dear, kindly old Skipper who advised me on the conversion and kept me out of trouble.

William Webb was a great admirer of the Wyllie's and declared there was nobody who could depict a barge with so few strokes. I must have been infected with his enthusiasm for I have never ceased to delight in Mrs Wyllie's description

Tubby Blake.

of their life both ashore and afloat in the charming book she wrote shortly before she died: "We were One."

We never lacked visitors during our second winter at Hoo, and we saw quite a lot of our old friend Tubby Blake who had left Wakeley's *Lancashire* to take the Thames Barge Sailing Club's *Arrow*. He and Peter were great friends and one Sunday afternoon Peter demanded he should draw him a barge.

"You don't want one o' them old things," said Tubby, with a fine display of scorn.

"Yes I do, Skipper. Really I do."

"All right then," said Tubby, seating himself at the table. "Give us a pencil and a scrap o' paper and we'll see what we can do."

With Peter kneeling on the table and watching intently, Tubby grasped the pencil in his great maw and firmly sketched the outline of a barge under full sail. Like his father whose water colours are said to adorn many a pub around Northfleet and Shoebury, Tubby was no mean artist.

Presently he drew back and cocked his head on one side.

"How's that?" he demanded.

"But she hasn't got an anchor, Skipper."

"She's a-sailing. She don't want no anchor."

"But she might want to bring up, Skipper."

"All right. Here's yer anchor. Now what else?"

"Where's her flag, Skipper?"

Tubby looked at Peter with mock severity. "You want everything you do," he exclaimed, then proceeded to draw a bob at the topmast truck. "Now let's have a look. Why, there ain't no smoke from the cabin chimney. That won't do."

"No," echoed Peter. "That won't do or their mother won't cook any dinner."

A few pencil scrawls smudged with a dubious looking forefinger soon produced a most realistic impression of smoke.

"Reckon the mate has jist stoked up to cook the duff."

Tubby chuckled to himself as he held the drawing at arm's length for both of them to study with a critical air. Peter was quiet; he was still somewhat over-awed by a bargeman's magic finger that could produce such a wealth of smoke.

"Can't get but half the boat in. Ain't no room fer more."

Peter was satisfied; he called to Elizabeth to fetch her crayons and the picture was duly coloured. Peter was still perched on the table and stopped every now and then to blow the dust away.

"Now put in a buoy, Skipper. One with a light on it."

Tubby meekly did as he was bid and Peter studied the brightly-coloured picture for some moments in silence. Then he turned and looked up wistfully into Tubby's face.

"Can you draw trees, Skipper?"

Elizabeth, who was standing by the table, burst out laughing.

"You don't get trees at sea, silly."

"Yes you do, Liz. I know you do 'cos I've seen them."

We all smiled but Peter was not to be put off. "You know what I mean. Trees with things crawling up them."

Tubby understood. He started to chuckle; his stomach quivered and shook with emotion. "I know what he wants," he roared, and picking up the pencil, quickly sketched a few withies of the sort to be seen marking the channel in any Essex creek. "Winkle trees is what my old gran'dad used to call 'em. That's what he wants — winkle trees!"

The thought of winkle trees put Tubby in a reminiscent mood. As a young man he was mate in the *Six Sisters*, a flush-deck, tiller-steering little barge working from the Jubilee Brick Works just above Shoebury. "Wicked place, that was, in any sort o' weather. Barges pretty often got swamped there," and he related how he spent three nights astride the collar lashing. "They'd take the bricks out at low water, put 'em ashore to dry, load you up with fresh ones and off you'd go."

Bill Bowman, who had the *Hawk*, brought a bottle of rum off with him one afternoon. "That *Hawk* — only had to show her a black cloud and down she'd go. Didn't take much of a popple to put her under. You'd a-laughed to see Bill Bowman sitting astride the collar lashing with the bottle o' rum in his hand a-singing: 'A life on the ocean wave.' "

Later Tubby went into the *Elwin* with Jack Grundy. She was much the same type of barge as *Six Sisters*, with chines drawn right out to her stem, but *Elwin* had a wheel. "Both carried bowsprit and jib. You needed a jib coming off Southend."

Jack Grundy was a much respected old barge master and very religious. "He was what they called a Peculiar. Bit too peculiar for me. He'd taken a fancy to me and wanted to adopt me, but I used to go along with the other mates to the pub and he didn't like that."

Tubby thought he would make a change and went across to Strood and enquired of a man at the pier, who turned out to be Lucky Brown, the huffler, if anybody wanted a barge mate. It happened that a new barge, the *Bobs*, had just loaded at Borstal and was short of a mate.

"Up I paddles to Borstal. Wasn't no buses nor nothing those days. Going across the fields I meets a chap in a light suit and brown polished gaiters. Looked like a farmer to me.

" 'Seen the *Bobs*, Gov'nor?'

" 'What do you want with the *Bobs*?' he says in a gruff sort o' voice.

" 'Why. I heard she was short of a mate.'

" 'I'm skipper of the *Bobs*,' he says. 'Can't say you look much like a barge mate.'

" 'I've been well trained, Gov'nor. Come to think on it, you don't look much like a barge skipper yourself.'

" 'All right,' he says. 'I'll give you a trial. Be aboard to-night and we'll shoot the bridge first thing.'

"Next morning he tells me to loose the tops'l and up I goes.

174

" 'I don't know much about shooting bridges,' I says. 'Never had no call for that before.'

" 'That's all right,' he says. 'We'll be picking up Lucky at the bridge. He'll take the wheel and I'll lower down. All you have to do is to smack the spreet down.'

"We shoots the bridge, and brings up and rigs. Then I was made to clear up. Had to get spudger and deck scrubber and paint scrubber and mop out o' the fo'c'sle. Scrub! Scrub! Scrub! At it all the way down the Medway. Soon as I lay me tools by he'd pick 'em up and have a go. He washes the mizzen rigging down with hot water, and after I've done washing down the cabin top, blowed if he don't start on it with hot water and soda.

" 'You'll mess it all up again, Gov'nor,' I says, but he would do it. I never see a man so particular. Used to come aboard, pull out his pocket handkerchief and wipe round the cabin panelling to see if there was any dust. Mind you, she was a fine looking barge, that *Bobs* — but scrub! I've never scrubbed so much in me life before nor since.

"We sailed a-Sunday. Up the docks Monday. Unloaded. Up we goes Albert Docks fer coke and we're back Borstal Wednesday. Wasn't bad for a start! He wasn't a bad sort o' chap apart from his scrubbing. Charlie Anderson, he called hisself, but I knew that wasn't his real name. Been left here as a boy. Come ashore from a Norwegian barque and worked the Borstal *A.B.C.* barges and finished up Commodore skipper.

"One day up in the docks the Customs come aboard after some particulars for the census. Wanted to know where he was born.

" 'Christiania.'

" 'Then yer name can't be Charles Anderson,' they says and that's when he brought out his papers and I see his full name: Carl Augustus Anson."

Tubby stayed in the *Bobs* until the Borstal works fell on bad times and were taken over by the Syndicate. That upset the barge work and the *Bobs* started working from Nickelpits up at Aylesford with sand. "That was queer sailing in them upper reaches o' the Medway. Down fores'l — up fores'l. 'Bout-O all the bleeding way."

Tubby left the barges then for a spell in the little single-topsail schooner *Druide*, which he saw loading at Rochester over by the Gasworks Point. Next day the newly-built sailing barge *Estelle* came alongside and Tubby had the job of heaving 2-cwt. bags of cement aboard on the *Druide*'s dolly winch.

"I was cook in her and drops the duff once in the grate, so I scrapes the worst off and smacks it on a plate. Down the cabin the skipper looks at me and then at the duff, takes his knife, cuts the end off with the ashes and hands it back. 'That's your share, boy.' "

The *Druide* loaded at Derwenthaugh for Strood with fire bricks, which so scratched and cut Tubby's hands when it came to working cargo that he soon had his fill of schooners at £3.10.0 per month. He went back to Shoebury and joined the little *Mary Jane*.

175

"That was the only barge as ever I knew to turn to wind'rd without leeboards. She caned the crack Kentish barges that come over for the Southend Regatta in 1900. The first leg was over the tide down to Shoebury. All the others were out in the tide — all except us and we turned away down in the slack water."

Mary Jane had flared sides — big on top and narrow on the bottom — and although built to carry some 40,000 bricks, once carried an extra 5,000 from Halstow to London so as to qualify for the return freight of rough stuff at £5, which was 10/- more than the smaller barges got. There were no freeboard restrictions in those days. "Couldn't sail on her. She just crawled up to London that time. Light barge, though, or properly trimmed, she'd go about like a deer. But even she couldn't do the *Champion* me and my wife took away when we went under Parker in February nineteen twenty-three after I lorst the *Isabella*. Parker bought the *Plantagenet* really for the sewage work and I was to have had her, but Cliff French jumped in, so I took the *Champion* instead. There was a barge for you! Rochester-built and well nigh sixty years old with real saucer bows an' all. But handy! Winded just like she was greased. Beat out o' Lion Crik once and she come bouncing off the banks.

"Same as turning up the Medway along with Jumbo Clegg in the *Verona*, we showed him, and him a racing barge an' all. It was 'Bout-O all the way up. More you went about, faster she'd go.

" 'Tubby,' says Jumbo after we're brought up. 'I never see a barge make so many boards. Must've made enough to build a bleedin' house!' Clem Parker had us on the blocks at Bradwell and got Walter Kemp to come over from Paglesham and double her. Kemp pulled up the rail and sheathed her all over with 1½-in. pitch pine. "There wasn't a butt anywhere in her deck planking. The Gov'nor was so proud of his decks that he had 'em varnished and kept 'em so for some years. Slippery! Just like glass, they were.

"Another time we come away from Beckton blowing a gale southerly, I had Jack Syfret along o' me that trip. When we get down to the top of the Swatch wind come westerly.

" 'Jack,' I says. 'I'm damned well not going to sea in this,' so we brings up and I gets out me old hoop net to do a bit o' fishing.

" 'Better by half get our passage,' grumbles Jack.

"That was enough. 'Up anchor!' "

By the time they fetched the Blacktail the wedges on the weather side were washing out and the hatch cloth lifting. *Champion* was going too fast. They tried to check her by holding the sprit in the middle, but she ran on till she stopped on the Ridge. The seas went right over her and the cloths washed off. Tubby and his mate had to take to the rigging while the barge bumped and jolted across the sands.

" 'We'd better bring up on the flats somewhere when she does come clear,' I says, but blessed if she don't start hauling her luff. She never made no more water so we beat up into Maldon River an' turned in.

"Next morning old Dale comes off from the *Boomont Belle* and gives a hand

176

Tarring *Henry* at Hoo.

into Bradwell. 'She's made a drop or two o' water, ain't she?' but when we'd taken off the hatches and he looks down the hold, he said he'd never a-come in with us if he'd known how much she had in her.''

Tubby used to carry stacks for Parker, loading at one or other of the outfalls on the Main.

" 'I'd like you to get to London a-Monday, Tubby,' he said one time.

" 'Righto, Gov'nor. We'll be off tonight.'

" 'Have you seen the glass?'

" 'Mustn't look at no weather glass — not if you want us there a-Monday.'

" 'Weather looks bad.'

" 'Can't help that.'

"We went down and sounded for the Spitway. Found it in the dark and over we goes. Then the old sails start going a-pieces. Tawps'l splits from head to sheet. That was a night, that was!

" 'There you are, Gov'nor,' I says when I gets back. 'You wanted your damned barge there. Now she wants some new sails in her.'

"Parker never said much, but he gave orders to Yankee Bill to make a new suit. He never could make a good mains'l, though. They were always too baggy — but strong! We had three feet off the spreet that time 'cos we couldn't never get under way without bowsprit an' jib.

177

"Parker said we'd better dress the jib while we're about it. I used to set it on the stay with a downhaul so's it was easier for Mother, but Clem never did like to see a jib on a stay.

" 'I don't reckon you stow that on the bowsprit end,' he said.

" 'Oh yes I do. Still, have it dressed if you like. Don't make no difference to me.'

"But Clem Parker was a decent old chap. Same as we're on the yard a-dressing sails. I'd be up the yard working on 'em, but Mother 'ud stay aboard. Come Friday I'd go up to get me money.

" 'Here you are, Tubby. And here's a couple o' quid for your wife. Can't leave her out of it.' And whenever we were in Bradwell he'd come down in his pony and trap with fresh vegetables from his garden. 'Here you are, Mother,' he'd say. 'Something for you to cook.' "

Joe Kirby was Commodore Skipper of Parker's barges and according to Tubby did his best to get him the sack. "That time o' day there was a good fleet working the Medway an' some on 'em used to lay for weeks under the West Shore in the Ness.

"I'd come down from Beckton with sludge and make me passage, and Clem 'ud say: 'Seen anything of the others, Tubby?'

"I'd have to say: 'No I ain't seen 'em,' and Clem 'ud shake his head. 'Holding up the West Shore again, I'll be bound.'

"Joe Kirby's uncle was ship's husband to Parker's barges and and puts aboard a hundredweight of deck dressing. I gets to Rochester and picks up some tar and gas oil. Tarred the decks all over. We tows up to Allington along o' Joe Kirby and he writes to the Gov'nor and tells him Tubby's tarred his decks and flogged the paint.

"I gets to hear of this, so I sits down and writes to Clem. 'Sir, the tar I got cost nothing and gas oil nothing, I thought it would be better for the work we're a-doing. Some of the paint I took home to paint the caravan,' And the Gov'nor replies: 'Don't blame you neither.' What's more, it was Joe what got the sack, not me."

Tubby and his wife made their home aboard the barge with their two boys Charlie and George, who were growing up and proving quite useful.

"Joe Kirby was on at the Gov'nor for my eldest boy to go in the *Water Lily*. Said I'd got two boys. ' 'Tain't fair to Charlie,' he said, 'a-keeping him back.'

"The gov'nor mentions it to me. 'What! And be starved out?' I says, for Joe crawled about and the boy couldn't earn nothing, but the Gov'nor had his way.

"Come Christmas time, *Water Lily*'s a-loading oats for Maldon. We're up at Beckton. It's no use us chasing away down as they wouldn't be starting on us over the holiday. Better be half wait up at Beckton. But Joe, he has to load whether he likes it or not, so he writes Parker to say Tubby's laying at Beckton, and sowing discord with his son. Parker 'phones through to me and asks what I'm playing at.

" 'All right,' I says, and away we go, holiday or no holiday. Joe Kirby and a lot of the others are laying in Yantlet. All Francis's get under weigh. Joe, he goes back to the Hope and sends the boy to Cliffe for bread.

"I went for Parker like a tiger. 'There's us half full o' stinking water and nobody to unload us. We ain't fit to be aboard of. Why take notice of Joe Kirby? I tell you my boy's a-coming out o' that barge of his. He ain't stopping along o' Joe Kirby.'

" 'No, he ain't,' says the Gov'nor. ' 'Cos I've sacked Joe Kirby up at Maldon. Juggy Gosling's taking her.' Bill Kirby, though, what had the *Duchess*, he kicks up a row, for he reckons *Water Lily*'s his barge, so Juggy took the *Lurline* instead.'

"But that *Champion* was a goer an' no mistake. We're away over Spitway one time and it comes on to blow a gale o' wind. The *Boomont Belle* was with us and a lot more besides.

" 'Hard up, Tubby,' he shouts. 'It's Harwich for us.'

" 'Bugger Harwich! I'm going in here.' "

Champion and *Oak* were the only two barges to make Maldon River, and the *Oak* wetted forty tons that trip.

"We hove up the mains'l in the lee of a four-masted ship called the *City of Manchester* laying off Bradwell. 'In with her, quick, Mother,' I shouts and it hung in the middle just long enough to get sail off."

Tubby had been sitting all this time in the big arm chair, with his hands clasped across his great stomach that heaved and rumbled as he laughed. His reminiscent mood was passing. He was growing sleepy but allowed himself one last fling.

"That *Champion* was the only barge as ever put Jack Waterhouse in a plight, and you know what a smart bargeman he was. He tried his damnest to come up past us once in his *Harold Margetts*. Damn nigh caught us at the top o' Chatham Reach, but I jest got in that bit of up tide under the Point to slip through and out acrorst Jack's bows. He pulled off his cap, chucked it on deck and stamped on it. An' that was the only time as ever I see Jack Waterhouse in a plight."

Tubby's eyes were red-rimmed as he hove himself out of the chair. He permitted himself yet one more diatribe on the *Champion*.

"What's happened to her?" he echoed. "Why, she got run down and sunk by a collier by the Mid Blyth ... Broken up? Not her! Too strong fer that. They got her up and she went as a roads barge at Swanscombe. Never a pump shipped in her, so I'm told. They knew how to build barges in the old days."

Cereal (renamed *Lyford Anna)* and *Edith.*

Chapter Twenty-Two

THE WHITSTABLE BARGES

Whitstable from seaward merges into the dark, wooded Canterbury hills beyond. But skirting the Columbine Shoal as we did in April 1951, and standing inshore over the flats where the oysters lie, the long, low shingle-fringed coastline of the bay takes on shape and character for the gaily painted cottages intermingle with the boatyards and tarred, weatherboarded fishermen's huts.

The harbour was always difficult for the stranger to pick up but for the top-masts rising high above the red-painted warehouses, and the entrance itself is slow to open up.

Poor old Bill Carpenter, the huffler, died soon after the war. Albert Fryer, one of a large family of bargemen, took his place, combining huffling with inshore fishing.

It was nearly low water when we made Whitstable, and the harbour was dried out, so we brought up just to windward of the oyster yawls in a bare fathom of water. Seventy years ago there would have been eighty smacks here. We found but five.

On the first of the flood the fishing boats began to motor in from sea. An hour or so later, as soon as there was water, Albert and his hefty mate, Stuart Eldridge, came off. There was quite a strong breeze westerly.

"We won't worry about the tops'l," said Albert, "Fores'l and a cloth or two of the main's about all she'll want to-day," and so it proved.

The small 'L'-shaped harbour was much the same as when it first opened in 1832 to serve the merchants of Canterbury in conjunction with the newly-built Whitstable and Canterbury railway. The original wooden ticket office still stood on the quay, close to the spot where the old broad gauge track was unearthed.

Most of the small trading craft, however, continued to moor off the town, and horses and carts came over the seawall at low water by way of the Horse-bridge. It was so with the locally-owned hoys on the London run. Even in 1790 there were six local colliers and six hoys. A new steam packet was put into service in 1836; the combined ship and rail fare from London to Canterbury was five shillings and although the railway age put paid to the paddle steamers, the Whit-stable Hoy Company continued in existence until 1936.

The earlier hoys were cutter-rigged and later, when spritsail barges were found more suitable for the work, at least one hoy — the *Good Intent* — was cut in two and lengthened to become the brigantine barge *Tankerton Tower*. Among the hoy barges were the *Reindeer, Excelsior, Onward, James & Harriet* and the Ipswich barge *Aveyron*, renamed *Gozby Solly* by Harry Solly.

There were usually two sailings each week, with a third barge held in reserve.

They called at a number of Thameside wharfs; Angerstein's and Black Eagle for general cargo; Fenning's, close by London Bridge, for tinned milk; Brunner Mond's for soda; Silvertown for sugar. Like the Sandwich, Ramsgate and Margate hoys, they made their passages with wonderful regularity.

Another of Solly's barges was the 60-ton *Sally*, built in Holland in 1859. Her mast was very nearly amidships; she was boomsail-rigged and carried two forestays. She was so shallow that her skipper had to stand in the cabin hatch to put on his trousers. In her later days she was working the dredger in the Lower Hope loading ballast for Whitstable.

Sally's remains served as a groin on West Beach for many years; she must have been strong, for it was not until soldiers started cutting doors in her bulkheads and hacking away planking here and there that she started to go to pieces. When we had a coffee table repaired, the furniture maker went to the old *Sally* for his seasoned oak.

Although the billyboys, barges and other small craft preferred to use the flats, a considerable fleet of locally-owned brigs, brigantines, barquentines, ketches and topsail schooners crowded into the harbour. There were practically no discharging facilities, but each craft used her own gear and coal was discharged by the time-honoured method of jumping it out. Under railway ownership the harbour prospered for nearly a hundred years.

It was a period of great expansion for Whitstable. In addition to the trading craft — and some three hundred were locally owned over the years — there was a great number of oyster yawls and smacks. In the days before the Royal Navy had its own deep-sea divers, Whitstable men acquired a considerable reputation for salvage work around the coasts. The five shipbuilding yards built smacks and trading vessels, the largest being the 500-ton barquentine-rigged barge *Nellie S* trading to the Caribbean and South America.

But times changed. By the turn of the century steam was ousting the larger foreign-going sailing craft; the collier brigs and billyboys dropped out; only the more economical ketches and schooners contrived to eke out a living on the coast under the ownership of the Whitstable Shipping Company. The sailing barges, of course, still held their own. Cheap to run with a crew of two, they were ideal for dock work with free access alongside the steamers, and as the Whitstable foreign trade declined they were more and more employed in trans-shipment cargoes of grain, timber, fertilizers and animal feeding stuffs.

In 1916 H. K. Daniels, manager of the Whitstable Shipping Company, left to found the firm of Daniels Bros. (Whitstable) Ltd., taking over the warehouses and the sailing barges. There was the Ipswich-built *Champion* that acted as blockship for the harbour in the 1914/18 war, and the little 80-ton *Sibyl*, one of the first of the Shipping Company's barges, a stumpy barge with a bowsprit, but later converted to topsail rig. She was in the Ramsgate work mostly, carrying 300 quarters or some 66 tons, but went away lightering during the war and never returned.

There was the *Whynot* that went ashore off West Beach with Quaker Oats, making the good folk of Whitstable who were not above beachcombing porridge minded. She was later cut down by an Orient Liner in Sea Reach and finished up at Black Jack's place at Rosherville, where an old chap built a bulkhead in her hold and lived aboard for several years. Yet another was the 200-ton *Eucrete*, built at the Whitstable Shipping Company's First Yard that once belonged to Gann, and she was so square that as often as not the anchor had to be touched down to get her to come about. She was sold away from Whitstable years ago and was reported to be trading under the French flag in the late 'twenties.

Another of the original barges was the *W. H. Randall*. She was run down off Greenwich whilst laying on the buoy in company with the Whitstable barges *Duluth* and *Kathleen*. They were repaired and doubled — 'put in a box' as the bargemen used to call it — but the *W. H. Randall* was old and too far gone. She was broken up and a great deal of her timbers went to the new Chestfield housing estate, where her stern frame was said to be erected in its entirety.

The little *Thomas & Frances* was another since gone. She was sailing up to the last war, when she was stripped of her gear and held in readiness as a block ship for the harbour entrance.

Three of Daniels' barges were lost during the war; *Duluth* hit a wreck; *Globe* and the coaster *H.K.D.* were both mined.

The shapely, deep-sided *Lord Churchill*, one-time boomy and the sole survivor of Walker & Howard's famous fleet of *Lords*, was sold away for a yacht after the war. She was never the same, so they said, since eighteen inches were cut off the sprit and thirty inches off the topmast. She was over deep for Whitstable work for she really wanted 8-ft. 6-in. of water. The 90-ton *Cereal* became a yacht barge, too, renamed *Lyford Anna*. *Vicunia*, jointly owned with Harold Andrews of Sittingbourne, traded for a number of years with an auxiliary engine before being cut down to a full-powered, twin-screw motor barge.

In 1951 Daniels Bros. owned seven sailing barges; *Kathleen*, a well-kept auxiliary; *Savoy*, bought from Crundall's, Dover; the ex-Sandwich hoy barge *Trilby; Violet*, formerly belonging to E. Marriage & Son of East Mills, Colchester, and for a while jointly owned with Francis & Gilders; *Azima*, built at Whitstable in 1898, one of the few sailormen with wheelhouse and mizzen; *Colonia*, purchased from Cranfield's, Ipswich; *Ardwina*, bought from Metcalfe's.

Another Whitstable-owned barge was the fine old Channel banger *Major*. She belonged to Anderson's and worked with Daniels' fleet on a percentage basis. Other regular Whitstable traders were the last of Cremer's Faversham barges: *Edith, Esther, Nellie, James & Ann* and *Pretoria*.

There were three barges in the harbour when we came in — *Major, Edith* and *Violet*. The *Major* was lying empty alongside the East wall, waiting to get away. We fetched in past her, then Stuart ran off our dolly wire and we warped slowly up harbour past *Edith* discharging wheat under the sucker, past the fishing boats and yachts to a snug berth inside *Violet* at the far end of the Steam Packet Quay, sometimes known as Big Ben from the standard crane that used to be there.

Beatrice Maud, Violet and *Henry.*

Shifting craft about a crowded harbour is a work of art, with a check line here and there but rarely the need for a fender. Albert Fryer laughed when I mentioned it. "It's what we're used to," he said. "Us chaps have been at it all our lives."

He was in Daniel's *H.K.D.* when she blew up on a magnetic mine January 19th 1942. "It had just come daylight. There was us and *Kathleen* and the *Savoy*. We'd all come through the boom first light and were racing down together. It had been snowing and I'd just told the mate to get a broom and sweep some of it off the deck when up she went. Never thought a wooden craft would set off one o' them things, but that's what they reckoned it was. She sliced through like a potato and a blooming great lump of her starboard quarter went up into Garrison that tide.

"I come to in the water and grabbed at a cupboard door. Shoey, the mate, he was on top of some wreckage and we were both picked up by my brother George in the *Savoy*, who downed tops'l and anchored, and I remember hearing him and Alf cursing as the thole pins kept all on breaking as they pulled across in the boat." The mate was badly smashed up, but Albert escaped with pneumonia, and afterwards took the *Duluth*.

184

London River and the Thames Estuary were unhealthy waters to sail in during the war, and although there were comparatively few casualties, most bargemen have stories to tell of near misses and yarns enlivened with touches of humour.

One time Albert Fryer was lying at Erith in the *Duluth* when bombs began to fall. "Pegs jumped from the clothes line over the cabin stove as her arse lifted out o' the water. Never done us a mite o' damage though it blew the plug out o' the boat."

Another time they lay at Woolwich waiting to be towed up river. There was a blitz on the docks and they saw their tug slipping by on the far side keeping out of trouble. "She was taking no notice of us — giving us a miss — till a bomb landed slap ahead of her and that reminded her to come round for us in double quick time!"

He eventually lost the *Duluth*, too. "Six ships got sunk in the Thames the night before. We were coming away down next morning and saw some of 'em. But there was one we didn't know anything about till the leeboard knocked up and I felt her scrape over something with her bottom. I didn't know whether she'd damaged herself, so I told the mate to try the pump. Couldn't fetch it, so he said, but I could tell right enough she was making water, so we stood in towards Shoebury till the decks were awash, then she just sank down a couple of feet and settled on the bottom. We made up the tops'l and afterwards unbent jib and fores'l and brought 'em home along with her spars and oars and boat.

"The barge couldn't have been all that damaged and I reckon she'd have been raised easy enough but for the salvage craft being kept so busy. Time they got round to us she'd sanded down."

The *Globe* was lost February 25th, 1941. Vic Rowden was taking the usual way up between the fourth and fifth pylons of the boom off Warden Point when she touched off a mine and disappeared without trace, even to the boat that was towing astern. Yet five barges had been up through the previous Saturday and five the Saturday before.

Life went on during our stay in Whitstable Harbour. *Edith* completed discharge and sailed light for London on the day tide while the *Major* took her berth under the sucker. High water is always a busy time. Jack Wills, railway foreman and harbour master, used to attend in person for two hours on each side of high water. Craft were not supposed to be left unattended, for there was often a general post involving much shifting from one berth to another. More often than not it was the small boat that got in the way; the yachtsman who paid ninepence per week mooring fee and only put in an occasional appearance at weekends was not popular here. It was surprising that small craft were so rarely damaged.

Chris Merritt and his son brought *Trilby* in light from Queenborough on the same tide and berthed just astern of us. Chris was one of the younger bargemen brought up in the old school; short, cheery and not afraid of telling a story against himself.

185

They had gone into Queenborough with a hundred tons of potash for the Chemical works. Sailing out, with a huffler aboard, the line to the shore to give them a start parted in the snatch. "There wasn't much we could do about it except keep going and hope for the best. Just couldn't get her to wind though, and there we stuck. Tides taking off, but we stayed aboard on the off chance of a sneak tide. You know how that does often come of a night tide with the wind in the no'west."

"And it did," I suggested.

"Not this time, it didn't. We stopped three days on the spit." Chris grinned happily. They had only got off that morning after three days beneaped on the mud, and a less pleasant berth could hardly be imagined with the evil-smelling glue factory for a close neighbour.

"One thing, we weren't long coming down here when we did get out and just when the breeze took off a bit down by the Cheney Range, a launch came after us and wanted to know how long we'd be there.

" 'If the breeze fails we'll be here all day,' I said and when he pulled a bit of a face I held up the end of a rope. He took the hint and brought us down well nigh to the Columbine."

We were chatting aboard *Henry*. Outside lay *Violet*, a pretty model of a barge, built at Maldon in 1889 by John Howard. The children found her wide decks made a perfect speedway track and they took turns at circling the mainhatch on Peter's tricycle until Peter overturned on a corner and all but fell overside into the mud.

He got to his feet rather ruefully, and tears were not far away.

"You're all right," said Chris.

"Barge boys don't cry," I added.

Peter rubbed his hands together, then remounted his tricycle.

"We don't cry, do we Liz?" he called. "Us bargemen don't."

"He'll do," said Chris with a laugh.

Chris knew *Violet* well, for he was in her until quite recently, shifting into *Trilby* with his son Colin as mate.

"I suppose she's that much bigger?" I said.

"Looks it, I know, but funnily enough there's not much in it. I've loaded 111 tons into the *Violet* and she's only 43 net register; *Trilby* goes 115 tons on 50 net register. To tell you the truth I'd as soon have the *Violet*. I reckon she's the better barge, but the gov'nor's short of a crew and he says he'd sooner get rid of *Violet* if he's got to. There's not much wrong with her either — a few shaky frames and the inwale wants looking to — but she'd make a lovely yacht for someone. Seen her cabin? All panelled out in mahogany. Gets along too with the wind free, though she's not so fast to wind'rd as I thought she'd be. Soon after I took her Horlock's *Portlight* gave us a beating to wind'rd, so I tried raking her mast for'rd to see if that would do the trick. Made no difference to wind'rd but she went even faster on a reach so we left it like that.

"Another thing, she's a handy barge, that *Violet*. I got caught up at the docks one time without a mate. Two minds whether to come away down on my own. While I thought it about I got the lamps ready just in case. Nice breeze no'therly and ... well, it was too good to miss. Got down all right, taking it nice and easy, but coming into the harbour here early morning and nobody about I began to wonder how I was going to stop her. In the end I made a line fast on board, jumped for a ladder as we sheered in alongside the East wall and managed to get a quick turn round a rung. Just pulled her up in time."

Colin Merritt, his son, was originally apprenticed to a local shipbuilder, but he begged his father to let him come barging. "Now he's telling me how to do things," said Chris with a grin.

Trilby had come in to load barley — Persian barley that had been brought down from London by barge to go into store only a fortnight earlier. It reminded me of another barge that took wheat to Great Yarmouth only to be told on arrival to take it back to London.

Across on the other side, discharging under the sucker, lay the *Major*, quite a different type of barge, with well-cambered decks and small hatchways, and rails that were almost bulwarks. She was built at Harwich in 1897 for Major Groom and sailed originally as a boomy barge. Later she passed to Brightlingsea owners and was laid up there during the depression of the 'thirties. She was bought by the late Abbie Anderson, one-time chairman of the now defunct British Sailing Ship Owners Association.

George Barker came out of Shrubsall's *Veravia* to take *Major* away when she came off the ways again after the war; after he went ashore George Faint became master — a Sittingbourne man, tall, well dressed and quietly spoken. He was in Wood's barges until the Milton Creek work fell away, then he became associated with Colonel Bingham's auxiliaries *Castanet* and *Bankside*, later merged in the firm of Francis & Gilders.

"I was in *Bankside* at the time," he told me. "I went with the barge but I knew I wouldn't suit Josh Francis. Although I was born near Colchester, I'd lived long enough this side of the Thames to be classed as a Kentishman." So he went skipper of Alan Baker's ocean racer *Thalassa* and won the R.O.R.C.'s award in 1939 for the most successful skipper.

Kent and Essex bargemen were traditionally poles apart. In the old days there was a great deal of rivalry between them. The Essex man's life was largely bound up with the mills and farms, and loading freights of corn and stacks and mangels and stable manure. He lived at a slower tempo as befitted a man of the land. He was slower of speech and more obdurate, maybe. Sailing the open waters of Swin and Wallet, there were times when even the thrustful had to lay for weather and be patient.

Kentishmen traded more in bricks and cement — Thames and Medway river work mostly, with no more of an open sea trip than the comparatively sheltered waters of Jenkin's Swatchway and Sea Reach.

Although barge work changed in character after the war, the differences were still apparent. When the 150-ton Ipswich barge *Colonia* came to work on the

Kentish side, the bowsprit very soon disappeared, for the Whitstable man had no love for such things. A steeved-up bowsprit was a nuisance in the docks and to unship it took time. As Harry Blaxland, head of Daniels Bros. said, his men didn't waste much time in the docks once loaded, and even begrudged a 'phone call to the office. *Kathleen* had been seen coming down the dock with the mate struggling with the hatches and the skipper dashing out of the wheel-house every now and then to lend a hand with the more awkward ones.

But the Ipswich and Mistley barges used to find themselves a quiet corner to cover up and batten down. And while the mate sluiced the decks, the skipper would dress for shore and go to town to clear his barge at the Customs House. When they put to sea they were taut and trim, with the bowsprit ready to be bowsed down when the wind served.

☆ ☆ ☆ ☆

Savoy was weatherbound in Ramsgate; George Fryer had left her there until the strong easterly wind had moderated, and come back home. He joined the other bargemen — some still active and others long since retired — on their regular morning constitutional under the lee of a shed on the quay.

Bill Foster was one of them, tall and portly, with a bushy, white moustache and dressed in the invariable blue reefer jacket and cheese-cutter cap. He and his father before him had the nickname 'Gooseberry'. Commodore skipper of Crundall's once famous fleet of Dover coasters, he used to sail *Savoy* many years before she came to Whitstable with her muley rig and bowsprit. It was ideal for cross channel work, and Bill Foster had traded in her to practically every port between the Hook of Holland and St. Malo, but it was too cumbersome a rig for river work with only an occasional trip round the Foreland to Ramsgate or Dover. The big mizzen had to come out and the bowsprit followed.

George Fryer was mate in the *Globe* in 1914 when, together with others from the Whitstable Shipping Company's barges, he joined the navy and served in sweepers out of Taranto. He had been skipper of *Savoy* for over twenty years and his brother Alf sailed as mate. Recently fitted with a new steel keelson, *Savoy* was well found and beautifully kept.

There was a barge anchored out by the Columbine. Some thought she was the *Azima*, but with the stong easterly wind blowing it was hardly likely that a sailorman would have attempted the passage. Sure enough as the tide made she came motoring in, rolling and wallowing in the cross seas — Sully's powerful auxiliary *Beatrice Maud*. There were plenty of willing hands to check her round the knuckle, but there was a following wind and plenty of it. Harold Smy, tough, big featured skipper with a voice to match, roared from the wheelhouse to "clear that lot out o' the way." He wanted the smacks and yachts shifted, but the hufflers took no notice. Stuart Eldridge's face was a study as he passed across our decks with a line, and as Smy roared he turned an impassive face towards us and winked. Within a little the big 200-tonner was coaxed into her

Savoy.

berth. *Violet* came back alongside us. The smacks returned to their berths.
Everybody relaxed.

Beatrice Maud was built at Sittingbourne in 1910, the last barge to come
from Alfred White's yard. Powered with an 88 H.P. Kelvin, she took part in the
Dunkirk evacuation and spent the rest of the war trading in the Bristol Channel.
Harold Smy had two great hates — river work and timber — as he told us, leaning
against his boat davits, hand in pocket. Suddenly he stopped, stared intently at
me for a few moments, then ejaculated to my utter dismay: "I've got you now!"
But his face broke into a broad smile. "Didn't you have a little old thing called
the *June?*" he demanded. "And didn't you git aground one time opposite Shotley?"

"Why yes," I said. "That's true. Strange you should remember that. Which
barge were you in then?"

"I had Paul's *Orwell* that time o' day. We were brought up under Stoneheaps
and come across in the boat to give you a hand."

"I remember the boat coming across," I said with a grin. "I couldn't say who
was in it though. I know I was feeling a bit ashamed of myself until somebody
told me not to worry for one of Everard's big coasters had been up on that very
same spot."

189

"That's right. And so she did. You weren't there for more'n a half-hour, but she went up top o' springs and got benipped for a fortnight."

Thereafter we became great friends and I heard many stories from Smy — of foolhardy, ignorant, bumptious and parsimonious owners, all of which were entertaining but too scurrilous for cold print. Besides, Harold Smy was an Ipswich man and his barge London-owned so that his incursion into the story of Whitstable craft is purely incidental.

Whitstable is open to the north-west and quite a sea comes rolling in during an onshore gale. Before the war I watched the little *Thomas & Frances* running in from the flats. The young skipper got sail off her and she drove up along the East Wall; a man caught her line and made fast. The skipper barely had time to take a turn when it parted and she surged on towards another barge moored ahead. The skipper snatched a line from the hatch top and had to wait what must have seemed an eternity while the man on the quay made fast again. The *Thomas & Frances* brought up eventually with her stem overlapping the other barge's rudder.

I happened to mention this to Chris Merritt. "That was me," he laughed. "I went skipper of her in 1935. We'd been lying alongside one of Goldsmith's ironpots on the Horsebridge and began to rub badly when it come on to blow. That's how we come to be running for shelter. Near thing, that was.

"She wasn't a bad little barge, that *Thomas & Frances*. Had fine high coamings for a little 'un that didn't go more than three hundred quarters. She used to leak through her topsides though. Up in the docks once they loaded hundred and fifty quarters into us aft, then knocked off. It wasn't long before the mate came to say there was water over the cabin floor. We pumped her out but she was still taking water through her plank ends, so I went and asked them to give us the rest of our cargo quickly so's to trim her up.

" 'Not likely,' they said. 'We're not putting any more on board if she's sinking.'

"I tried to explain but they wouldn't listen, so in the end I went ashore and got some clay and plugged the holes as best I could. Only got a couple of hours sleep that night, but I was able to go and tell them she was all right. That seemed to satisfy them, so they got cracking with the rest of our cargo, and we levelled up and came away down."

☆ ☆ ☆ ☆

Azima came in with a stack of Moroccan sheanut cake that smelt and tasted vaguely like ginger. Bargemen did not think much of it for it stowed too light to make a decent freight.

Trilby finished loading her dusty Persian barley and sailed for Silvertown. The breeze was still easterly but not quite so fresh. Chris warped out along the East Wall, hung on while he set sail, then slipped and sped out of the harbour like a scalded cat.

190

The next day *Colonia* came in with wheat. She was a Kentish-built barge from Felton's Sandwich yard in 1897, but had been trading for Cranfields, Ipswich, until just after the war when she joined Francis & Gilders' fleet. Then Daniels Bros. bought her. She was a pretty barge with steel sprit and loftier rig than most of the others.

Edith, distinctive with wheelhouse and mizzen, came in again with more sheanut cake. She was Charlie Ward's barge for many years and a regular trader to the powder works in Hamford Water at the back of Walton-on-the-Naze. Tall, lanky Charlie Frake came out of *Pretoria* to take her when Charlie Ward retired.

☆ ☆ ☆ ☆

There is a social life in a small harbour where everybody knows each other by Christian name. A few like Stuart Etheridge and Albert Fryer, who rejoiced in the nickname of Bloody Fryer and had a habit of repeating sentences, went from barging to the fishing or oyster dredging, but in general there seemed to be quite a distinction between the two fraternities. Frank Nicholls, manager of Daniels' Whitstable office, had the nickname of 'Dolly', and his father before him. He, too, had served in the barges and was one-time Master of the coaster *H.K.D.* The office faces the harbour gates and the ground floor was a meeting place for barge skippers, so that Frank Nicholls must have found it difficult at times to get on with his desk work.

I was in the office the Saturday before we sailed. Fred Wraight, master of the *Kathleen*, was standing just inside the door. He had been to Dover with wheat, then loaded scrap iron for Fords at Dagenham, and was now in Whitstable again with wheat. He started in the *Lord Churchill* as third hand and had been master of the 155-ton *Kathleen* for over 25 years. His son was mate and looked after the 66 h.p. diesel which had given no trouble for the six years it had been aboard. It pushed her along well enough, except for a dead plug to windward in the chop of a sea, but as soon as sails were set to help her the engine started revving up and away she used to go. Like *Savoy*, the *Kathleen* was always kept in tip top condition and a credit to her crew.

Chris Merritt was home for the weekend, having discharged his barley and loaded wheat back for Chatham. "We came down the Albert Dock with *Gertrude May* and locked out stern first, then *Thalatta* was social like and gave us a pluck down Gallions. First of all there was too much breeze for the jib, then it fell light and we drove down past Gravesend and had to touch the anchor down with twenty-five fathoms out. Anyway, we're up at Chatham now."

As usual, talk turned on the Whitstable barges. I was keen to know more of the little *Cereal*, now the yacht barge *Lyford Anna*. Apparently a ship foundered off Whitstable and baulks of teak were washed up the beach at the time *Cereal* was building in 1894 so she was launched with 3½-in. teak decks and rails of full 30-ft. lengths in the waist, as the surveyor was amazed to find after she got them flattened by a lighter in the docks.

Cereal washed ashore the wrong side of the piers at Ramsgate soon after she

191

came out and the crew of two had to be taken off. Fred Wraight reckoned she broke some of her main fastenings then, for he took her in 1913 and it was not until after the war when she went on the ways to be doubled and had a number of her keel bolts renewed that she really tightened up.

In the 'thirties Albert Fryer had her when she loaded wheat on top of oats and as she touched the mud coming into Whitstable Harbour she went over on her side, but so gently that she never even damaged a crosstree.

Chris was mate in her for four years and considered her somewhat cranky when loaded. "It was down tops'l — up tops'l — in anything of a breeze. Often had to let go the fores'l to get her up. In the early days she never had a crab winch for the main brails. Used the mast winch. Many a time I was up to my waist in water getting the mains'l off her."

Fred would not have it. "I tell you that *Cereal* was the liveliest little thing as ever I sailed. Nothing wrong with her. There never was a handier barge."

"I grant you that," conceded Chris. "Light barge she was handy. Screw her round anywhere."

A call came from the upper room for Fred Wraight and presently he came downstairs stuffing notes in his pocket. He had just had a settlement and was grinning widely as he made for the door.

"Hold on, Fred." Chris went up to him and rubbed shoulders. "Fair winds both ways, that's Fred. You want to keep in with him."

Fred Wraight laughed again as he opened the door. "I lay you wouldn't have said that if you'd been with us time we come out o' Dover and caught that there blow from the no'th-east!"

☆ ☆ ☆ ☆

Our fortnight was up. I turned out Sunday morning just before high water at 5.30 and walked round the harbour to take a look at the weather. *Vicunia* was in with wheat and Theobald's motor barge *Mary Ann*. On the East Wall, astern of *Edith*, lay *Savoy* with a torn topsail.

It was blowing a fresh westerly — a dead nose-ender up along the land. Charlie Frake, of the *Edith*, was already astir.

"Are you going out?" I asked.

"Reckon we'll have a look at it."

Albert Fryer joined us. "Ready? I said: Ready?"

"Just having a cup of tea."

"All right. I'll go and fetch the boat." Then turning to me: "I'll give Charlie a tow out first, then I'll come back if you're going. I said I'll come back if you're going."

We were going all right. It was no good waiting. As Charlie Frake said; "You have to keep turning over the ebb with the wind down else us bargemen don't get nowhere London River way."

I grinned happily to myself — Us bargemen!

POSTSCRIPT

The Bennets lived aboard *Henry* for ten years. Since they sold her the *Henry* has spent a chequered twenty years, but she is now refitted and based on the Medway.

Peter has emigrated to Australia and is now married with two daughters. Elizabeth is married with three sons and lives in Maidstone. Arthur and Dorothy retired to Christchurch in 1970, where Dorothy died four years later.

In 1976 Arthur married Joan, widow of Philip Hayes from Whitstable.

PUBLISHER'S ACKNOWLEDGEMENT

As the reader will be aware, many of the stories in the book were told to the author during long evenings aboard each other's barges. Although they are recorded accurately as told they may contain the usual embellishments to be found in 'oral history'. I am particularly grateful to four members of the Society for Spritsail Barge Research, Tony Farnham, Patricia O'Driscoll, Richard-Hugh Perks and Don Sattin for reading the proofs and checking the information about barges with written records such as Lloyds Register.

Many of the photos were taken by the author and others are acknowledged in the captions. Some, however, were given to the author without a note on them as to their original source. We regret these have not been acknowledged.

Hamish Mackay Miller

GLOSSARY

ADZE — Long-handled tool for trimming timber, like an axe with arched right-angled blade.

ANCHOR CHAFING PLATE — Galvanized iron plate nailed to bow planking to take the chafe of the anchor.

BARQUE — Square-rigged on all masts but fore-and-aft on mizzen.

BARQUENTINE — Square-rigged on foremast, fore-and-aft on mainmast and mizzen.

BOB — Owner's flag or burgee at topmast truck usually on a frame.

BOW BOARDS — Fitted on top of the rails. Usually painted white.

BILLY BOY — Boxy tiller-steering craft developed from Humber Keel.

BRIG — 2-masted vessel square-rigged on both masts.

BRIGANTINE — 2-masted vessel square-rigged on foremast and fore-and-aft on mainmast.

CARLINE — Beam other than main beam. Sometimes CARLING.

CEILING — Floor of the hold.

CHINE — Where the flat bottom meets the side. Sometimes spelled CHIME.

COLLAR LASHING — Secures throat of mainsail to mast.

CUPBOARD — Usually refers to space fore and aft of the hatchways difficult for cranes to plumb.

DEMURRAGE — Payment for extra time taken working cargo.

DOLLY WINCH — Fitted between windlass bitts. DOLLY WIRE used for running off to work barge in confined waters.

DOUBLING — Sheathing of sides and bottom. Sometimes termed PUTTING IN A BOX.

FLEET — Shifting cable from one end of windlass to the other. Also FLOAT.

FULL AND BY — Sailing close to the wind, but keeping everything full.

GUDGEON — Iron Socket on stern post to take rudder pintle.

GYBE — So much off the wind that it comes on the lee quarter, and causes the sail to shift over.

HATCH CARLINES — Oak beams on hatches.

HAWSE HOLES — Iron lined holes in the rail for mooring lines.

HITCHER — Long boat hook.

HOLE — Hold, or archway of bridge.

HOY — Barges sailing to schedule with goods and passengers.

HUFFLER — Boatman who assists in and out of port or through bridges. Sometimes spelled HOVELLER.

INWALE — Heavy strengthening timber between deck and sides.

IRONPOT — Steel barge.

JACKSTAY — Steel rod bolted to mainmast to which luff of mainsail is shackled.

KEELSON — Backbone of a barge — usually of pitch pine or steel.

KETCH — Vessel with mizzen stepped forward of rudder post.

LEEBOARD — Heavy, fan-shaped, iron-bound boards hinged forward and lowered from aft for windward work.

LEEBOARD CRAB — Small winch for working leeboards and sometimes fitted with a barrel for hardening in vangs and sheets.

LINING — Inside of hold.

MARLINE — Small line.

MIZZEN — After mast or sail.

MUZZLE — Iron band holding foot of sprit to mast.

PINCH BAR — Bar with flattened curve end for levering timber.

QUARTER RAIL — Usually white and capped with oak, fitted on top of the normal rail.

REEMER — Boring tool.

ROADS BARGE — Permanently moored fore and aft for craft to come alongside.

ROUGH STUFF — Household rubbish.

ROWING IRONS — Barge rowlocks.

SCARPH — Join.

SETTING BOOMS — 25/30-ft, steel-tipped for poling, or booming out sails.

SKEG — Protubing deadwood from heel of sternpost to prevent lines from jamming.

SPRIT — Pine, white wood or steel, 55/60-ft, rigged from mainmast heel to mainsail peak and stays permanently aloft.

SPUNYARN — Twisted yarns.

STAYFALL — Wire for lowering away.

STANLIFT — Wire taking weight of sprit.

STOP OUT — Clean out.

STRIKE TOPMAST — House or lower.

TACKLE BAND — Iron band mid-sprit to take weight of sprit especially when lowering. Usually pronounced YARD TAIKLE BAND.

TIE BEAM — Fixed or portable, bisecting main hold.

TOPSAIL SCHOONER — Fore-and-aft rig on both masts with square topsails on foremast.

TREENAIL — Wooden pegs used in older barges for fastenings.

VANG — Wire to control sprit. Pronounced WANG.

WELT — Hardwood strip on windlass barrel.

WIND — Tack. Come about. Sometimes spelled WEND.

WYEMARKS — River Blackwater shore between Bradwell and St Peters Point. Anchorage sheltered from South-west. Derives from Saxon Wyemarc.

YARMOUTH ROADS — Traditional name for aft end of cabin.

YAWL — Vessel with mainmast, and mizzen stepped abaft rudder post but Whitstable oyster smacks invariably called YAWLS.

INDEX OF BARGE NAMES

Cecil Rhodes (Faversham 1899) 62
Centaur (Harwich 1895) 23, 24, 141-143, 145, 157, 158, 160-163
Centaur (Rochester 1899) 41
Cereal (Whitstable 1894, later renamed *Lyford Anna*) 16, 29, 134, 135, 180 (photo), 183, 191, 192
Ceres (Battersea 1795) 171
Challenger (Rochester 1875) 40
Champion (Ipswich 1861) 182
Champion (Rochester 1865) 154, 176, 179
Charles & Isabella (Milton 1884) 154
Cheshire (Sittingbourne 1903) 46
Chieftain (London 1893) 42
C.I.V. (Sittingbourne 1901) 63-64
Clara (Sittingbourne 1896) 98
Colne (Ipswich 1890) 53
Colonia (Sandwich 1897) 71, 81, 183, 187, 191
Conqueror (Rochester 1876) 40
Conyer (Sittingbourne 1866) 170
Coot (Halstow 1894) 46
Crouch Belle (Hull Bridge 1901) 45
Cumberland (Halstow 1900) 47
Curlew (Halstow 1897) 51 (photo)
Cypress (unrigged barge Maldon 1887) 150

Daisy Little (Strood 1891) 116
D'Arcy (Maldon 1894) 145, 149, 151, 162
Dawn (Maldon 1897) 150, 151
Dawn (Rochester 1896) 42, 47
Defender (Maldon 1900) 145, 149, 151, 158, 165
Devon (Halstow 1901) 50, 51
Diamond, The (Greenwich 1897) 47
Dick Turpin (Otterham 1870) 45, 48
Diligent (Milton 1880) 62, 144, 162
Dinah (yacht barge, Rochester 1887) 115-117
Dipper (Halstow 1896) 115-117
Doric (Papendrecht 1903) 103
Dorothea (Ipswich 1880) 42
Dorothy (Harwich 1889) 56
Dreadnought (Sittingbourne 1907), 17, 36, 111
Druide (Schooner, France 1877) 175
Duchess (E. Greenwich 1904) 157, 179
Duluth (Whitstable 1895) 183-185
Durham (Conyer 1899) 49

East Anglia (Rochester 1908) 42
Eastwood (Southwark 1822) 41
Ebenezer (Milton 1879) 62
Edith (Sittingbourne 1904) 25, 26 (photo), 63, 180 (photo), 183, 185, 191-2
Edith & Hilda (Milton 1892) 111
Edmund (Rochester 1866) 41
Edward (Frindsbury 1856) 41
Elizabeth (Bankside 1809) 172

Ella (Faversham 1874) 62
Ellen (Ketch, Sunderland 1860) 63
Ellen Smeed (Murston 1872) 63
Elwin (Teynham 1878) 174
Emily (Milton 1883) 151
Emma (Grays 1845) 101, 102
Emma (Maldon 1897) 145
Emma (Schooner, Rye 1853) 21
Enchantress (Maidstone 1908) 42
Ernest Piper (Greenwich 1898) 109
Estelle (Rye 1899) 175
Esterel (Southampton 1899) 97, 98
Esther (Faversham 1900) 63, 183
Esther (Ware 1837) 102
Esther Smeed (Murston 1868) 18
Ethel (Conyer 1878) 154
Ethel (Faversham 1900 renamed *Pride of Sheppey*) 64 (Photo), 65
Ethel Ada (Paglesham 1903) 111
Ethel Edith (Ipswich 1892) 166
Ethel Maud (Maldon 1889) 144
Eucrete (Whitstable) 183
Eva Annie (Milton 1878) 151
Evelyn (brig, Portmadoc 1877) 59
Evening (Rochester 1903) 47
Excelsior (Harwich 1885) 142
Excelsior (Ipswich 1862) 181
Excelsior (Sittingbourne 1879) 155

Falcon (Paglesham 1868) 150
Falconet (Strood 1899) 155, 159, 166
Fanny (Sittingbourne 1872) 65
Federation (Brightlingsea 1900) 42
First Attempt (Rochester 1898) 49 (photo)
Five Sisters (Sittingbourne 1891) 54
Flame, The, M/B (Deptford 1914) 137
Fleur de Lis (Rochester 1890) 149
Flower of Essex (Ipswich 1890) 57, 81
Forth (Rochester 1885) 62
Foxhound (Conyer 1895) 42, 43 (photo)
Fred (Rochester 1893) 42

Gamma (Halstow 1891) 46
G.C.B. (Rochester 1907) 170
General Jackson (Ipswich 1896) 32 (photo), 34, 35, 161
George (Murston 1879) 53
George & Eliza (Rochester 1906) 42, 43 (photo)
George Smeed (Murston 1882) 18, 160
Gertrude May (Sittingbourne 1893) 48, 154, 191
Gillman (Lambeth 1865) 155
Gipping (Ipswich 1889) 36, 111
Giralda (Greenwich 1897) 145
Gladiator (Milton 1865) 101
Gladys (Harwich 1901) 165

196

197

198

Scone (Rochester 1919) 42
Scot (Southampton 1898) 93, 98
Scotsman (Sittingbourne 1899) 112
Scud (Shoebury 1898) 46
S.D. (MUrston 1902) 59
Sea Spray (Rochester 1893) 140 (photo)
Senta (Southampton 1899) 105, 107
Serb (E. Greenwich 1916) 166
Servic (Krimpen d'Ysel 1904) 100, 103
Severn (Rochester 1888) 62
Sextus (Ipswich 1849) 41
Sibyl (Sittingbourne 1872) 182
Sirdar (Ipswich 1898) 42

Sir Richard (Gravesend 1900) 42
Six Sisters (Limehouse 1864) 174
Snowdrop (Frindsbury 1879) 162
Sophie (Halstow 1866) 154
Sophy (Sittingbourne 1861) 170
Spinaway C. (Ipswich 1899) 71, 73, 77, 166
Spurgeon (Murston 1883) 115-118
Squawk (Strood 1914) 42
Stanley (Sittingbourne 1866) 47
Star (Lambeth 1836) 102
Sunbeam (Maldon 1888) 53
Sunrise (Rochester 1889) 43 (photo)
Surprise (Faversham 1878) 62
Surprise (Maldon 1879) 144, 145, 160
Surrey (E. Greenwich 1901) 41
Surrey (Milton 1903) 51
Swift (Northfleet 1871) 131
Swift (Rochester 1898) 62, 134

Tankerton Tower (Whitstable 1884) 181
Teetotaler (Sittingbourne 1906) 23
Thames (Faversham 1864) 62
Thalatta (Harwich 1906) 191
Thermopylae (Ship, Aberdeen 1868) 59
Theta (Halstow 1898) 46, 50, 51 (photo)
Thetis (Sittingbourne 1897) 36, 37 (photo)
Thistle (Glasgow 1895) 33, 42
Thoma II (Maldon 1909) 147-148
Thomas & Frances (Sittingbourne 1878) 53, 56, 183, 190
Three Brothers (Rochester 1886) 171
Thyra (Maidstone 1913) 42
Tovil (Rochester 1862) 41
Trilby (Rochester 1896) 55
Trilby (Sandwich 1896) 16, 25, 27, 183, 185-187, 190
Triton (Sittingbourne 1866) 154

Trojan (Southampton 1898) 84, 154
Twilight (Rochester 1898) 47
Two Brothers (Faversham 1878) 62
Tyne (Faverhsam 1869) 62

Undaunted (Frindsbury 1878) 48
Unity (Milton 1871) 155
Unity (Rainham 1897) 48
Uplees (Uplees 1897) 62
Utility (Rainham 1906) 48
U.V.W. (Borstal 1894) 42

Valonia (E. Greenwich 1911) 146
Venta (Maldon 1893 ex *Jachin*) 134, 147
Vera (Limehouse 1898) 42
Veravia (Sittingbourne 1898 ex *Alarm*) 25, 26, 28, 40 (photo), 84, 99, 104, 105, 110, 147, 158, 160, 161, 187
Verona (E. Greenwich 1905) 55, 56, 99, 147, 176
Veronica (E. Greenwich 1906) 145, 146
Victa (Rochester 1874 ex *& Co.*) 43 (photo), 167
Victoria (Sittingbourne 1897) 58 (photo)
Victory (Conyer 1901) 52
Vicunia (E. Greenwich 1912) 16, 56, 100, 117, 183, 192
Vigilant (Ipswich 1904) 39
Violet (Maldon 1889) 25, 28, 145, 149, 183, 184 (photo), 186, 189
Violet (Ipswich 1896) 170
Viper (Sittingbourne 1898) 36
Virocca (Southampton 1899) 45

Water Lily (Rochester 1902) 33, 162, 166, 178, 179
Waveney (Ipswich 1892) 52
Westall (Strood 1913) 43 (photo)
Westmoreland (Conyer 1900) 49 (photo)
Whaup (Halstow 1892) 51
Whimbrel (Milton 1882) 41, 43 (photo)
W.H. Randall (Sittingbourne 1876) 183
Why Not? (Faversham 1866) 62, 182
Will Everard (Yarmouth 1925) 23, 36
William Cleverley (Borstal 1899) 43 (photo)
William Stone (Sittingbourne 1864) 48
William Wood (Sittingbourne 1864) 170
Wiltshire (Milton 1908) 50
Winifred (Sandwich 1893) 115, 134
Woodside (brig. Hylton 1867) 18
Wouldham Court (Rochester 1899) 42

Zebrina (Whitstable 1873) 18

Meresborough Books

BYGONE KENT
A monthly journal on all aspects of Kent History. 95p per month. Annual Subscription £10.50. A free sample copy will be sent on request.

VILLAGES AROUND OLD MAIDSTONE by Irene Hales
Over 140 old postcards depicting the villages in a seven mile radius around Maidstone. £2.50 (£2.80 post free).

US BARGEMEN by A. S. Bennett
A new book of sailing barge life around Kent and Essex from the author of 'June of Rochester' and 'Tide Time'. £6.95 (£7.50 post free).

A VIEW OF CHRIST'S COLLEGE, BLACKHEATH by A.E.O. Crombie, B.A., Master, Headmaster and Tutor 1920-1976.
£6.95 (£7.95 post free)

A NEW DICTIONARY OF KENT DIALECT by Alan Major
All the words from Parish and Shaw's Dictionary of 1888 are included, but many more have been added from a wide variety of sources. Publication November, 1980. £7.50 (£7.95 post free).

THE GILLS by Tony Conway
A history of Gillingham Football Club. 96 large format pages packed with old photographs. Hardback. Publication, November, 1980. £5.95 (£6.95 post free).

KENT CASTLES by John Guy
The first comprehensive guide to all the castles and castle sites in Kent. The first part outlines the history of castles and castle building. The second part gives the history of over 60 castles in Kent with a guide for the modern visitor. 264 pages. Over 150 illustrations. Hardback. £7.50 (£7.95 post free).

THE CANTERBURY AND WHITSTABLE RAILWAY 1830-1980: A PICTORIAL SURVEY
(Published with the Locomotive Club of Great Britain.) 28 pages. Over 30 pictures and maps. 75p (95p post free).

MEDWAY MEMORIES by Norman Clout
A series of talks first broadcast on Radio Medway, Summer 1980. £1.50 (£1.80 post free).

ROCHESTER'S HERITAGE TRAIL
(Published for The City of Rochester Society). A useful guide for the visitor to most places of interest in Rochester. 95p (£1.15 post free).

OLD MAIDSTONE by Kay Baldock and Irene Hales
Over 100 old postcards from the early years of this century. 52 large format pages. £1.95 (£2.25 post free).

WATERMILLS AND WINDMILLS OF KENT by William Coles Finch
The classic book on all Kent mills reprinted at £10.00, now available at £4.95 (£5.95 post free).

STROOD A PICTORIAL HISTORY by Avril Bloomfield
Over 100 fascinating old photographs. Hardback £2.95 (£3.35 post free).

JUST OFF THE SWALE by Don Sattin.
The story of the barge building village of Conyer. £3.95 (£4.35 post free).

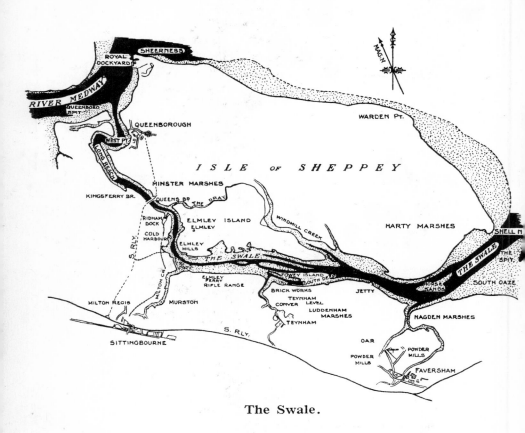

The Swale.